PLANET OF THE APES

THE HALF MAN

PLANE

ROSS RICHIE Chief Executive Officer • **MATT GAGNON** Editor-in-Chief • **FILIP SABLIK** VP-Publishing & Marketing • **LANCE KREITER** VP-Licensing & Merchandising • **PHIL BARBARO** Director of Finance
BRYCE CARLSON Managing Editor • **DAFNA PLEBAN** Editor • **SHANNON WATTERS** Editor • **ERIC HARBURN** Assistant Editor • **ADAM STAFFARONI** Assistant Editor • **CHRIS ROSA** Assistant Editor
STEPHANIE GONZAGA Graphic Designer • **CAROL THOMPSON** Production Designer • **JASMINE AMIRI** Operations Coordinator • **DEVIN FUNCHES** Marketing & Sales Assistant • **BRIANNA HART** - Marketing Assistant

A catalog record of this book is available from OCLC and from the BOOM! Studios website, www.boom-studios.com, on the Librarians Page.

BOOM! Studios, 5670 Wilshire Boulevard, Suite 450, Los Angeles, CA 90036-5679. Printed in China. First Printing.
ISBN: 978-1-60886-297-9

"THE HALF MAN"

WRITER
DARYL GREGORY

ARTIST
CARLOS MAGNO

COLORIST
DARRIN MOORE

LETTERER
TRAVIS LANHAM

"THE FIRST AND LAST DAYS"

WRITER
DARYL GREGORY

ARTIST
CARLOS MAGNO

COLORIST
DARRIN MOORE

LETTERER
ED DUKESHIRE

"A BOY AND HIS HUMAN"

WRITER
CORINNA BECHKO

ARTIST
JOHN LUCAS

COLORIST
STUDIO PARLAPÁ

LETTERER
ED DUKESHIRE

"OLD WORLD ORDER"

WRITER
JEFF PARKER

ARTIST
BENJAMIN DEWEY

COLORIST
NOLAN WOODARD

LETTERER
ED DUKESHIRE

"THE SCROLL"

WRITER / ARTIST
GABRIEL HARDMAN

COLORIST
MATTHEW WILSON

LETTERER
ED DUKESHIRE

COVER ARTIST
CARLOS MAGNO
WITH NOLAN WOODARD

EDITOR
DAFNA PLEBAN

TRADE DESIGNER
STEPHANIE GONZAGA

SPECIAL THANKS: LAUREN WINARSKI

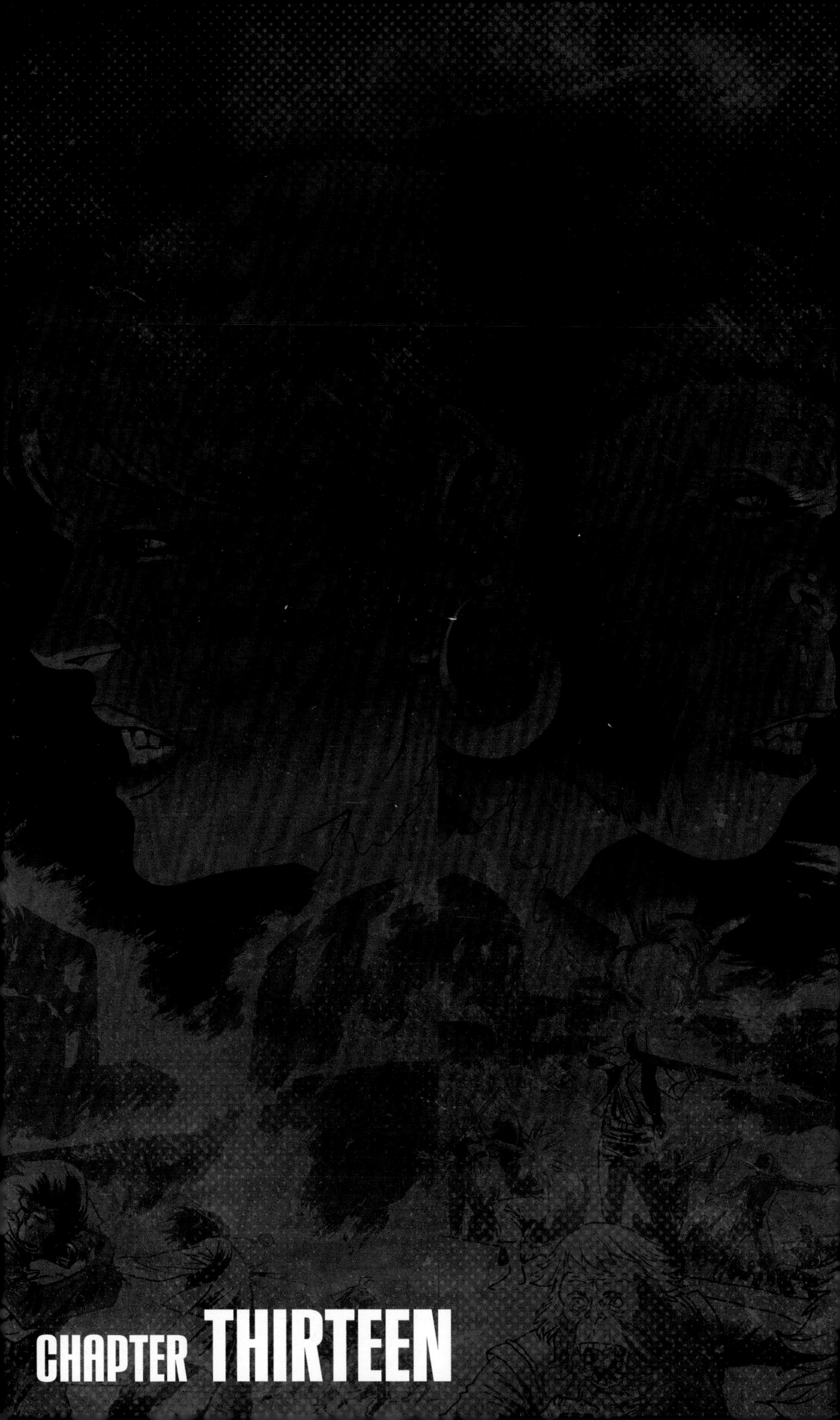

CHAPTER THIRTEEN

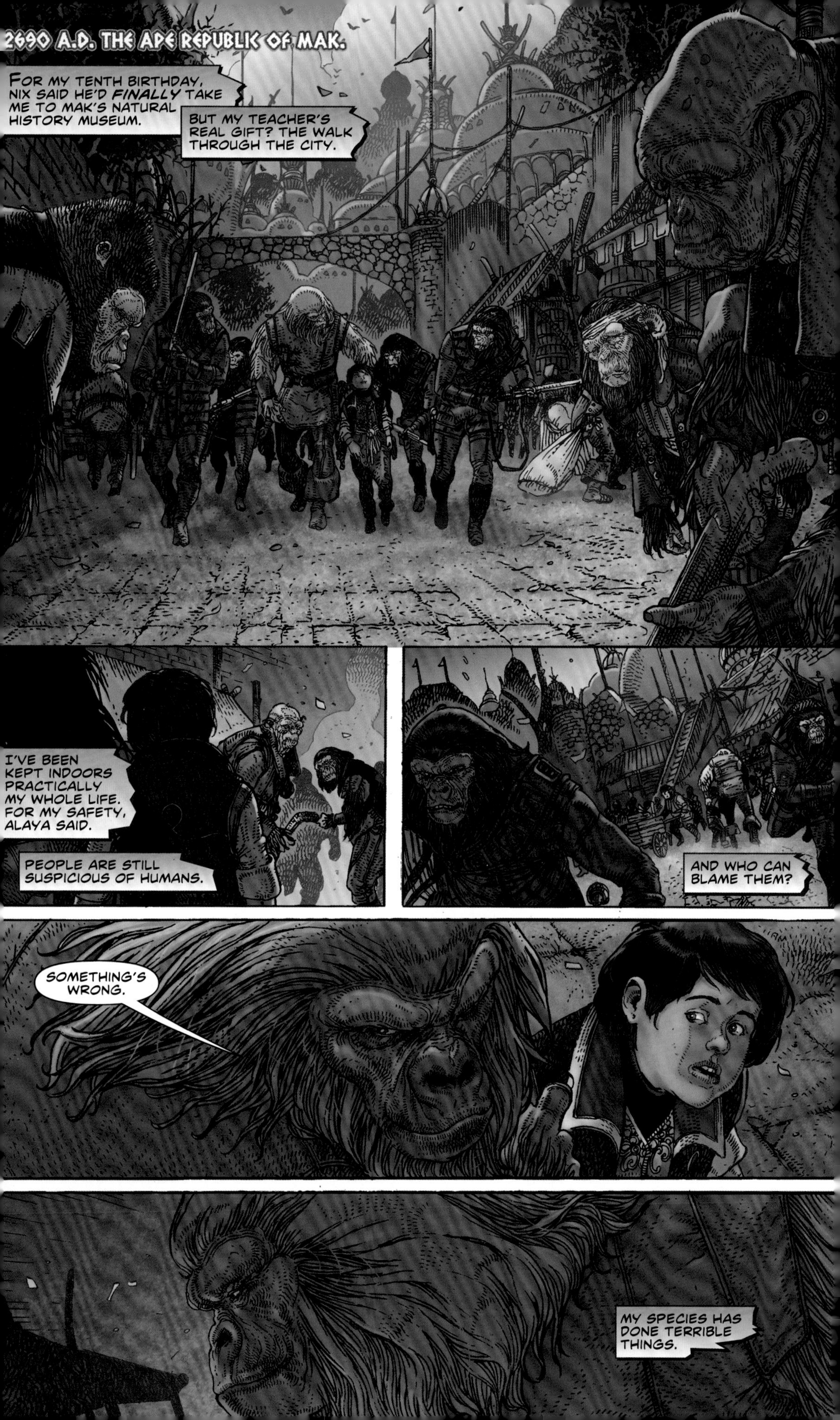
2690 A.D. THE APE REPUBLIC OF MAK.
FOR MY TENTH BIRTHDAY, NIX SAID HE'D FINALLY TAKE ME TO MAK'S NATURAL HISTORY MUSEUM.
BUT MY TEACHER'S REAL GIFT? THE WALK THROUGH THE CITY.
I'VE BEEN KEPT INDOORS PRACTICALLY MY WHOLE LIFE. FOR MY SAFETY, ALAYA SAID.
PEOPLE ARE STILL SUSPICIOUS OF HUMANS.
AND WHO CAN BLAME THEM?
SOMETHING'S WRONG.
MY SPECIES HAS DONE TERRIBLE THINGS.

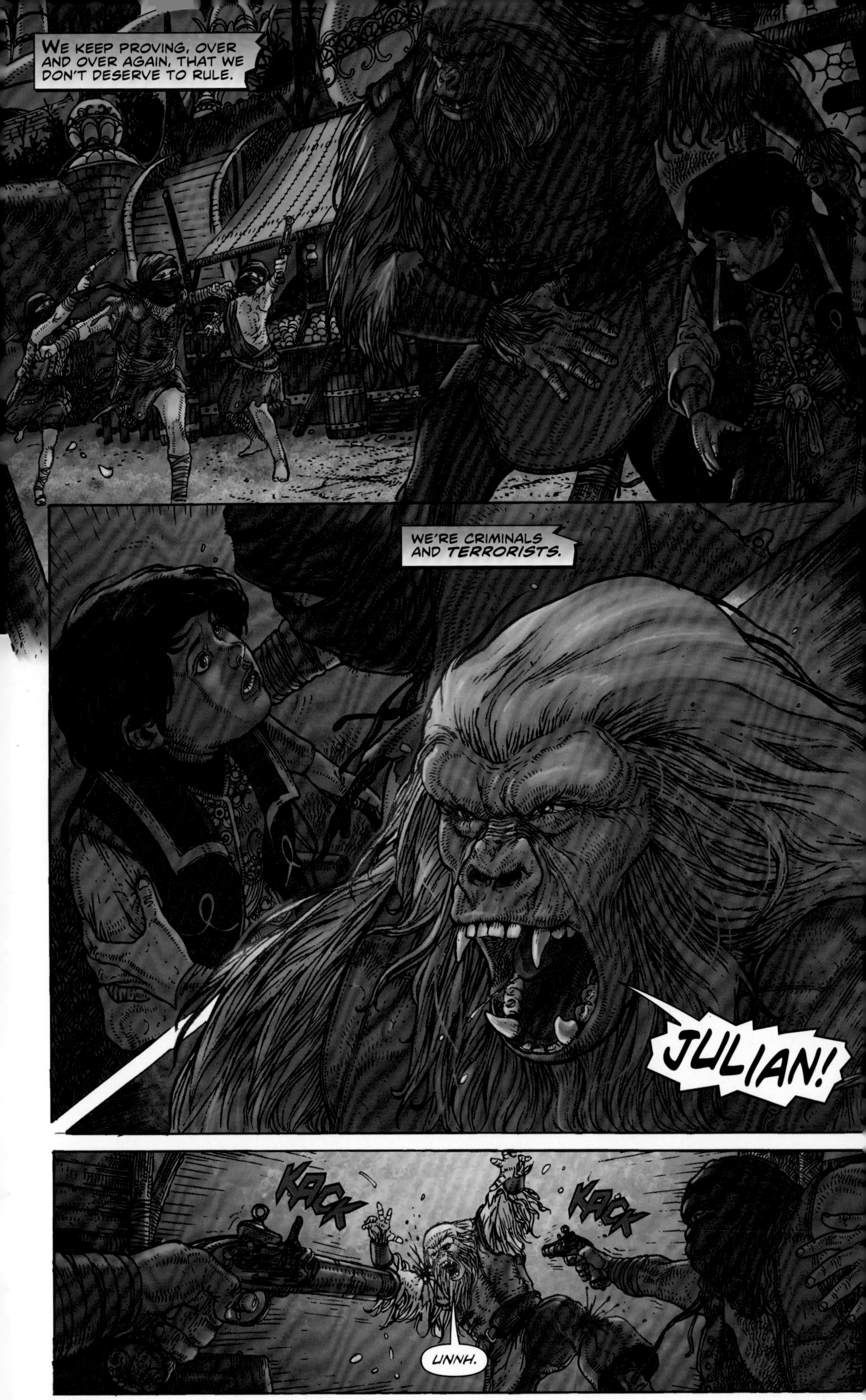
WE KEEP PROVING, OVER AND OVER AGAIN, THAT WE DON'T DESERVE TO RULE.
WE'RE CRIMINALS AND TERRORISTS.
JULIAN!
KACK
KACK
UNNH.

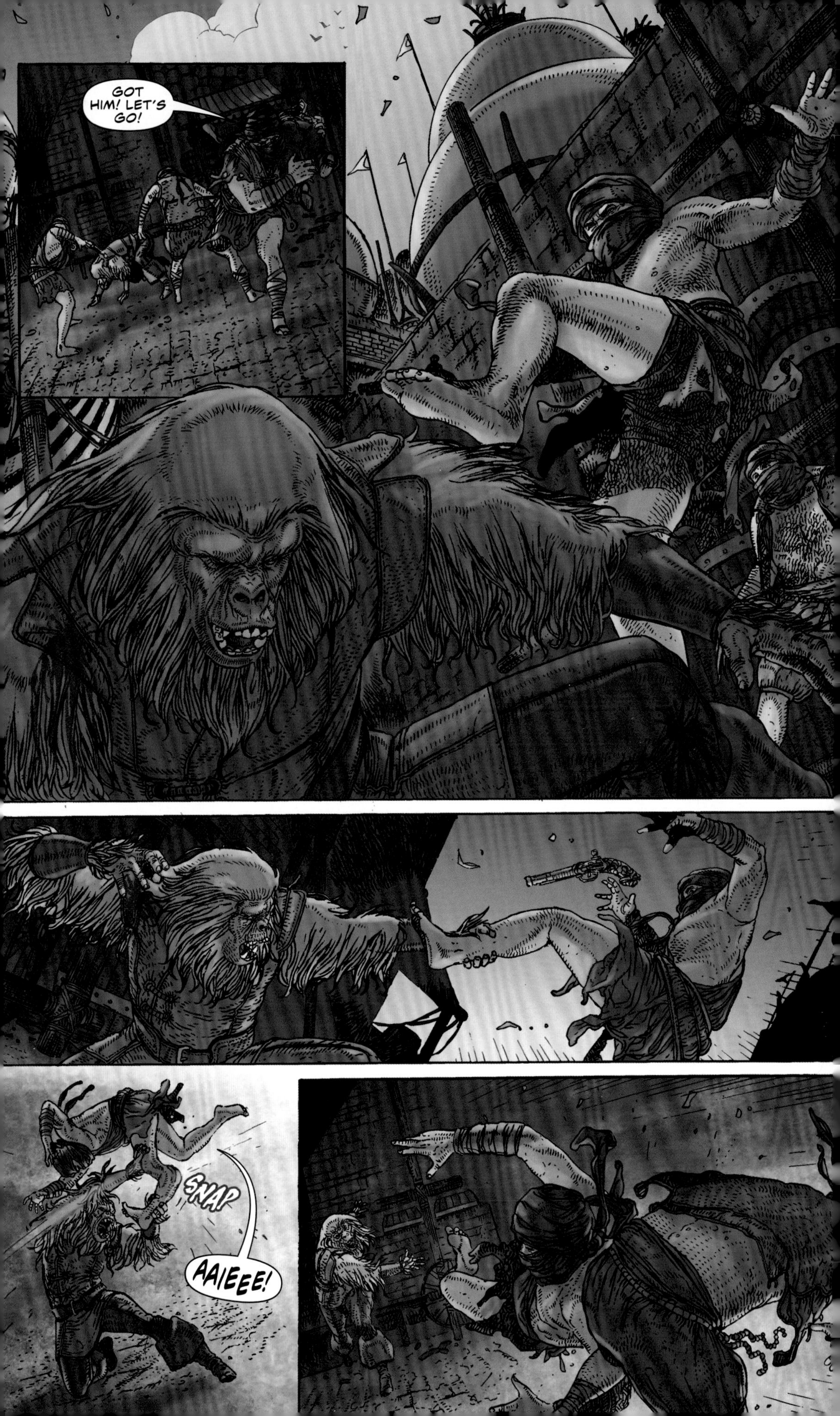
GOT HIM! LET'S GO!
SNAP
AAIEEE!

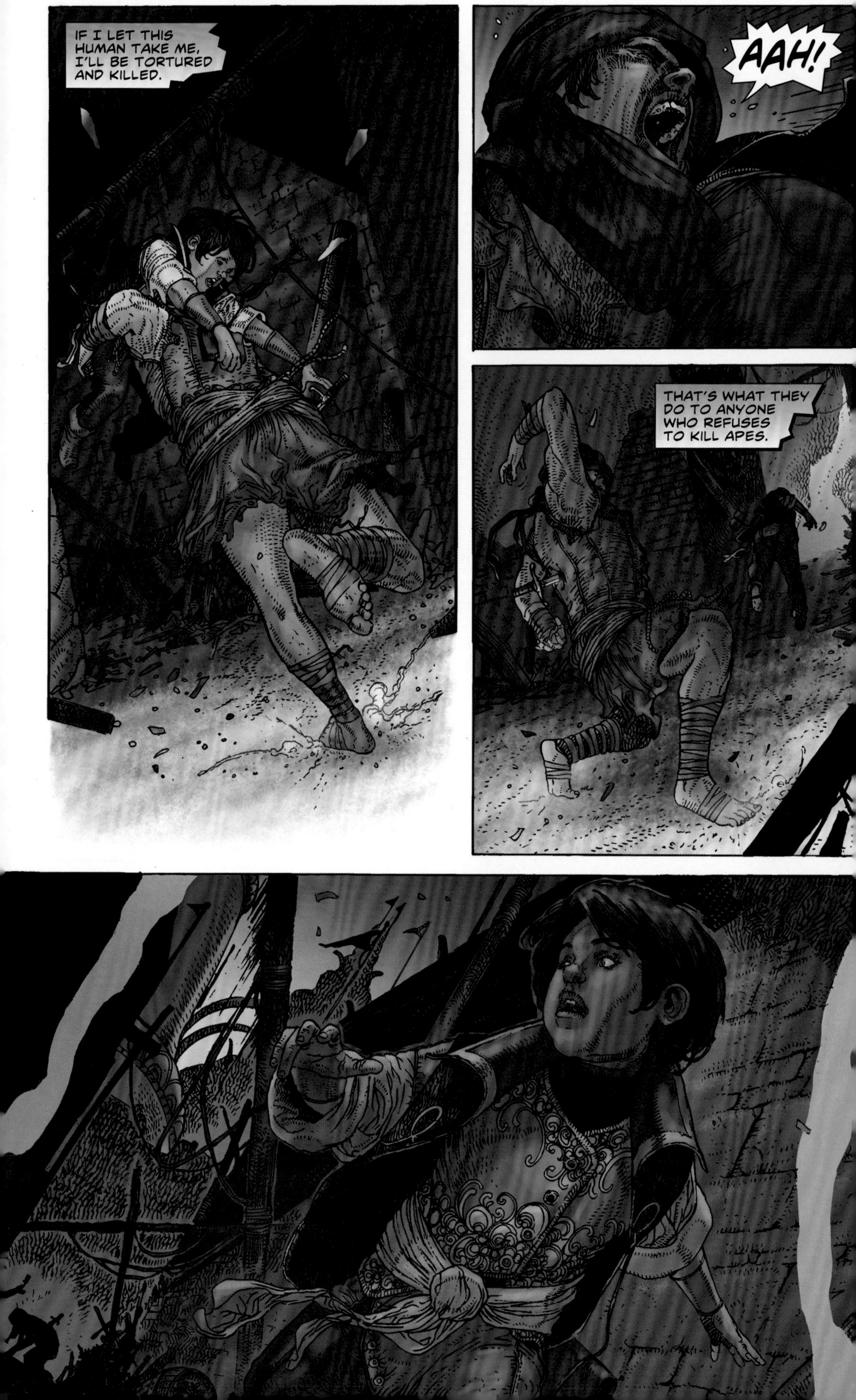
IF I LET THIS HUMAN TAKE ME, I'LL BE TORTURED AND KILLED.
AAH!
THAT'S WHAT THEY DO TO ANYONE WHO REFUSES TO KILL APES.

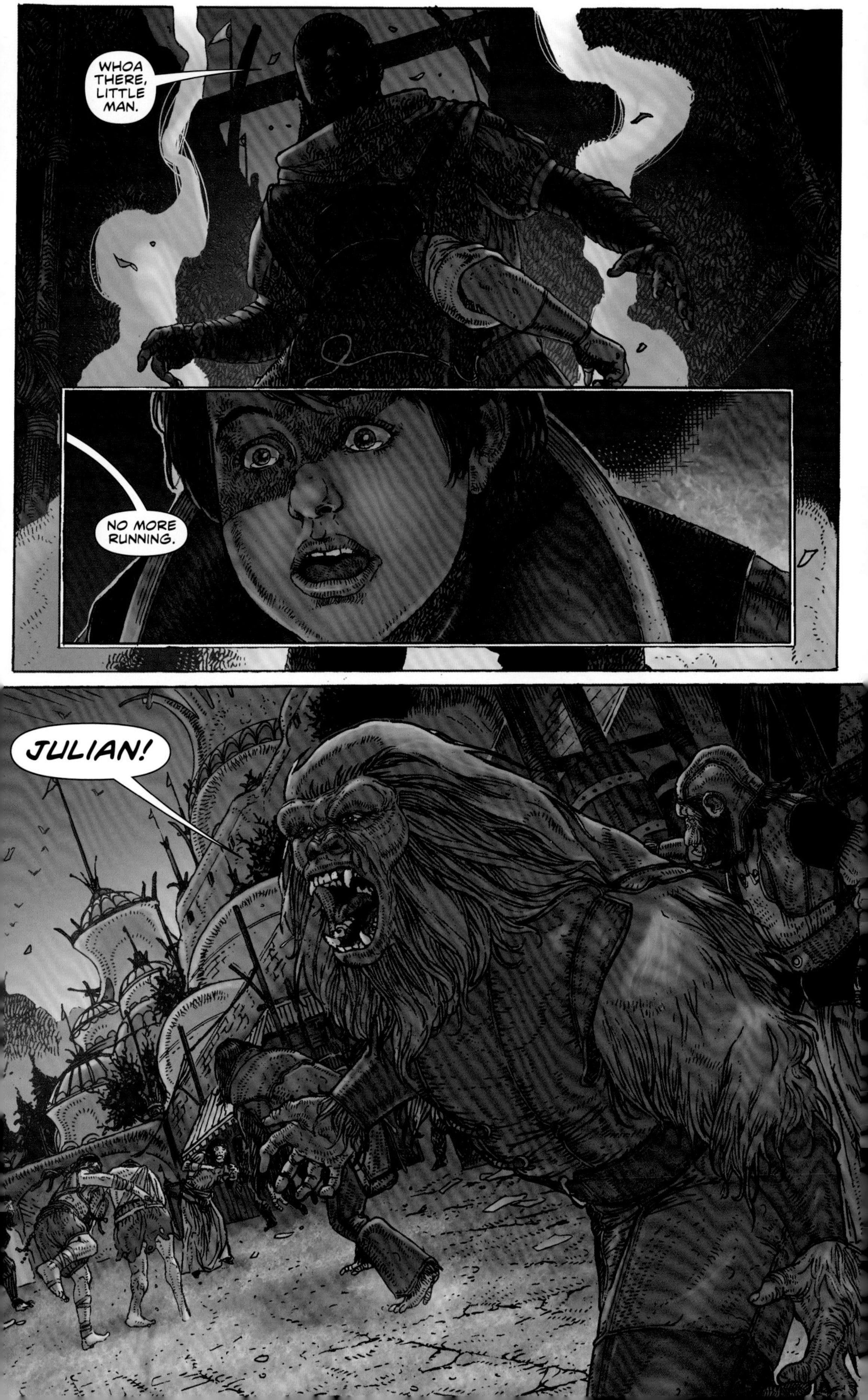
WHOA THERE, LITTLE MAN.
NO MORE RUNNING.
JULIAN!

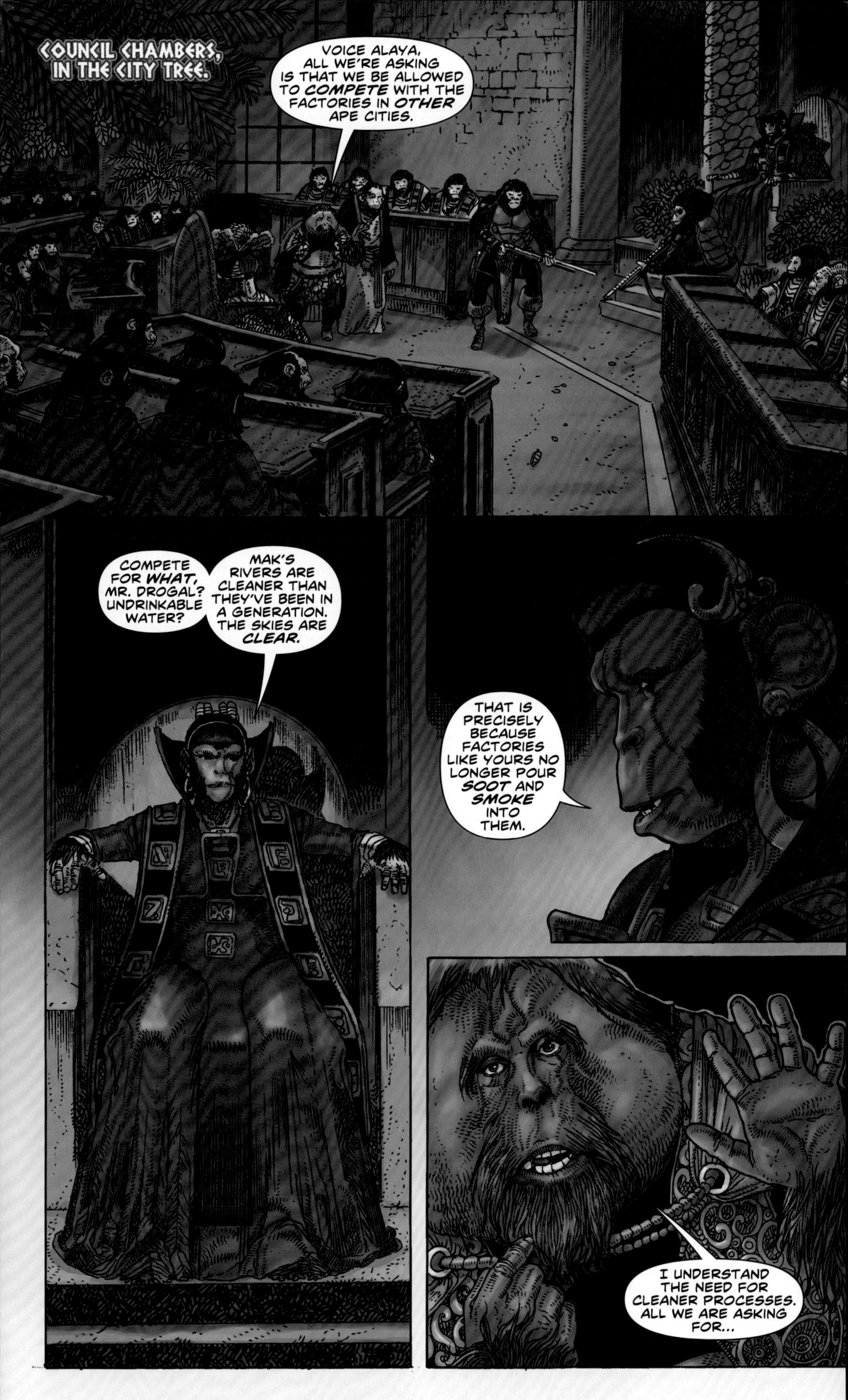
COUNCIL CHAMBERS, IN THE CITY TREE.
VOICE ALAYA, ALL WE'RE ASKING IS THAT WE BE ALLOWED TO *COMPETE* WITH THE FACTORIES IN *OTHER* APE CITIES.
COMPETE FOR *WHAT,* MR. DROGAL? UNDRINKABLE WATER?
MAK'S RIVERS ARE CLEANER THAN THEY'VE BEEN IN A GENERATION. THE SKIES ARE *CLEAR.*
THAT IS PRECISELY BECAUSE FACTORIES LIKE YOURS NO LONGER POUR *SOOT* AND *SMOKE* INTO THEM.
I UNDERSTAND THE NEED FOR CLEANER PROCESSES. ALL WE ARE ASKING FOR...

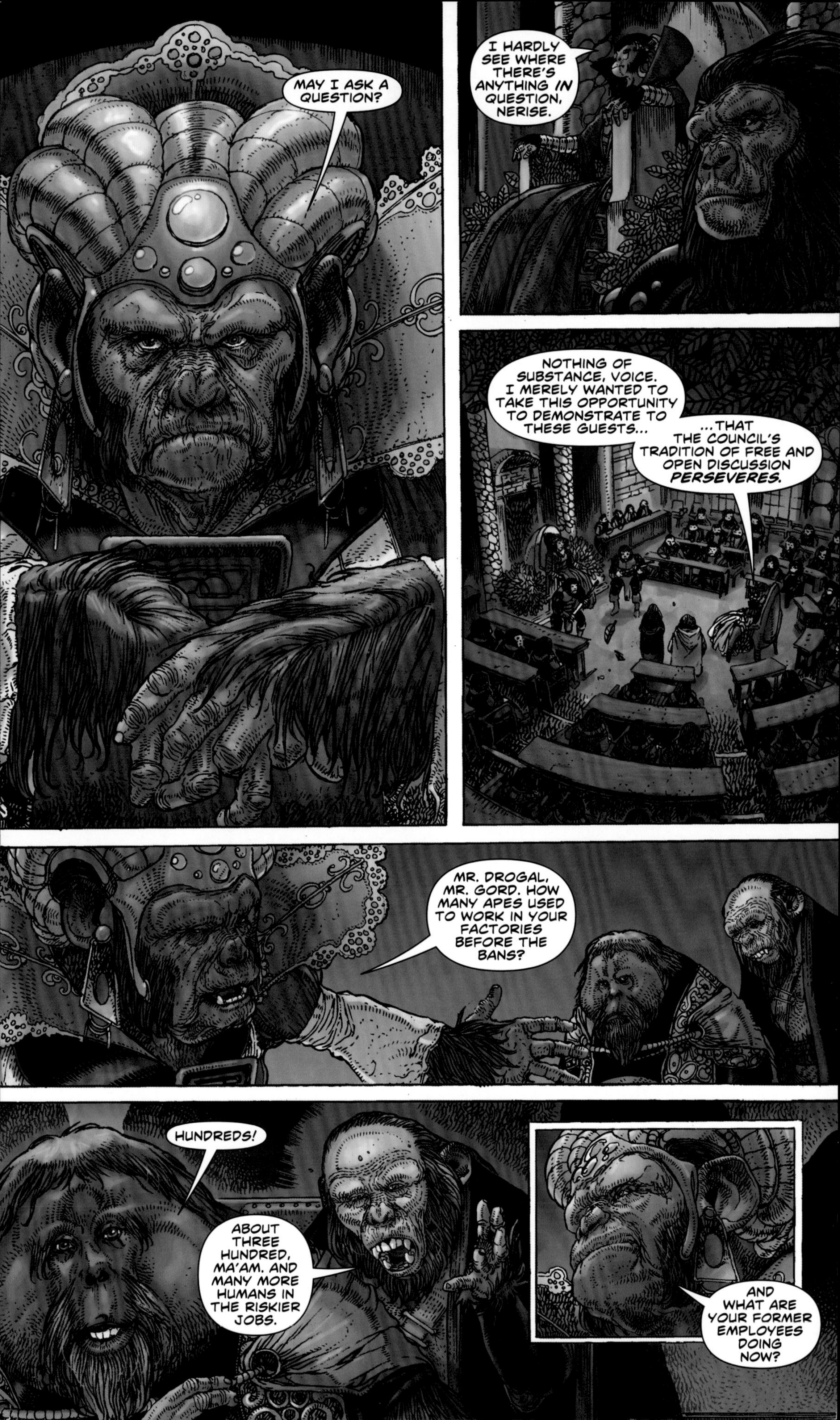
MAY I ASK A QUESTION?
I HARDLY SEE WHERE THERE'S ANYTHING *IN* QUESTION, NERISE.
NOTHING OF SUBSTANCE, VOICE. I MERELY WANTED TO TAKE THIS OPPORTUNITY TO DEMONSTRATE TO THESE GUESTS...
...THAT THE COUNCIL'S TRADITION OF FREE AND OPEN DISCUSSION *PERSEVERES.*
MR. DROGAL, MR. GORD. HOW MANY APES USED TO WORK IN YOUR FACTORIES BEFORE THE BANS?
HUNDREDS!
ABOUT THREE HUNDRED, MA'AM. AND MANY MORE HUMANS IN THE RISKIER JOBS.
AND WHAT ARE YOUR FORMER EMPLOYEES DOING NOW?

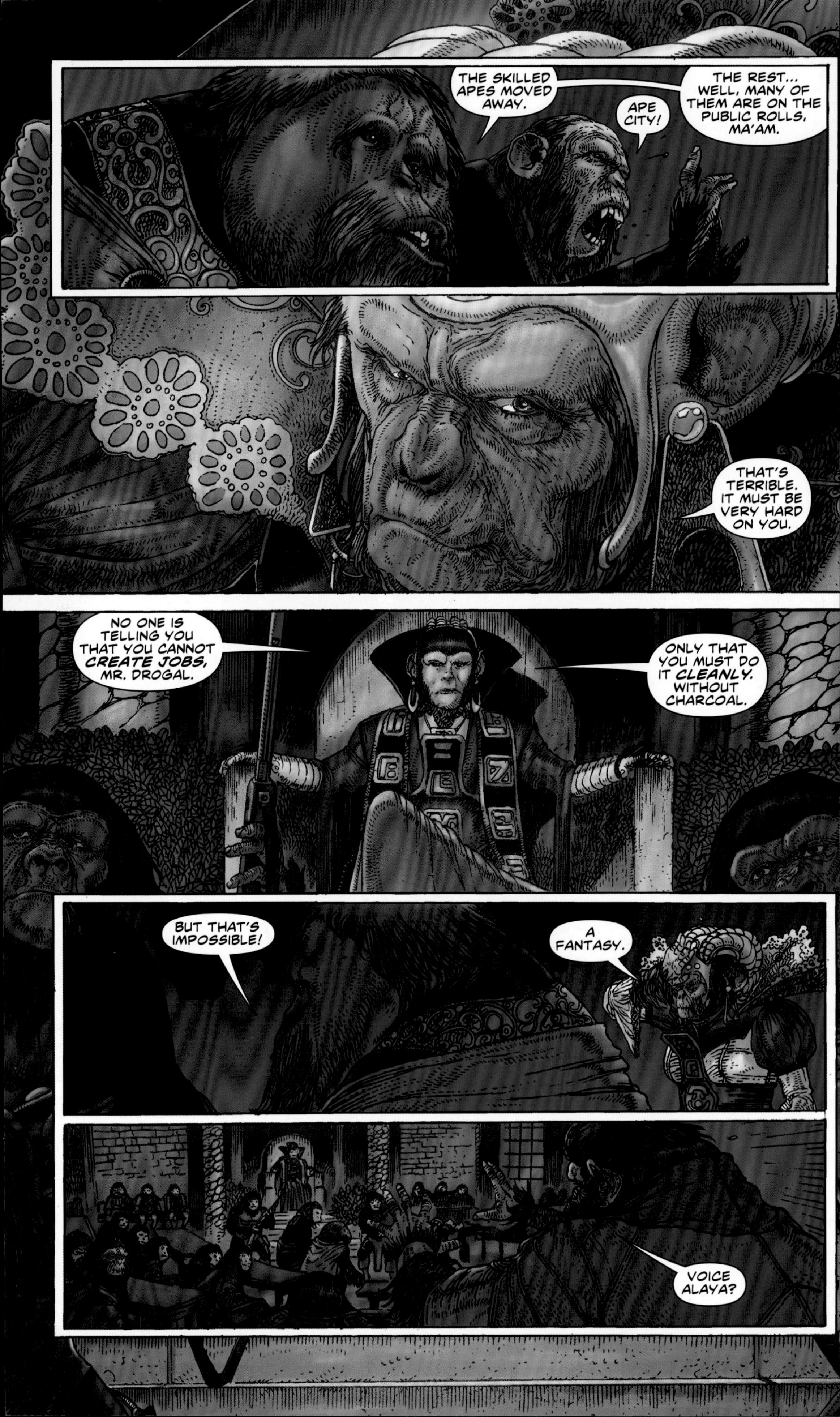
THE SKILLED APES MOVED AWAY.
APE CITY!
THE REST... WELL, MANY OF THEM ARE ON THE PUBLIC ROLLS, MA'AM.
THAT'S TERRIBLE. IT MUST BE VERY HARD ON YOU.
NO ONE IS TELLING YOU THAT YOU CANNOT *CREATE JOBS,* MR. DROGAL.
ONLY THAT YOU MUST DO IT *CLEANLY.* WITHOUT CHARCOAL.
BUT THAT'S IMPOSSIBLE!
A FANTASY.
VOICE ALAYA?

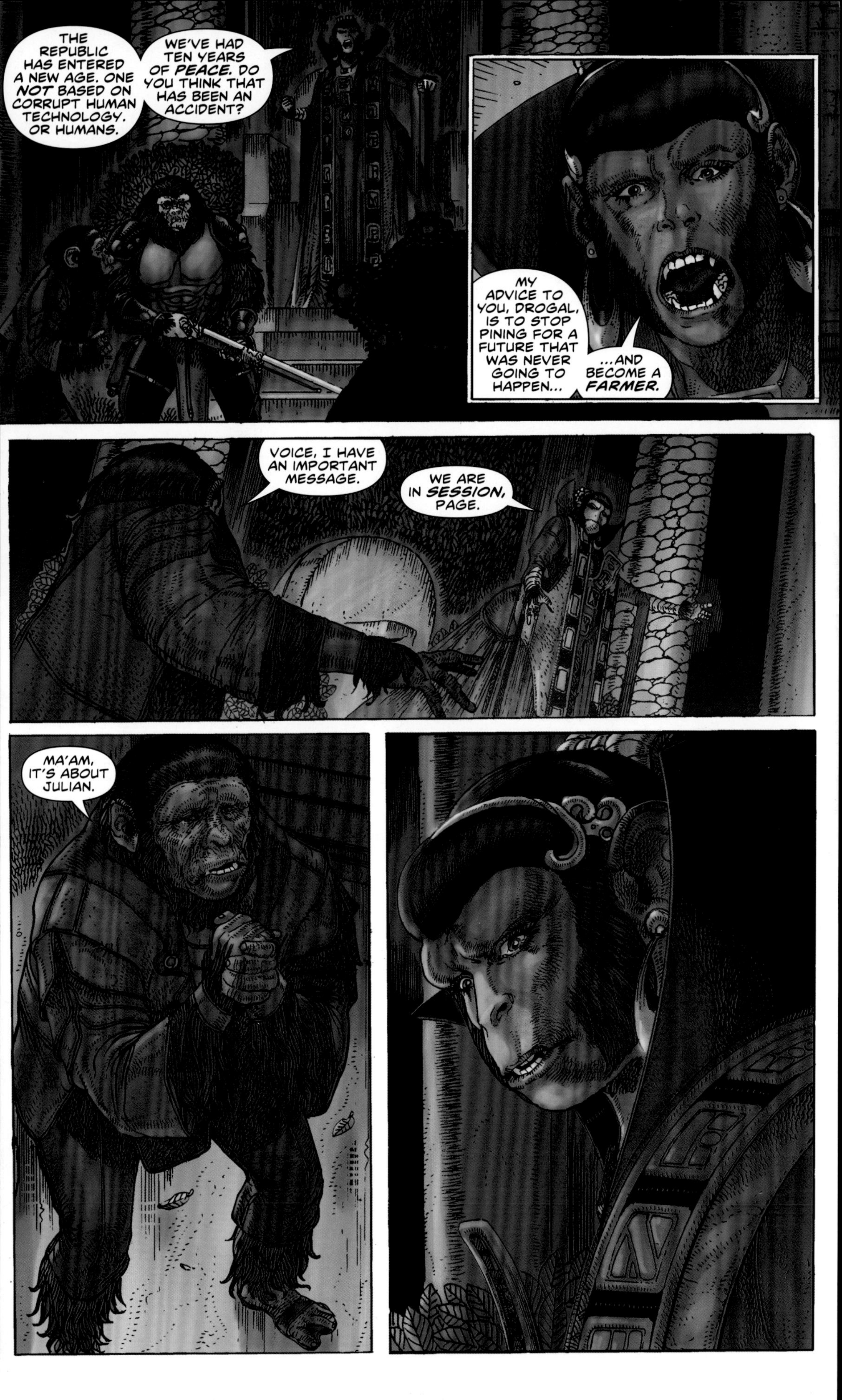
THE REPUBLIC HAS ENTERED A NEW AGE. ONE NOT BASED ON CORRUPT HUMAN TECHNOLOGY. OR HUMANS.
WE'VE HAD TEN YEARS OF PEACE. DO YOU THINK THAT HAS BEEN AN ACCIDENT?
MY ADVICE TO YOU, DROGAL, IS TO STOP PINING FOR A FUTURE THAT WAS NEVER GOING TO HAPPEN...
...AND BECOME A FARMER.
VOICE, I HAVE AN IMPORTANT MESSAGE.
WE ARE IN SESSION, PAGE.
MA'AM, IT'S ABOUT JULIAN.

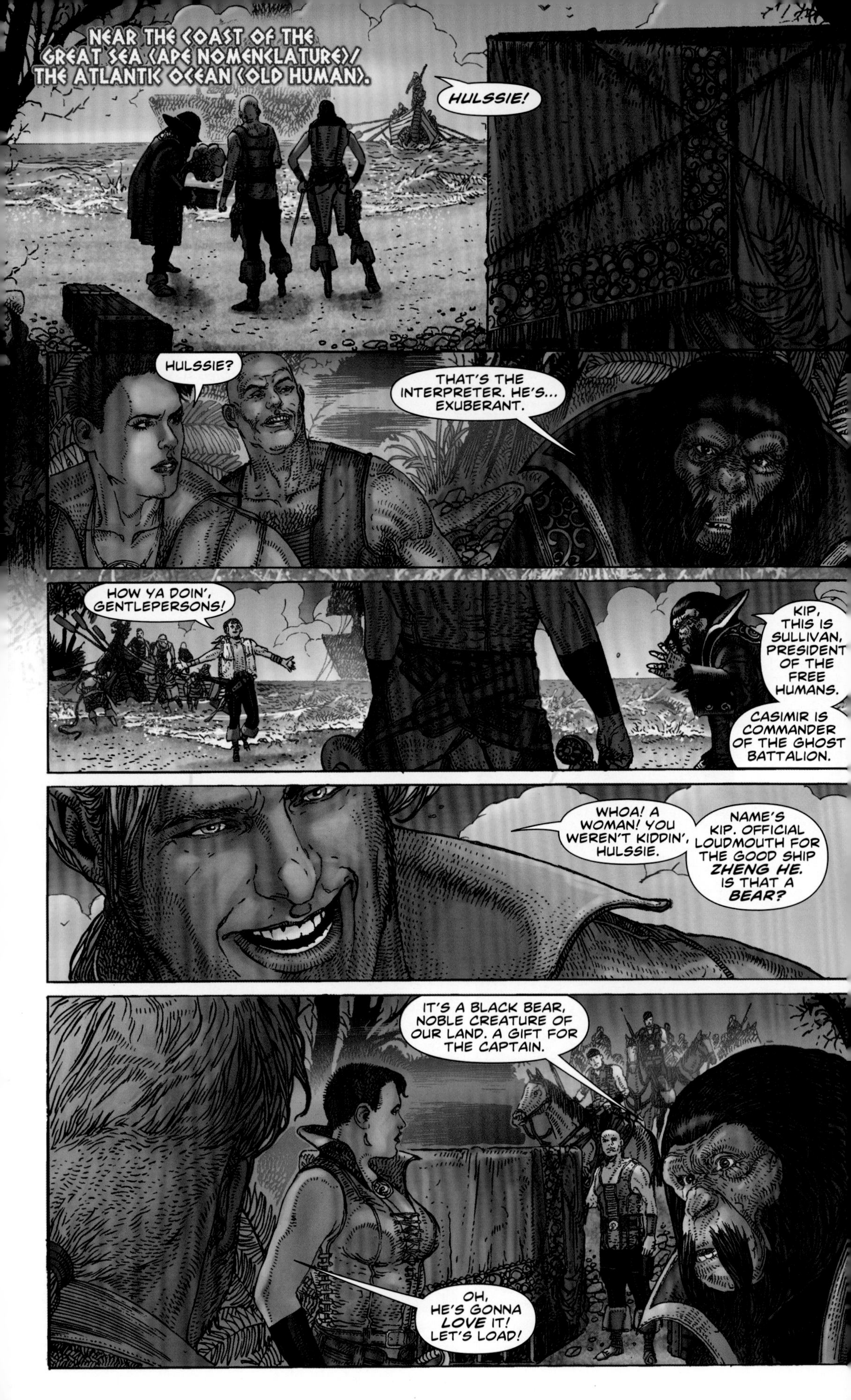
NEAR THE COAST OF THE GREAT SEA (APE NOMENCLATURE)/ THE ATLANTIC OCEAN (OLD HUMAN).
HULSSIE!
HULSSIE?
THAT'S THE INTERPRETER. HE'S... EXUBERANT.
HOW YA DOIN', GENTLEPERSONS!
KIP, THIS IS SULLIVAN, PRESIDENT OF THE FREE HUMANS.
CASIMIR IS COMMANDER OF THE GHOST BATTALION.
WHOA! A WOMAN! YOU WEREN'T KIDDIN', HULSSIE.
NAME'S KIP. OFFICIAL LOUDMOUTH FOR THE GOOD SHIP *ZHENG HE.* IS THAT A *BEAR?*
IT'S A BLACK BEAR, NOBLE CREATURE OF OUR LAND. A GIFT FOR THE CAPTAIN.
OH, HE'S GONNA *LOVE* IT! LET'S LOAD!

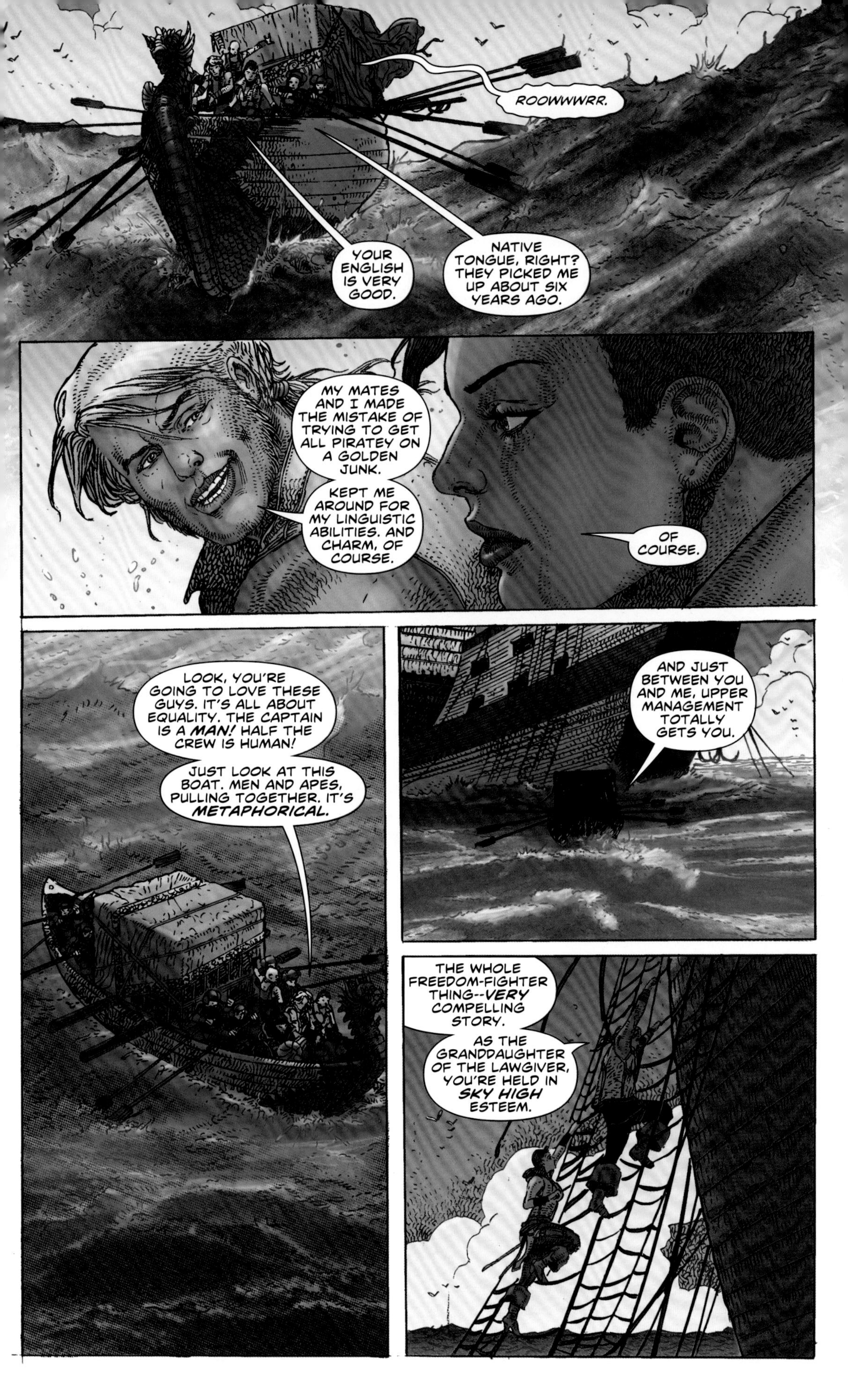
ROOWWWRR.
YOUR ENGLISH IS VERY GOOD.
NATIVE TONGUE, RIGHT? THEY PICKED ME UP ABOUT SIX YEARS AGO.
MY MATES AND I MADE THE MISTAKE OF TRYING TO GET ALL PIRATEY ON A GOLDEN JUNK.
KEPT ME AROUND FOR MY LINGUISTIC ABILITIES. AND CHARM, OF COURSE.
OF COURSE.
LOOK, YOU'RE GOING TO LOVE THESE GUYS. IT'S ALL ABOUT EQUALITY. THE CAPTAIN IS A MAN! HALF THE CREW IS HUMAN!
JUST LOOK AT THIS BOAT. MEN AND APES, PULLING TOGETHER. IT'S METAPHORICAL.
AND JUST BETWEEN YOU AND ME, UPPER MANAGEMENT TOTALLY GETS YOU.
THE WHOLE FREEDOM-FIGHTER THING--VERY COMPELLING STORY.
AS THE GRANDDAUGHTER OF THE LAWGIVER, YOU'RE HELD IN SKY HIGH ESTEEM.

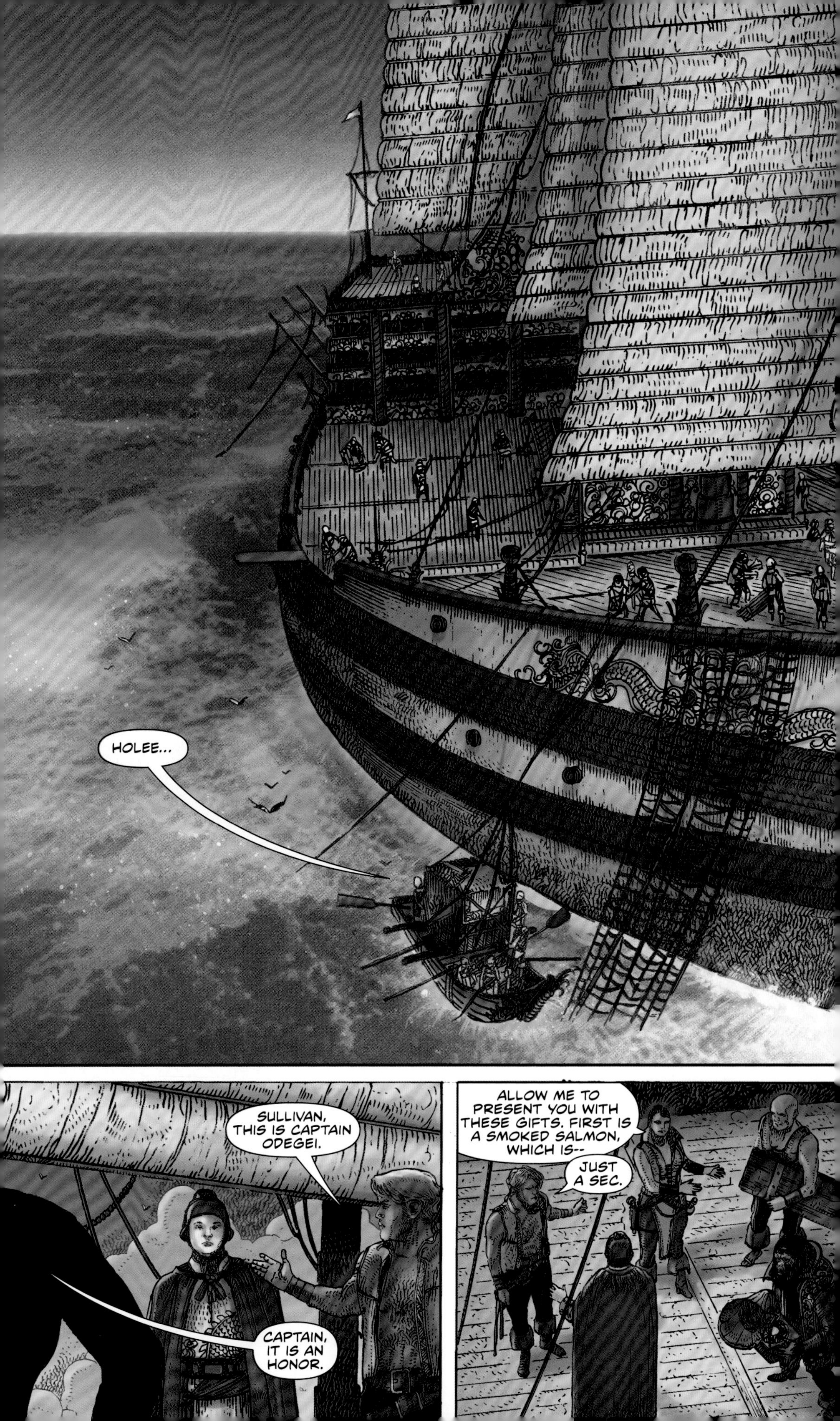
HOLEE...
SULLIVAN, THIS IS CAPTAIN ODEGEI.
CAPTAIN, IT IS AN HONOR.
ALLOW ME TO PRESENT YOU WITH THESE GIFTS. FIRST IS A SMOKED SALMON, WHICH IS--
JUST A SEC.

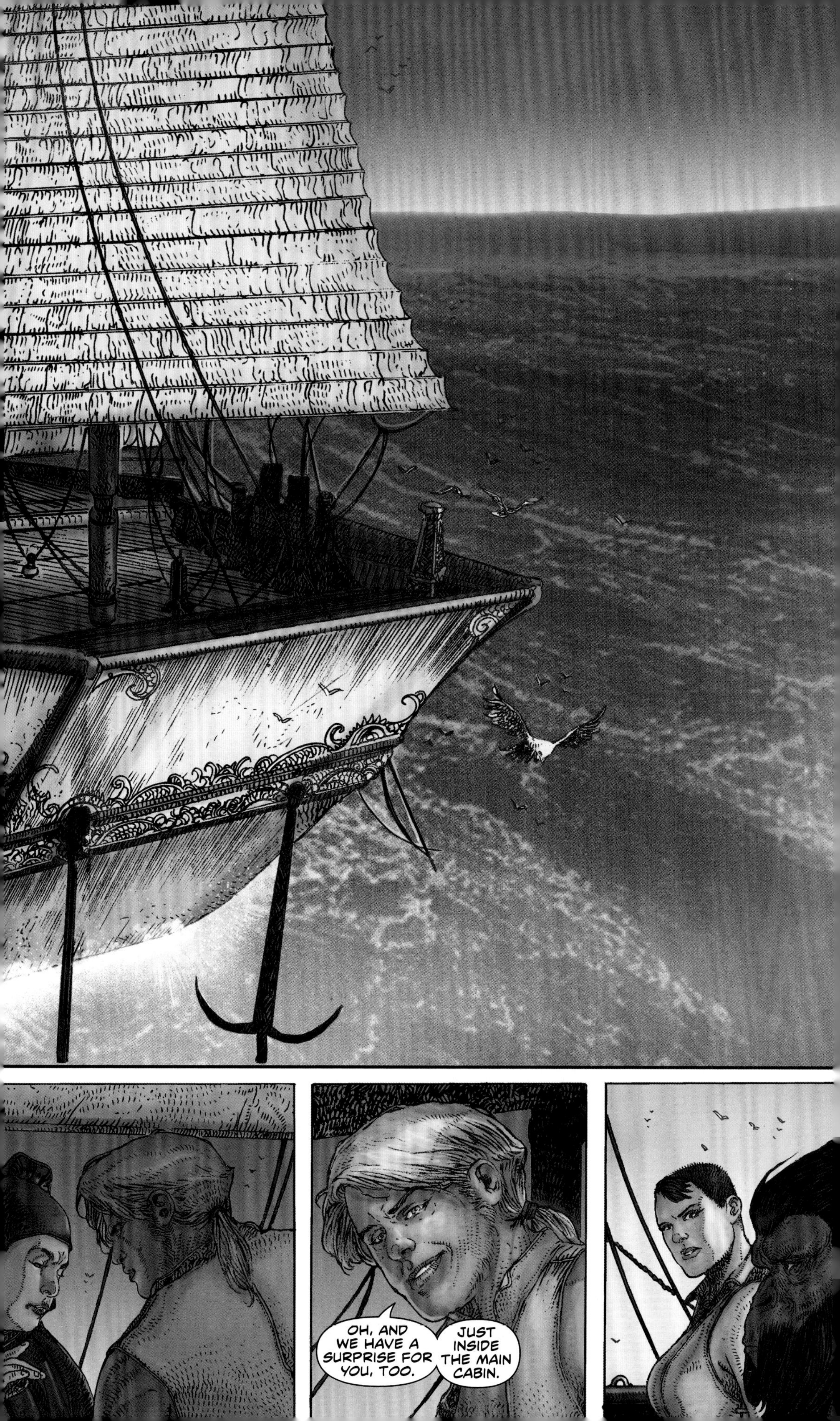
OH, AND WE HAVE A SURPRISE FOR YOU, TOO.
JUST INSIDE THE MAIN CABIN.

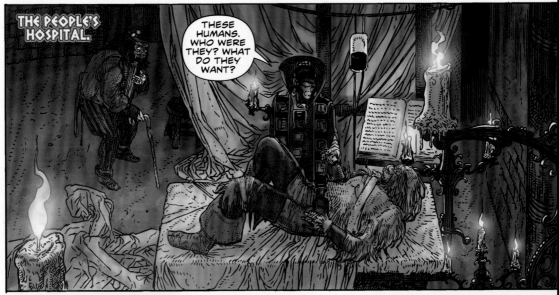

THESE HUMANS. WHO WERE THEY? WHAT DO THEY WANT?

LOOKED LIKE BEGGARS. BUT...TOO ORGANIZED.

MA'AM, YOU MUST LET HIM REST. WE JUST CAME OUT OF SURGERY. I CAN'T BELIEVE HE'S CONSCIOUS.

THE HALF MAN.

HA! YOU SEE, MA'AM? HE'S BABBLING.

JUST BECAUSE WE HAVEN'T CAUGHT HIM, DR. BARAN, DOES NOT MEAN HE'S A MYTH.

BUT WE RAZED SKINTOWN TO THE GROUND. THE ONLY HUMANS LEFT IN THE REPUBLIC ARE LICENSED HOUSE SERVANTS, OR IN THE CAMPS.

RIGHT?

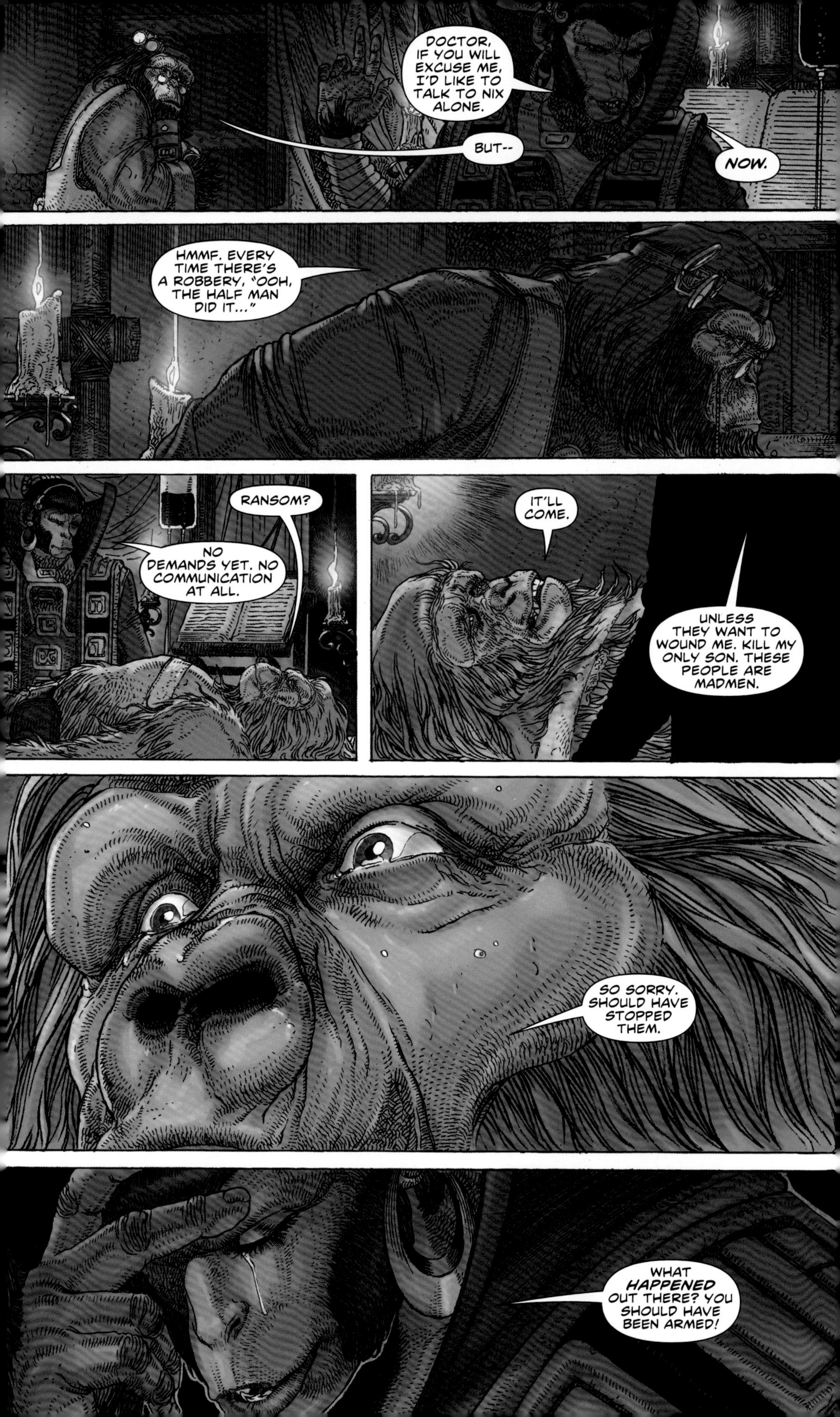
DOCTOR, IF YOU WILL EXCUSE ME, I'D LIKE TO TALK TO NIX ALONE.
BUT--
NOW.
HMMF. EVERY TIME THERE'S A ROBBERY, "OOH, THE HALF MAN DID IT..."
RANSOM?
NO DEMANDS YET. NO COMMUNICATION AT ALL.
IT'LL COME.
UNLESS THEY WANT TO WOUND ME. KILL MY ONLY SON. THESE PEOPLE ARE MADMEN.
SO SORRY. SHOULD HAVE STOPPED THEM.
WHAT HAPPENED OUT THERE? YOU SHOULD HAVE BEEN ARMED!

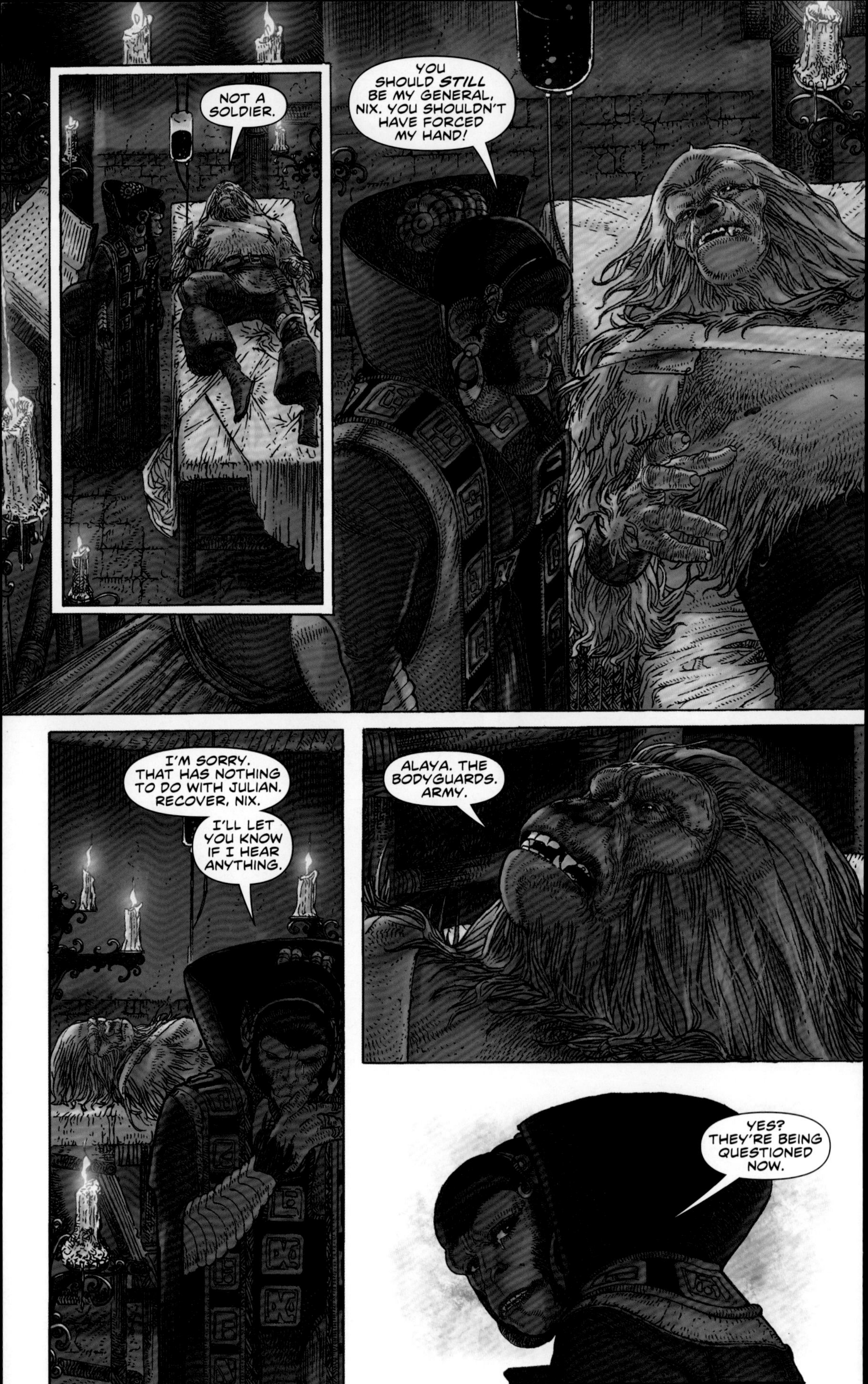
NOT A SOLDIER.
YOU SHOULD STILL BE MY GENERAL, NIX. YOU SHOULDN'T HAVE FORCED MY HAND!
I'M SORRY. THAT HAS NOTHING TO DO WITH JULIAN. RECOVER, NIX.
I'LL LET YOU KNOW IF I HEAR ANYTHING.
ALAYA. THE BODYGUARDS. ARMY.
YES? THEY'RE BEING QUESTIONED NOW.

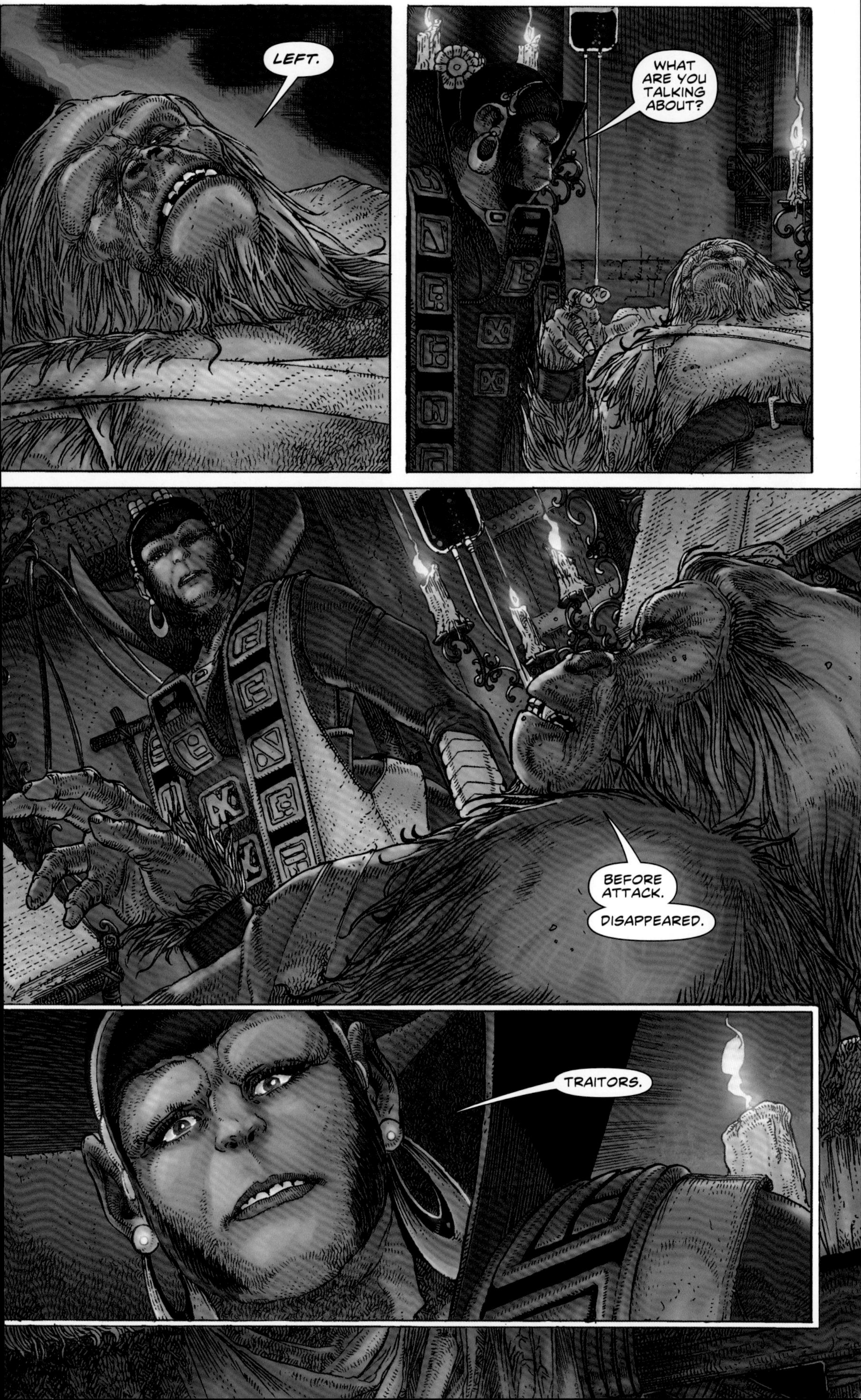
LEFT.
WHAT ARE YOU TALKING ABOUT?
BEFORE ATTACK.
DISAPPEARED.
TRAITORS.

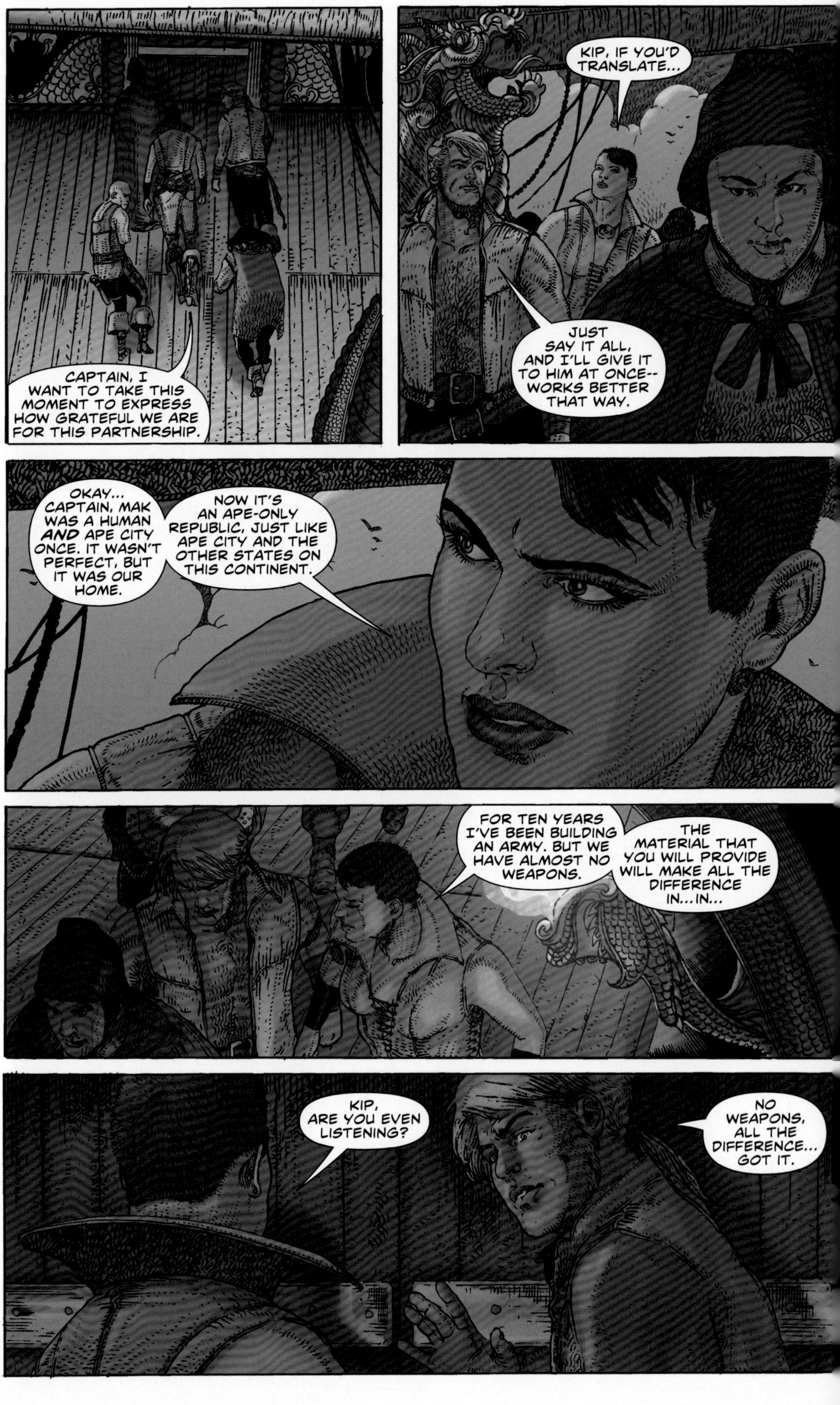
CAPTAIN, I WANT TO TAKE THIS MOMENT TO EXPRESS HOW GRATEFUL WE ARE FOR THIS PARTNERSHIP.
KIP, IF YOU'D TRANSLATE...
JUST SAY IT ALL, AND I'LL GIVE IT TO HIM AT ONCE-- WORKS BETTER THAT WAY.
OKAY... CAPTAIN, MAK WAS A HUMAN AND APE CITY ONCE. IT WASN'T PERFECT, BUT IT WAS OUR HOME.
NOW IT'S AN APE-ONLY REPUBLIC, JUST LIKE APE CITY AND THE OTHER STATES ON THIS CONTINENT.
FOR TEN YEARS I'VE BEEN BUILDING AN ARMY. BUT WE HAVE ALMOST NO WEAPONS.
THE MATERIAL THAT YOU WILL PROVIDE WILL MAKE ALL THE DIFFERENCE IN... IN...
KIP, ARE YOU EVEN LISTENING?
NO WEAPONS, ALL THE DIFFERENCE... GOT IT.

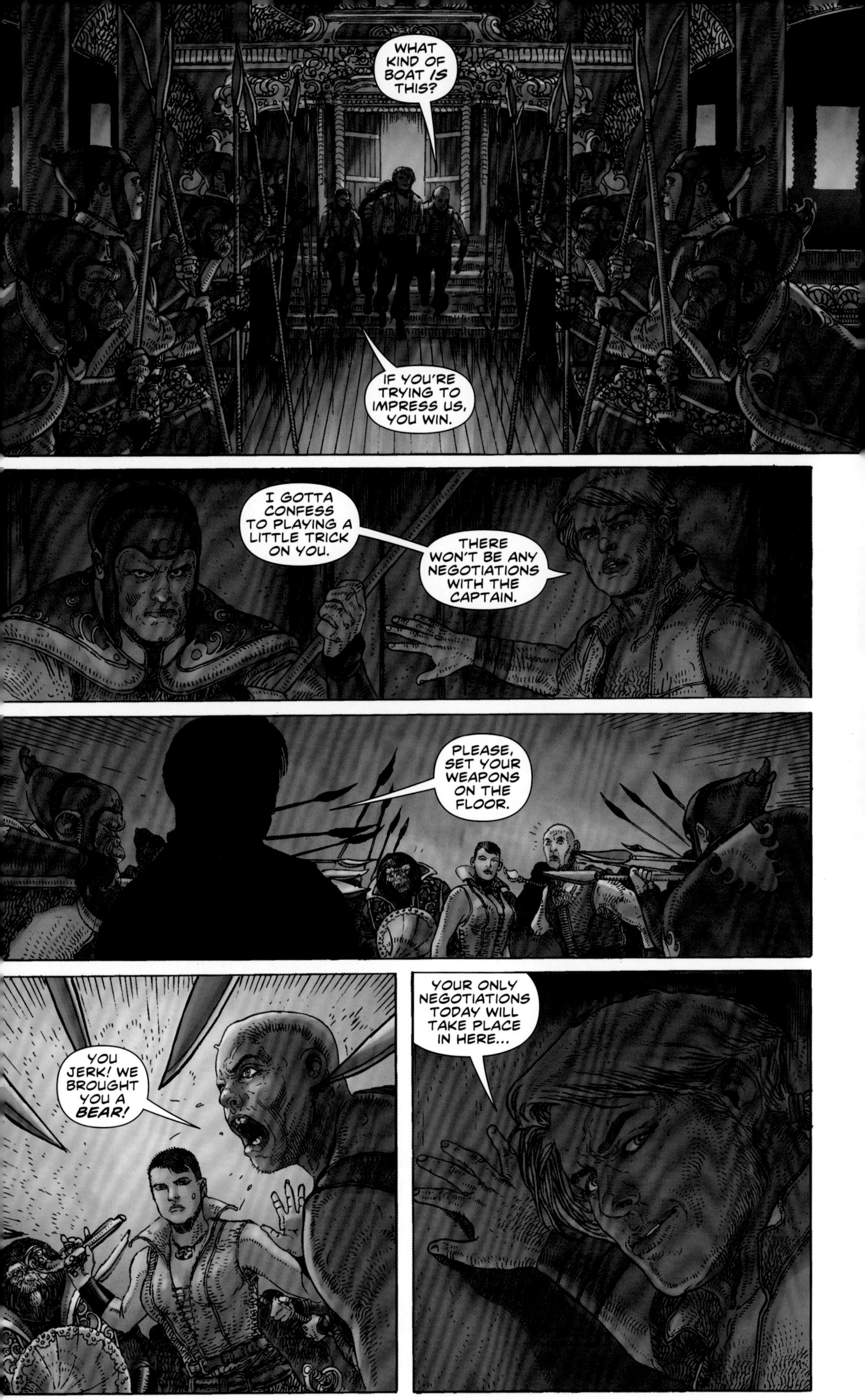
WHAT KIND OF BOAT *IS* THIS?
IF YOU'RE TRYING TO IMPRESS US, YOU WIN.
I GOTTA CONFESS TO PLAYING A LITTLE TRICK ON YOU.
THERE WON'T BE ANY NEGOTIATIONS WITH THE CAPTAIN.
PLEASE, SET YOUR WEAPONS ON THE FLOOR.
YOU JERK! WE BROUGHT YOU A *BEAR!*
YOUR ONLY NEGOTIATIONS TODAY WILL TAKE PLACE IN HERE...

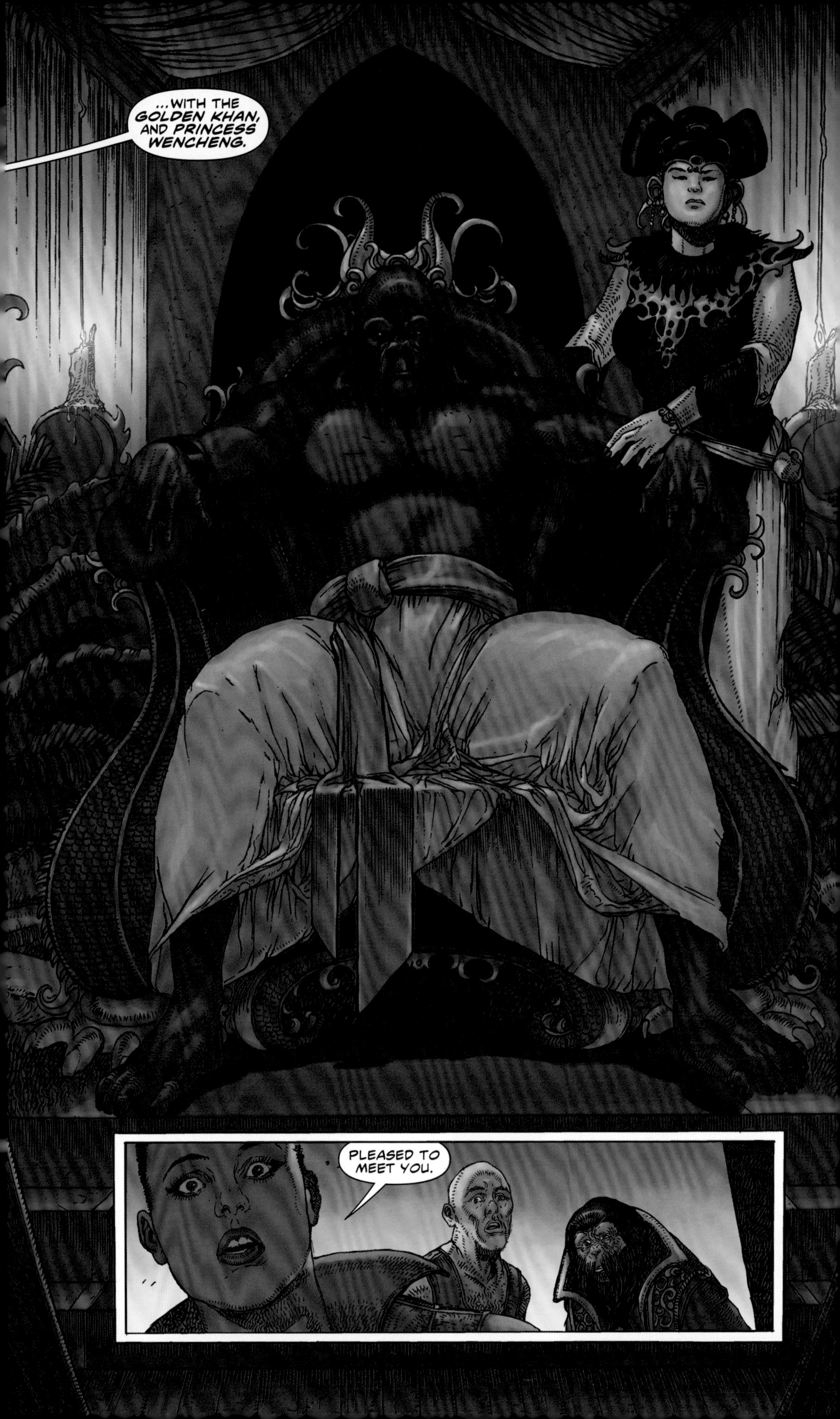
...WITH THE GOLDEN KHAN, AND PRINCESS WENCHENG.
PLEASED TO MEET YOU.

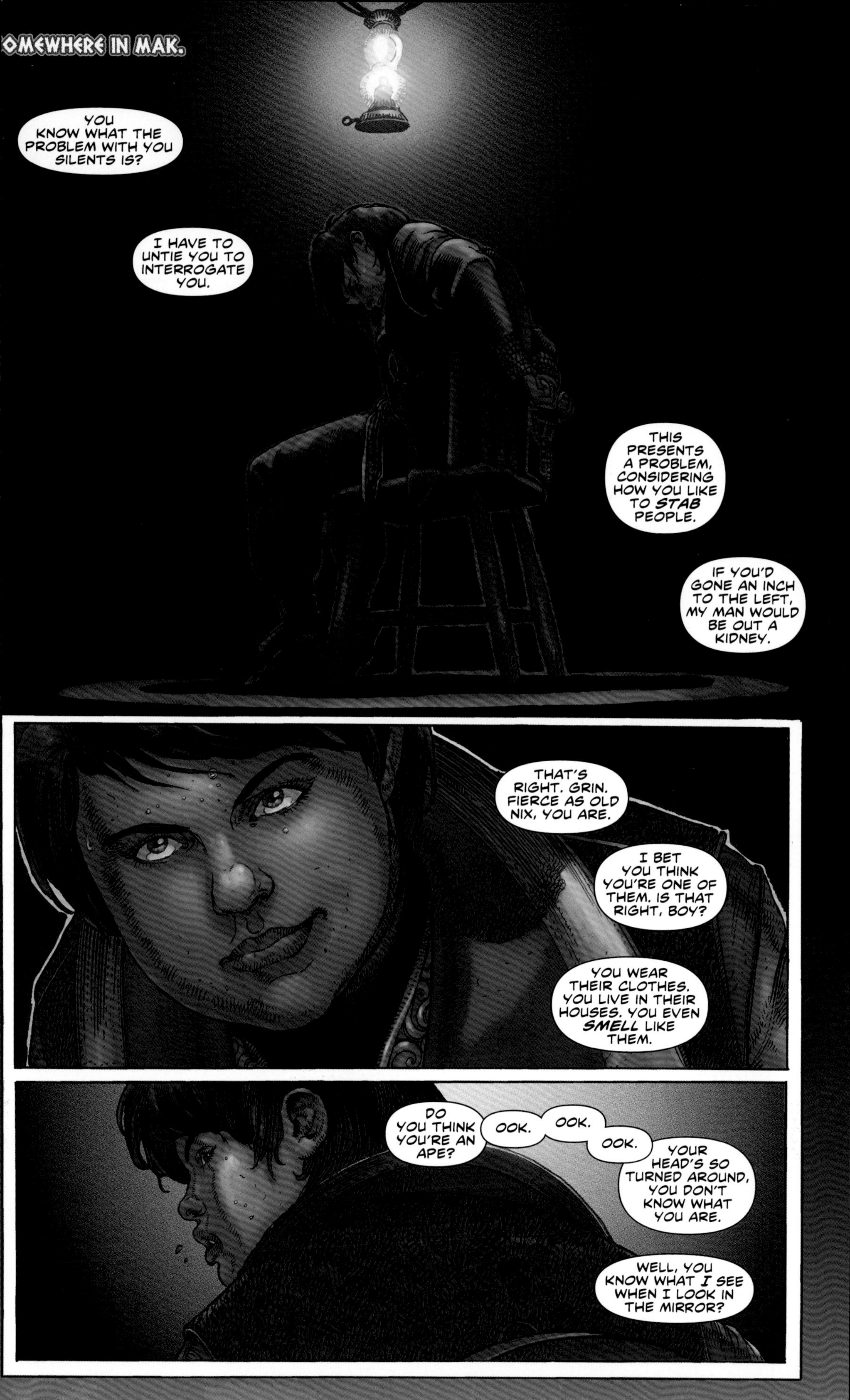
OMEWHERE IN MAK.
YOU KNOW WHAT THE PROBLEM WITH YOU SILENTS IS?
I HAVE TO UNTIE YOU TO INTERROGATE YOU.
THIS PRESENTS A PROBLEM, CONSIDERING HOW YOU LIKE TO STAB PEOPLE.
IF YOU'D GONE AN INCH TO THE LEFT, MY MAN WOULD BE OUT A KIDNEY.
THAT'S RIGHT. GRIN. FIERCE AS OLD NIX, YOU ARE.
I BET YOU THINK YOU'RE ONE OF THEM. IS THAT RIGHT, BOY?
YOU WEAR THEIR CLOTHES. YOU LIVE IN THEIR HOUSES. YOU EVEN SMELL LIKE THEM.
DO YOU THINK YOU'RE AN APE?
OOK.
OOK.
OOK.
YOUR HEAD'S SO TURNED AROUND, YOU DON'T KNOW WHAT YOU ARE.
WELL, YOU KNOW WHAT I SEE WHEN I LOOK IN THE MIRROR?

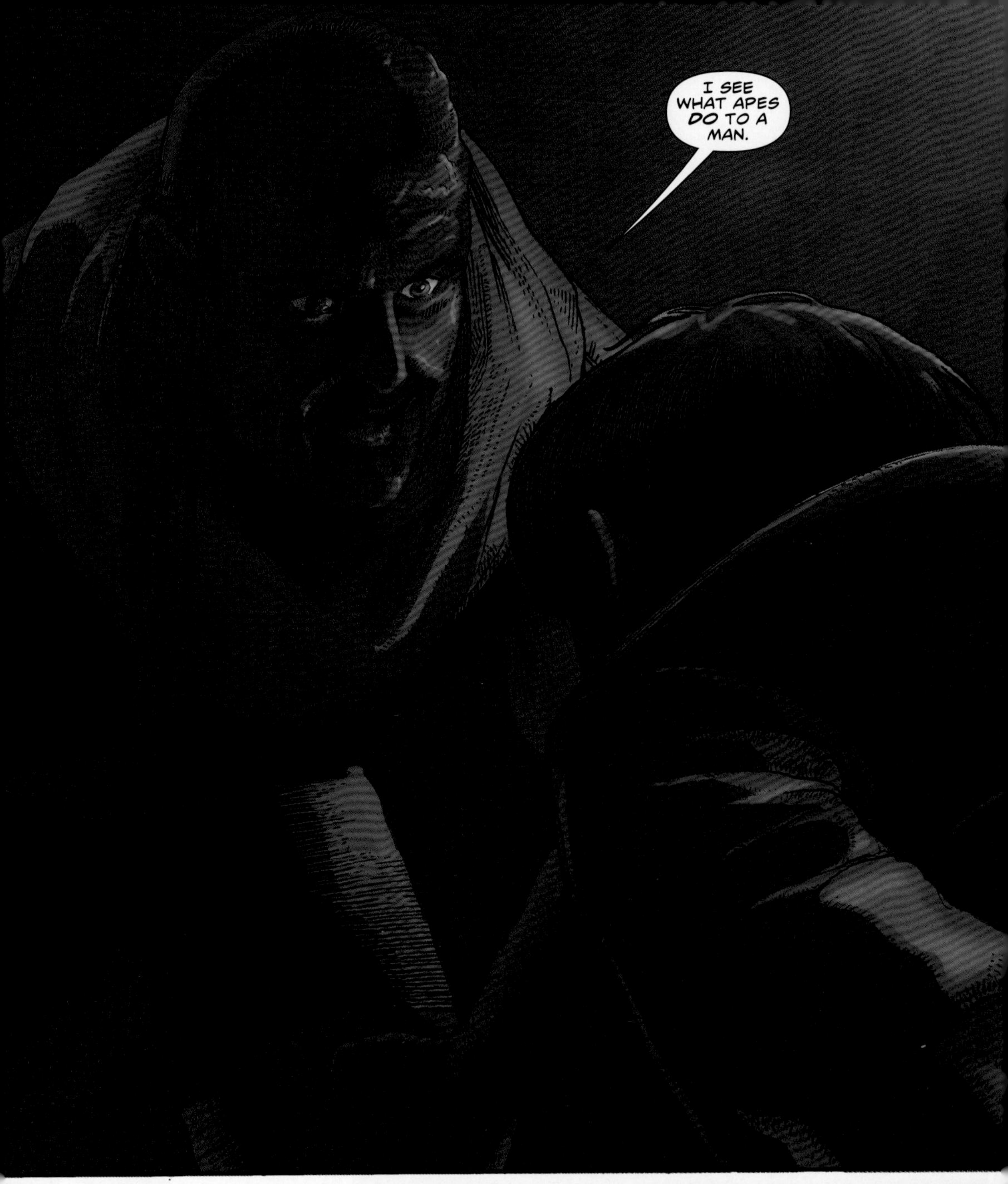
I SEE WHAT APES DO TO A MAN.

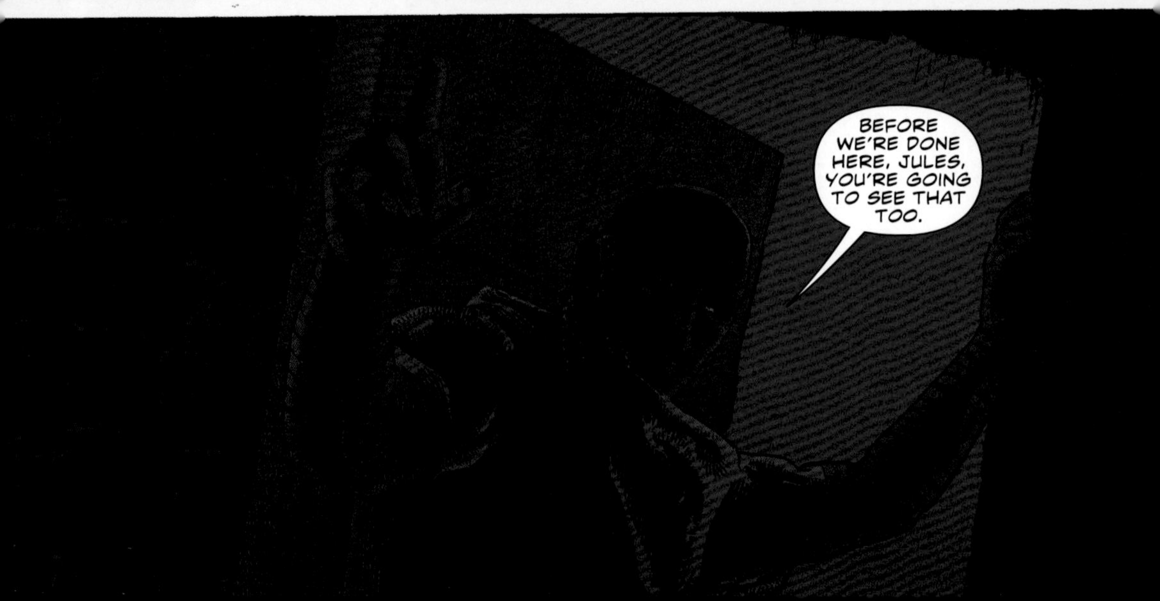
BEFORE WE'RE DONE HERE, JULES, YOU'RE GOING TO SEE THAT TOO.

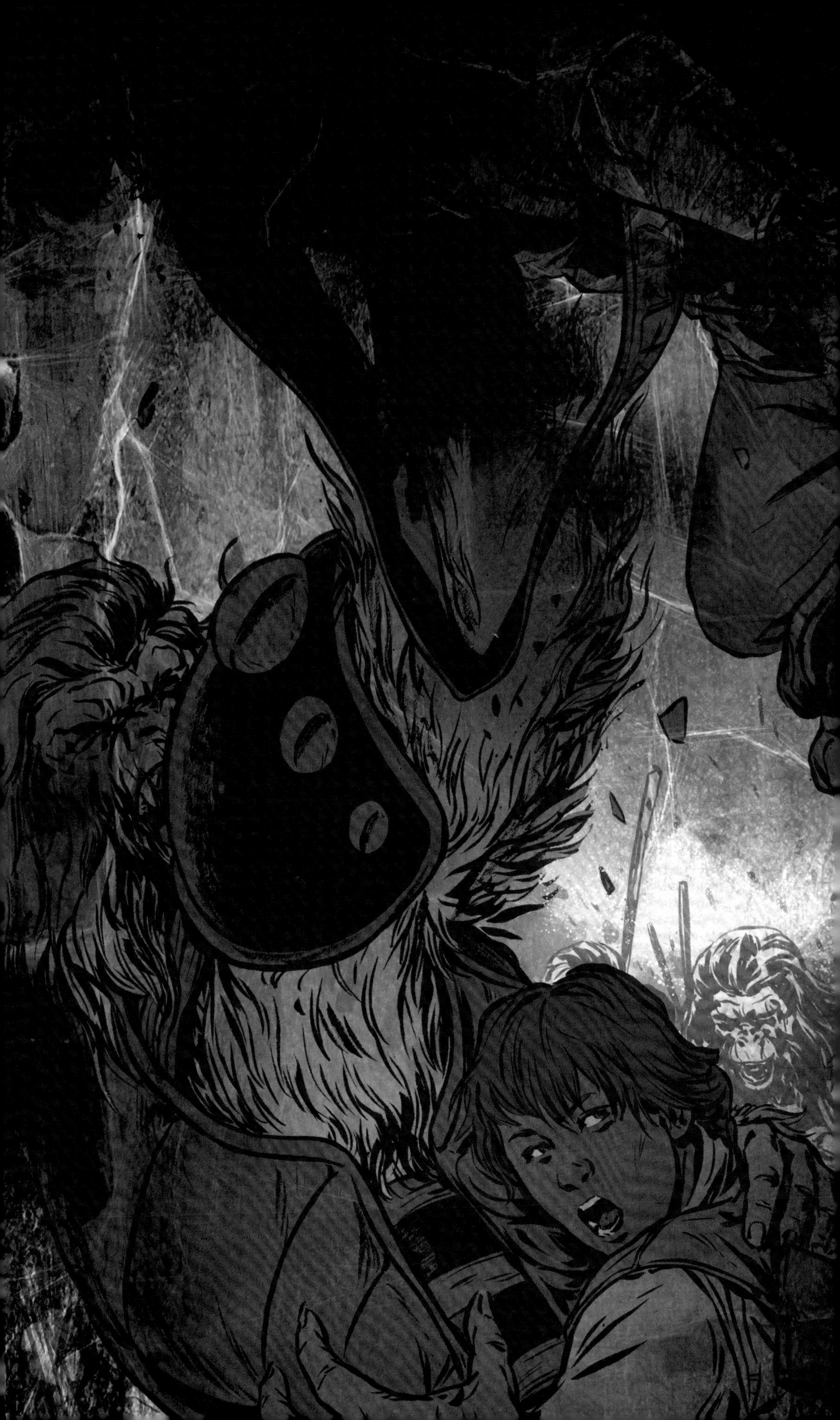

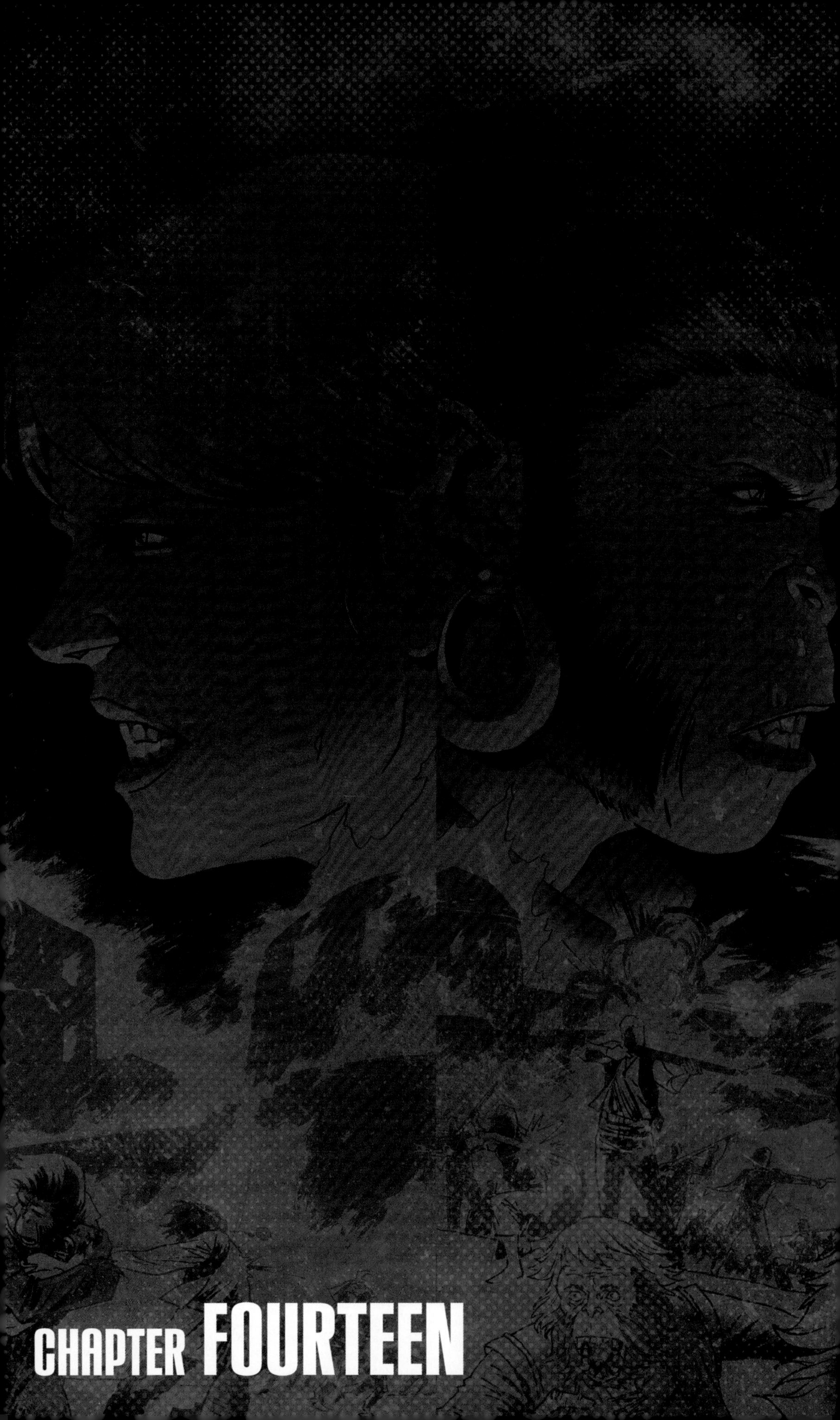
CHAPTER FOURTEEN

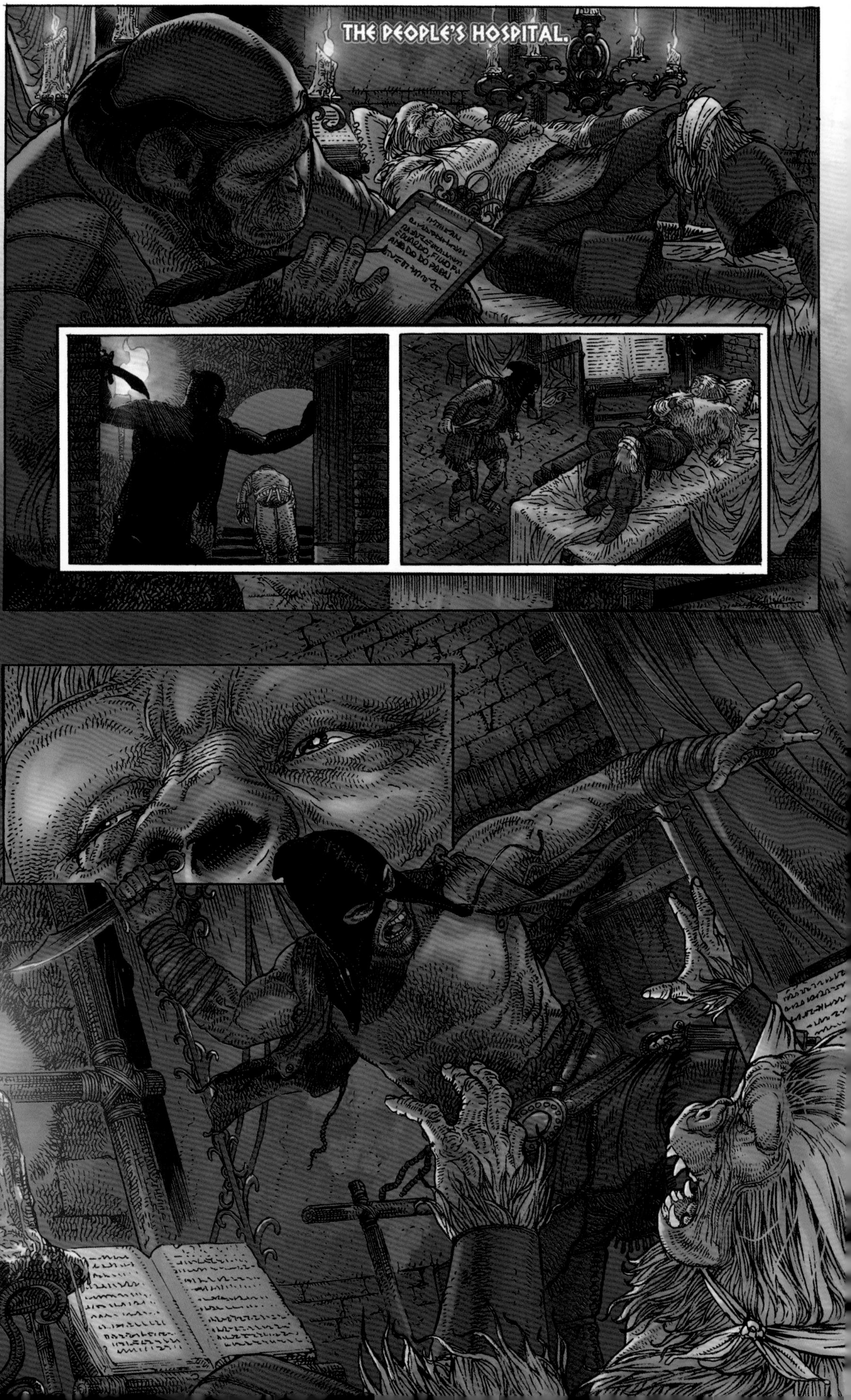
THE PEOPLE'S HOSPITAL.

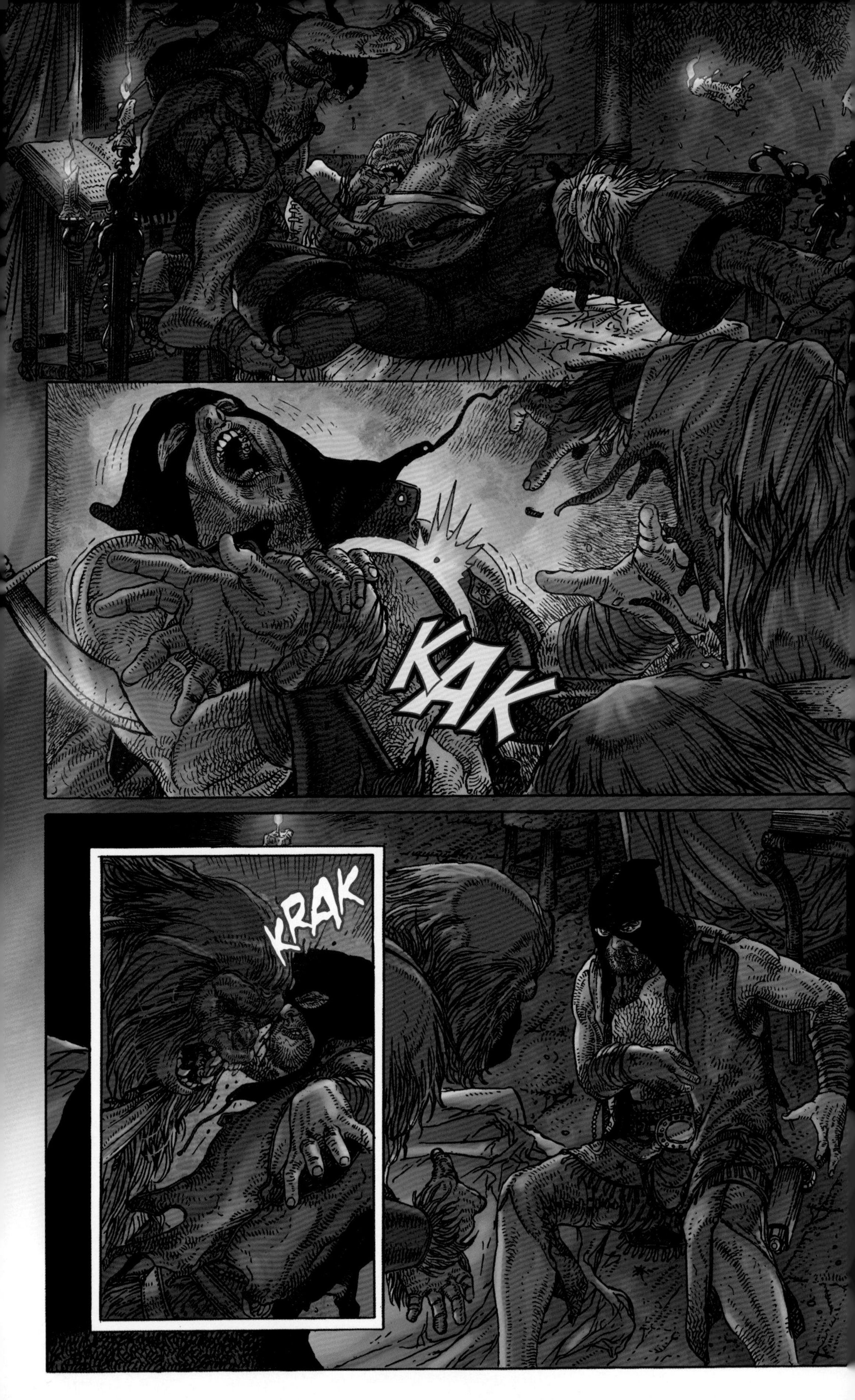
KAK
KRAK

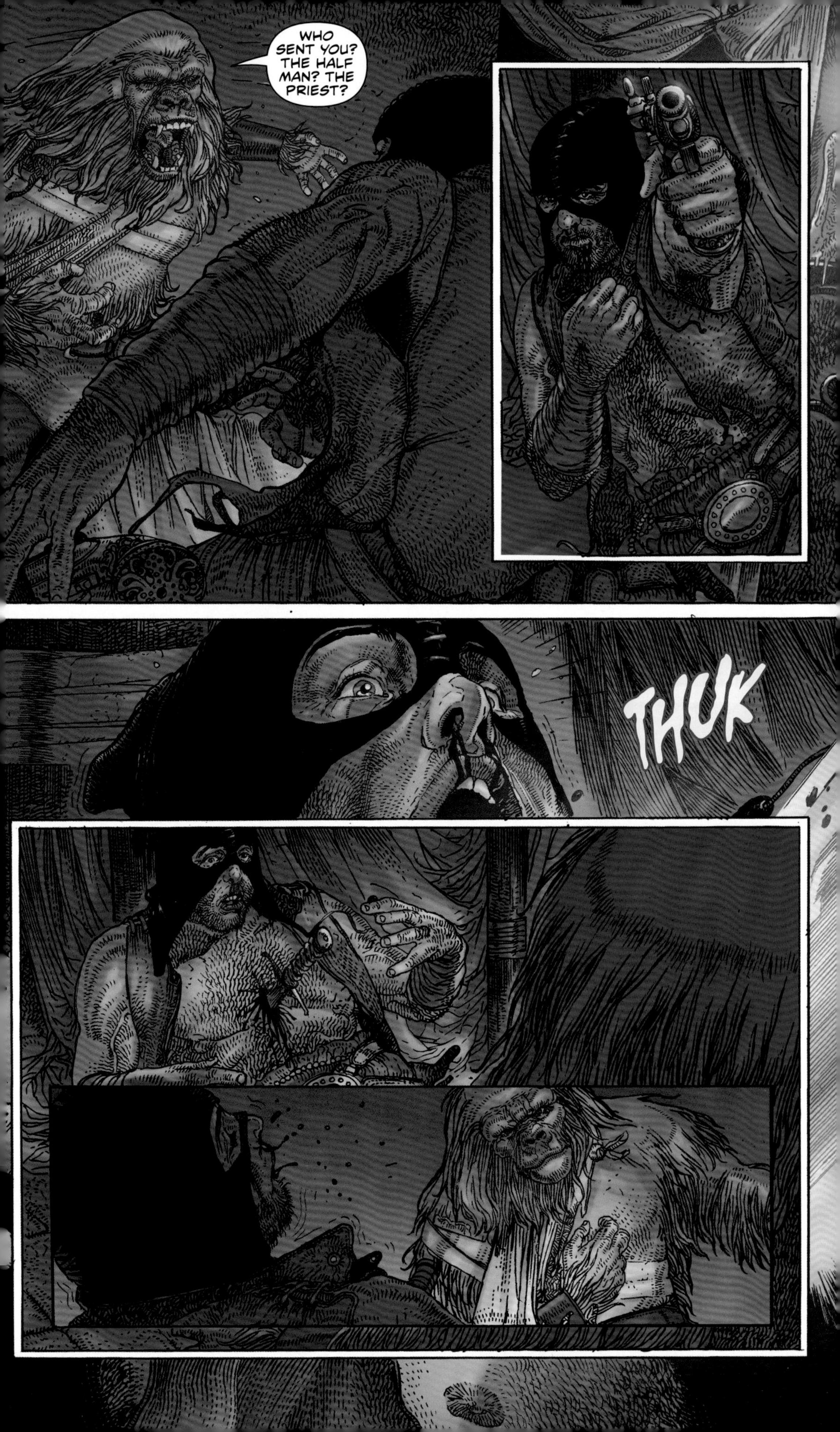
WHO SENT YOU? THE HALF MAN? THE PRIEST?
THUK

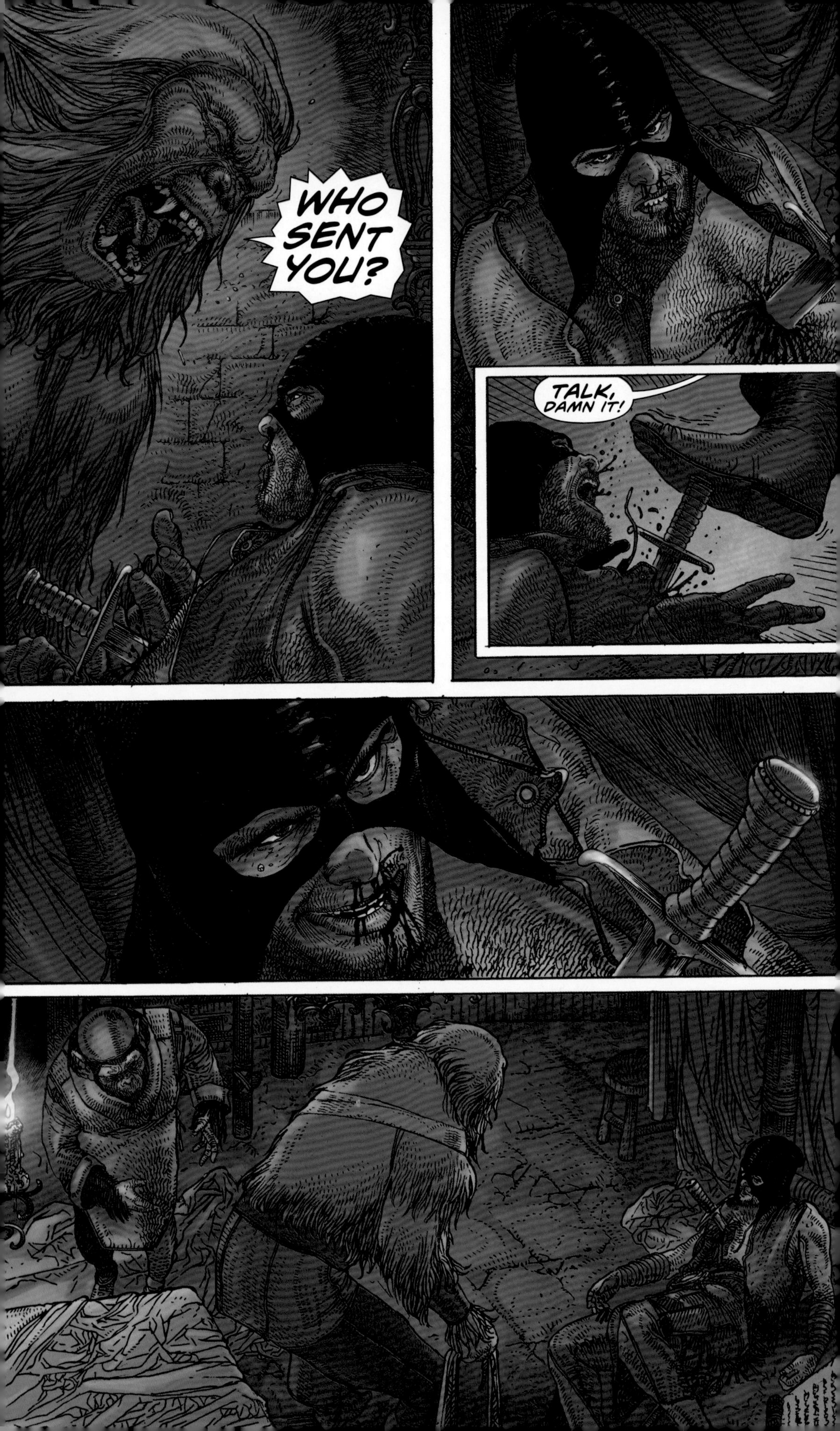
WHO SENT YOU?
TALK, DAMN IT!

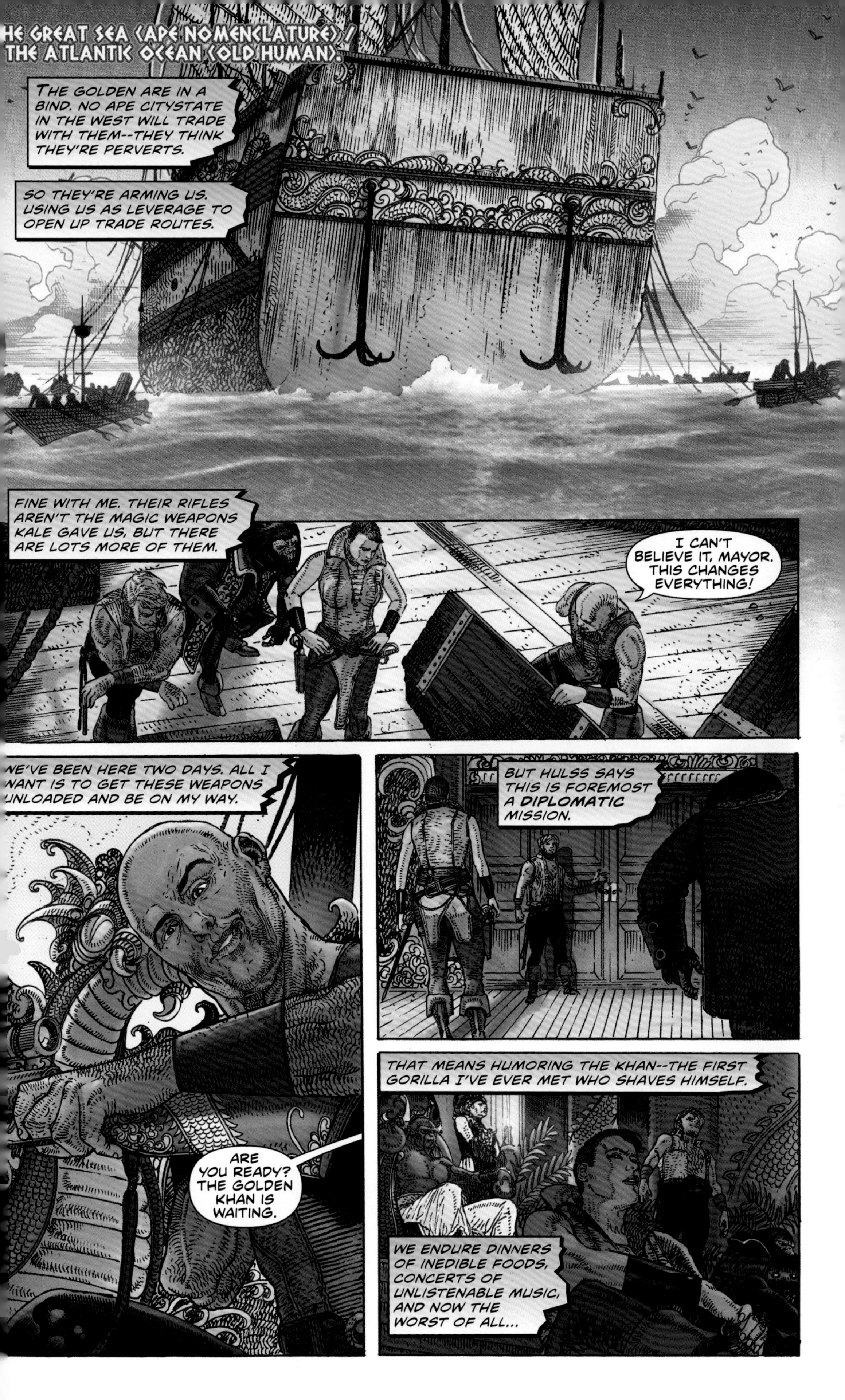
HE GREAT SEA (APE NOMENCLATURE) / THE ATLANTIC OCEAN (OLD HUMAN).
THE GOLDEN ARE IN A BIND. NO APE CITYSTATE IN THE WEST WILL TRADE WITH THEM--THEY THINK THEY'RE PERVERTS.
SO THEY'RE ARMING US. USING US AS LEVERAGE TO OPEN UP TRADE ROUTES.
FINE WITH ME. THEIR RIFLES AREN'T THE MAGIC WEAPONS KALE GAVE US, BUT THERE ARE LOTS MORE OF THEM.
I CAN'T BELIEVE IT, MAYOR. THIS CHANGES EVERYTHING!
WE'VE BEEN HERE TWO DAYS. ALL I WANT IS TO GET THESE WEAPONS UNLOADED AND BE ON MY WAY.
ARE YOU READY? THE GOLDEN KHAN IS WAITING.
BUT HULSS SAYS THIS IS FOREMOST A DIPLOMATIC MISSION.
THAT MEANS HUMORING THE KHAN--THE FIRST GORILLA I'VE EVER MET WHO SHAVES HIMSELF.
WE ENDURE DINNERS OF INEDIBLE FOODS, CONCERTS OF UNLISTENABLE MUSIC, AND NOW THE WORST OF ALL...

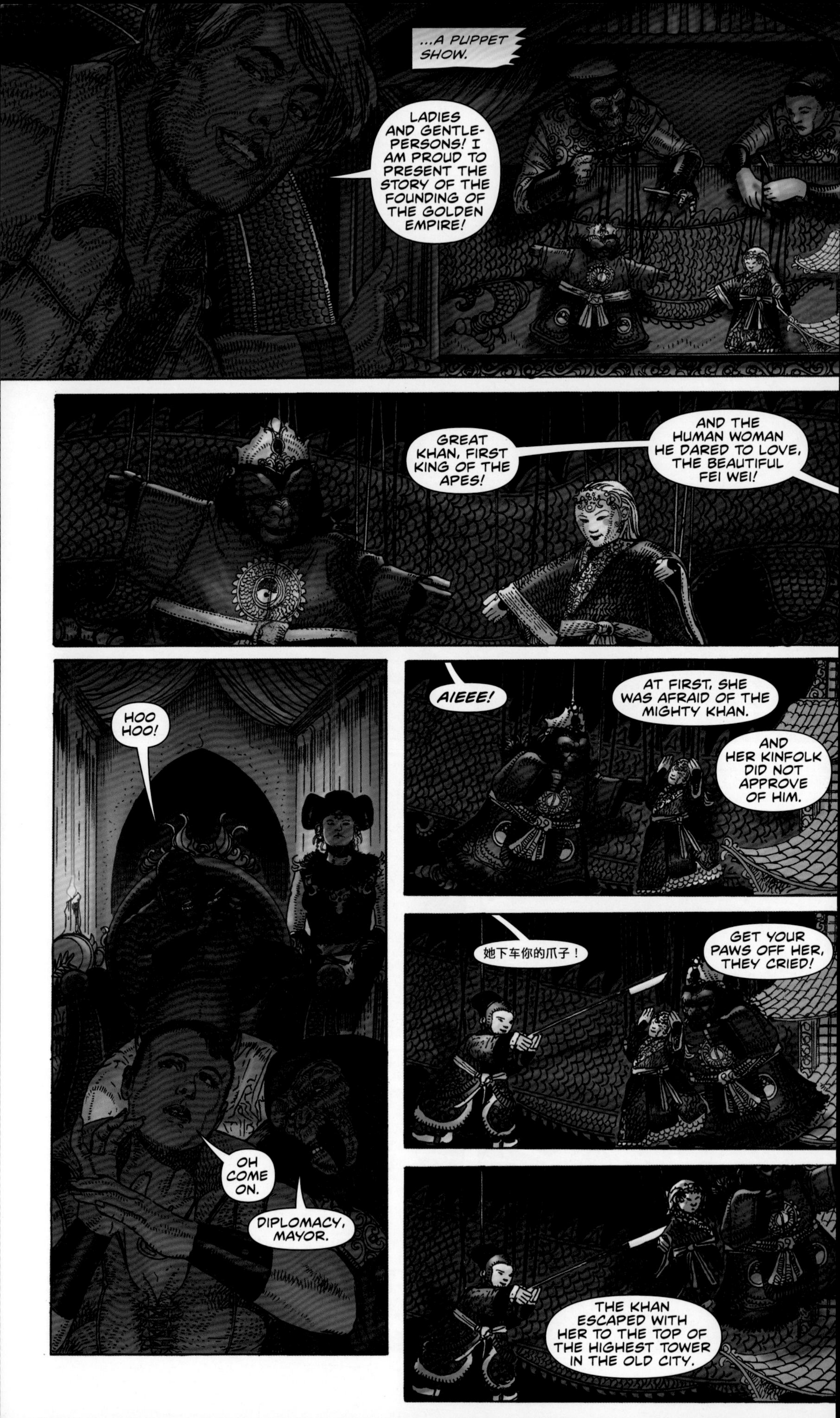
...A PUPPET SHOW.
LADIES AND GENTLE-PERSONS! I AM PROUD TO PRESENT THE STORY OF THE FOUNDING OF THE GOLDEN EMPIRE!
GREAT KHAN, FIRST KING OF THE APES!
AND THE HUMAN WOMAN HE DARED TO LOVE, THE BEAUTIFUL FEI WEI!
HOO HOO!
OH COME ON.
DIPLOMACY, MAYOR.
AIEEE!
AT FIRST, SHE WAS AFRAID OF THE MIGHTY KHAN.
AND HER KINFOLK DID NOT APPROVE OF HIM.
她下车你的爪子！
GET YOUR PAWS OFF HER, THEY CRIED!
THE KHAN ESCAPED WITH HER TO THE TOP OF THE HIGHEST TOWER IN THE OLD CITY.

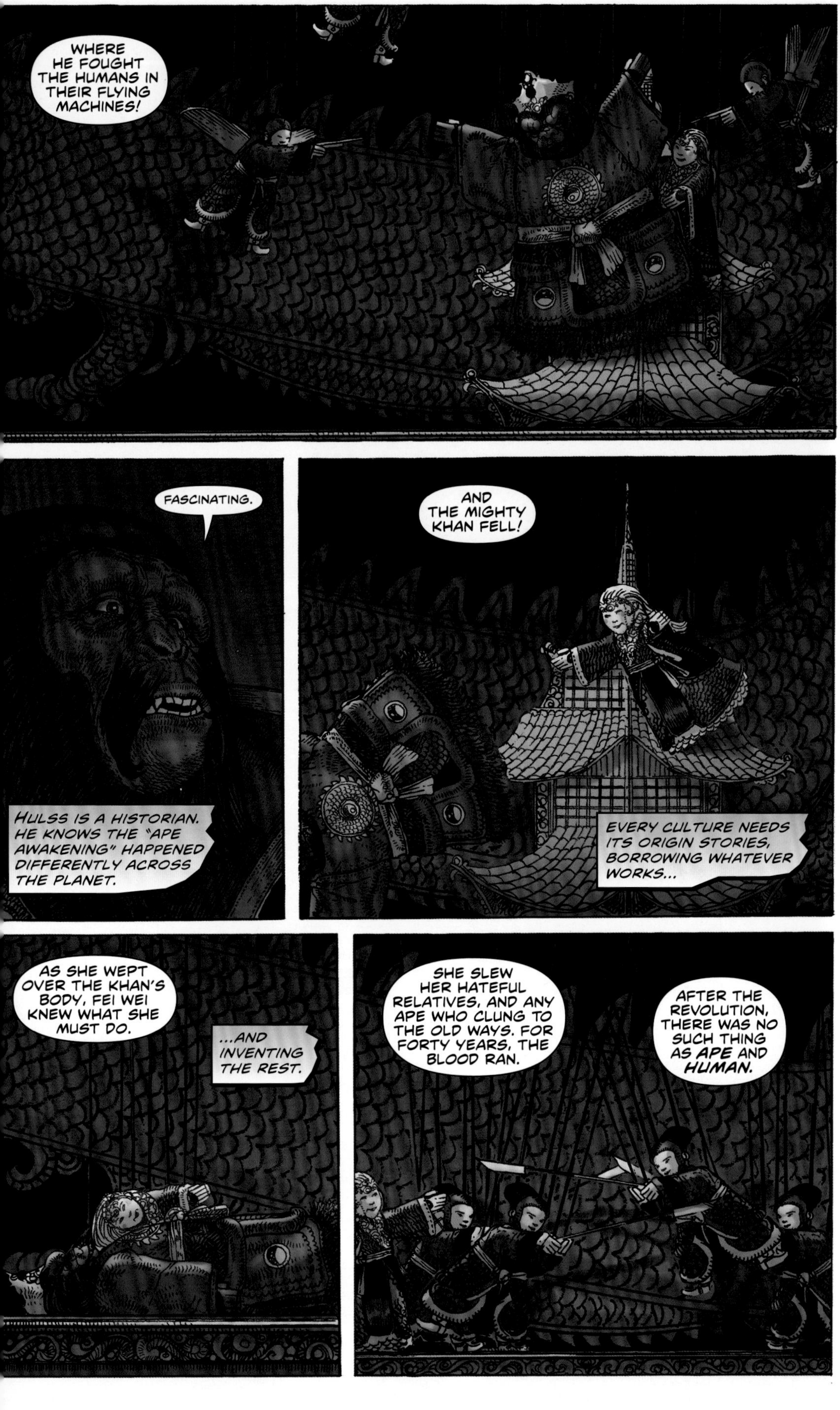

WHERE HE FOUGHT THE HUMANS IN THEIR FLYING MACHINES!
FASCINATING.
HULSS IS A HISTORIAN. HE KNOWS THE "APE AWAKENING" HAPPENED DIFFERENTLY ACROSS THE PLANET.
AND THE MIGHTY KHAN FELL!
EVERY CULTURE NEEDS ITS ORIGIN STORIES, BORROWING WHATEVER WORKS...
AS SHE WEPT OVER THE KHAN'S BODY, FEI WEI KNEW WHAT SHE MUST DO.
...AND INVENTING THE REST.
SHE SLEW HER HATEFUL RELATIVES, AND ANY APE WHO CLUNG TO THE OLD WAYS. FOR FORTY YEARS, THE BLOOD RAN.
AFTER THE REVOLUTION, THERE WAS NO SUCH THING AS APE AND HUMAN.

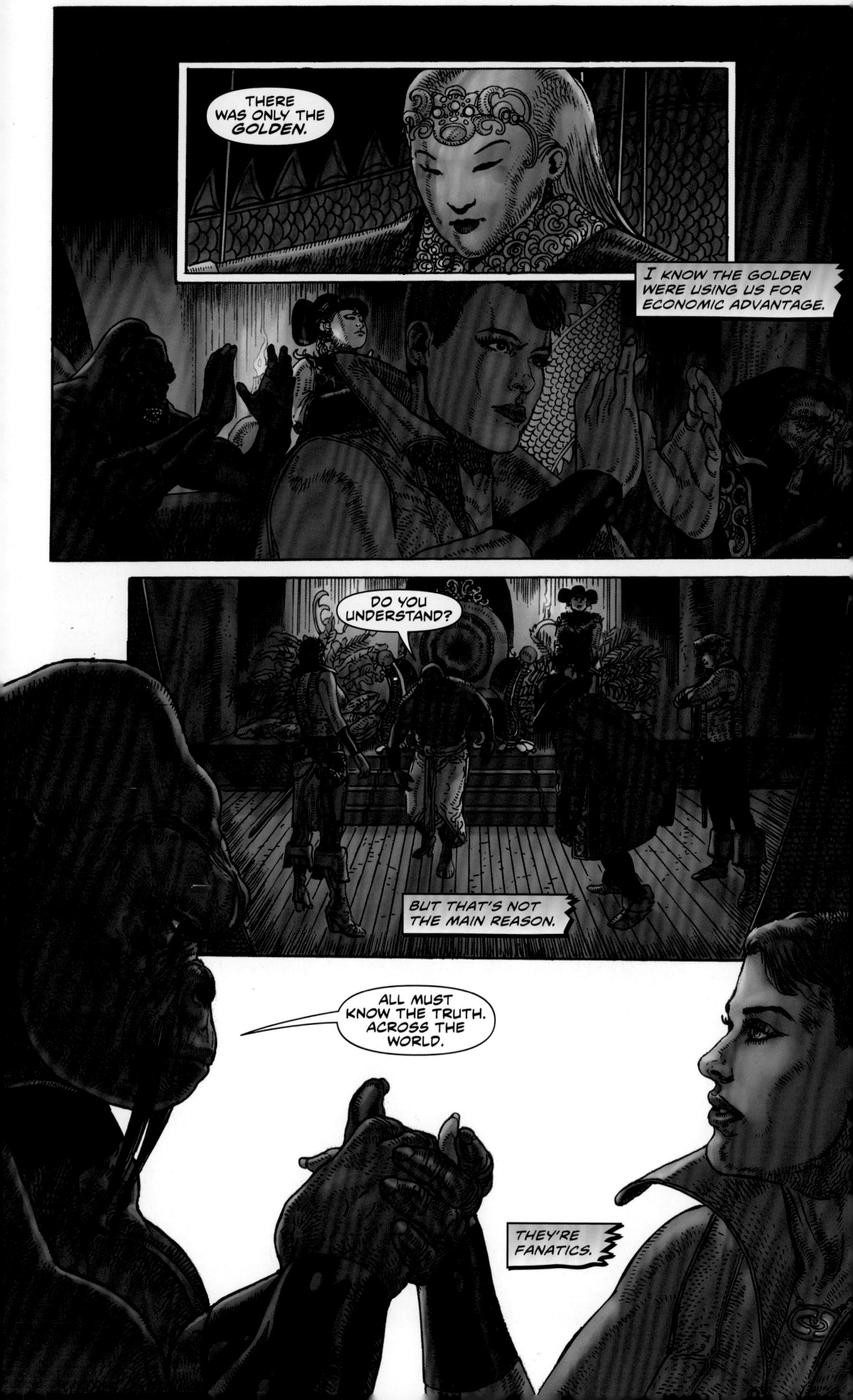
THERE WAS ONLY THE GOLDEN.
I KNOW THE GOLDEN WERE USING US FOR ECONOMIC ADVANTAGE.
DO YOU UNDERSTAND?
BUT THAT'S NOT THE MAIN REASON.
ALL MUST KNOW THE TRUTH. ACROSS THE WORLD.
THEY'RE FANATICS.

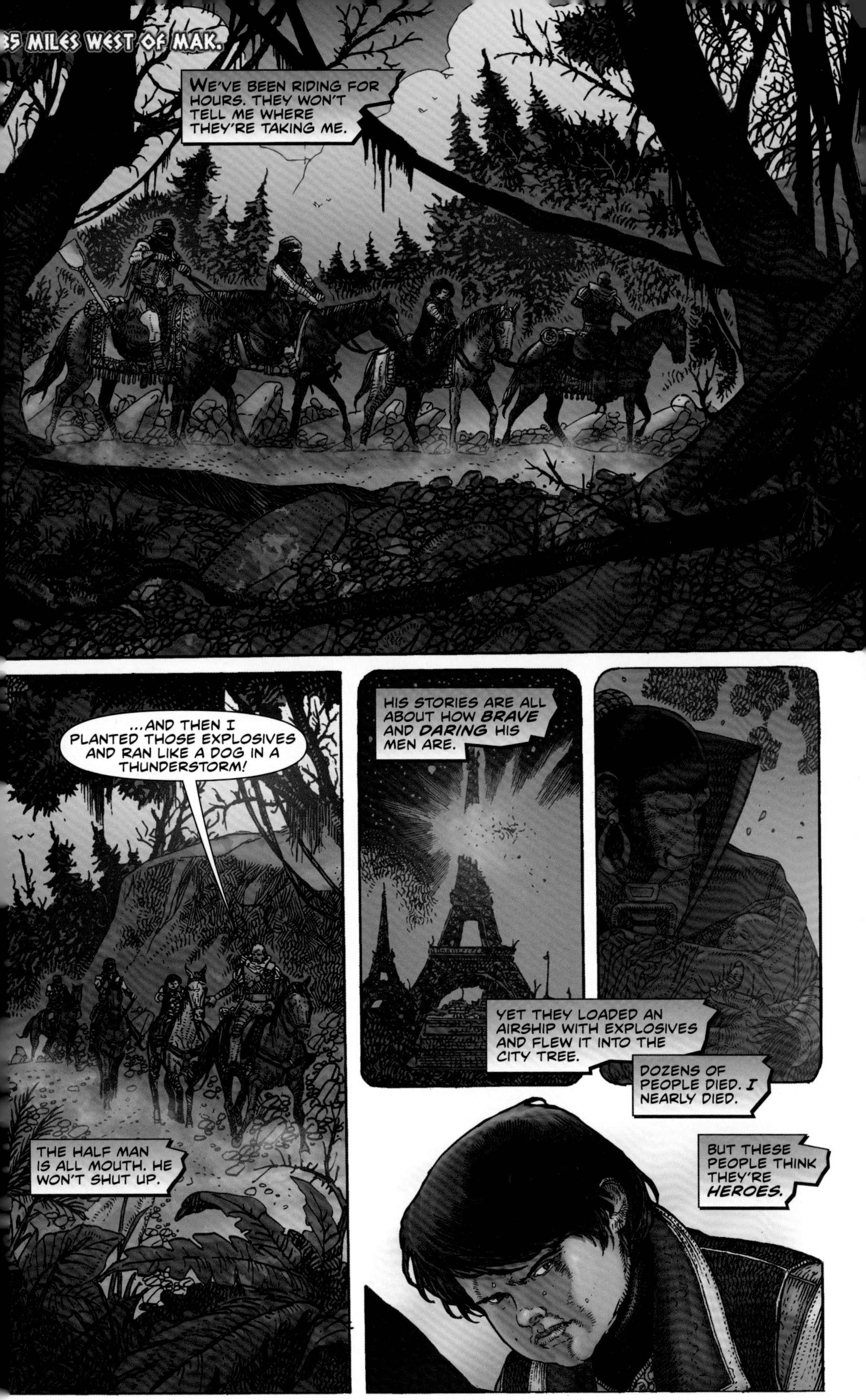

35 MILES WEST OF MAK.
WE'VE BEEN RIDING FOR HOURS. THEY WON'T TELL ME WHERE THEY'RE TAKING ME.
...AND THEN I PLANTED THOSE EXPLOSIVES AND RAN LIKE A DOG IN A THUNDERSTORM!
THE HALF MAN IS ALL MOUTH. HE WON'T SHUT UP.
HIS STORIES ARE ALL ABOUT HOW BRAVE AND DARING HIS MEN ARE.
YET THEY LOADED AN AIRSHIP WITH EXPLOSIVES AND FLEW IT INTO THE CITY TREE.
DOZENS OF PEOPLE DIED. I NEARLY DIED.
BUT THESE PEOPLE THINK THEY'RE HEROES.

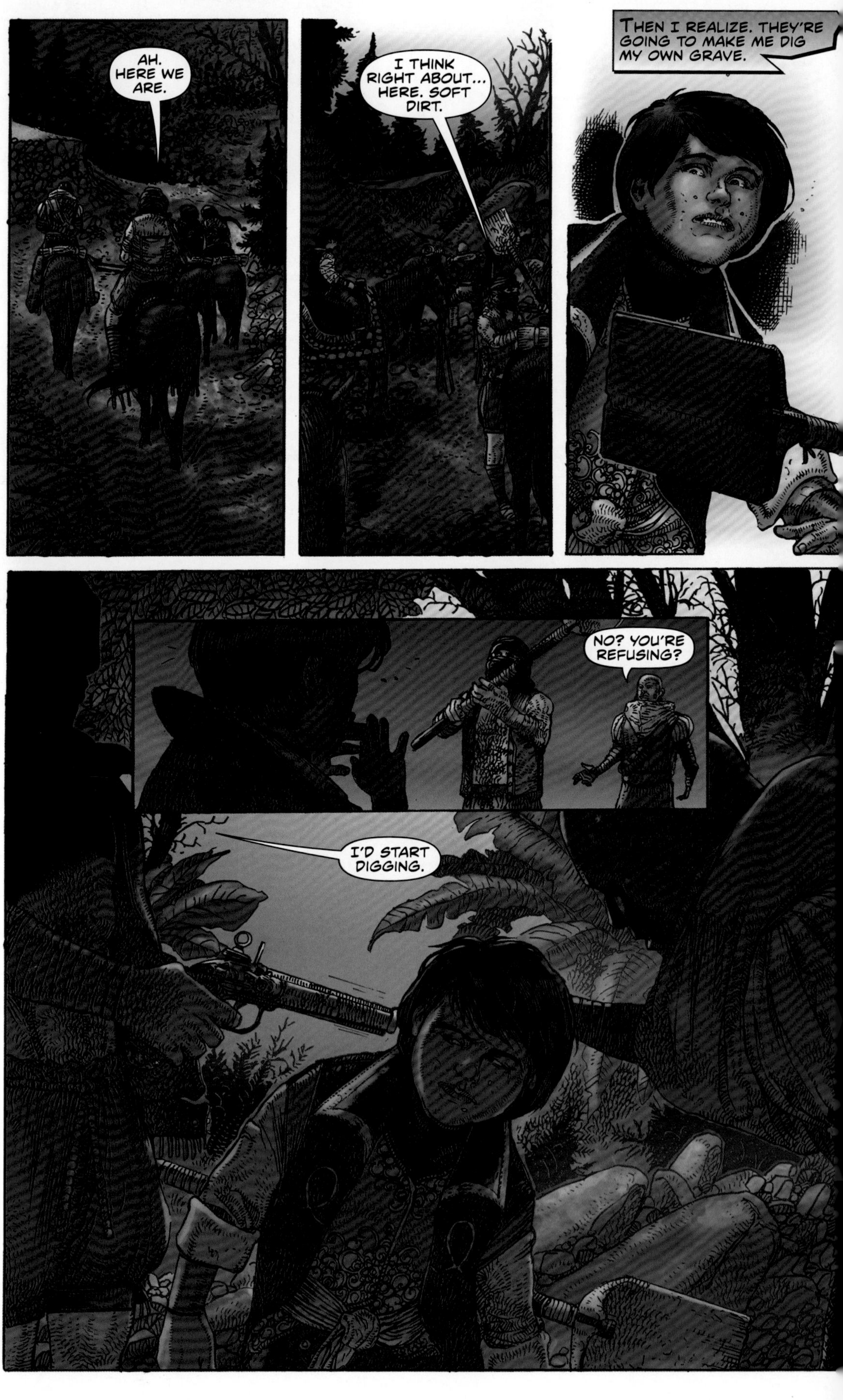
AH. HERE WE ARE.
I THINK RIGHT ABOUT... HERE. SOFT DIRT.
THEN I REALIZE. THEY'RE GOING TO MAKE ME DIG MY OWN GRAVE.
NO? YOU'RE REFUSING?
I'D START DIGGING.

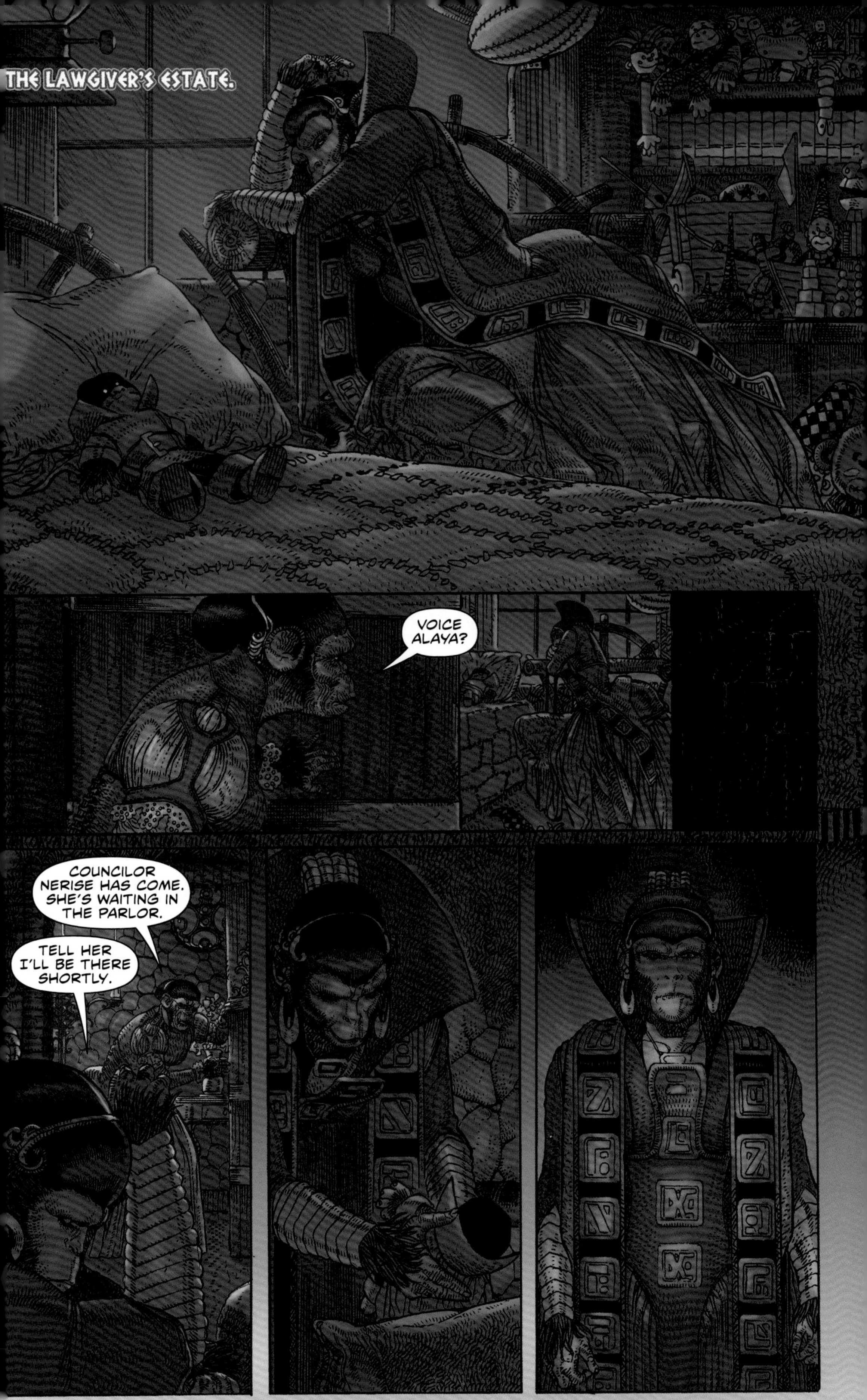
THE LAWGIVER'S ESTATE.
VOICE ALAYA?
COUNCILOR NERISE HAS COME. SHE'S WAITING IN THE PARLOR.
TELL HER I'LL BE THERE SHORTLY.

NERISE. SO GOOD OF YOU TO COME.

DO YOU FIND MY GRANDFATHER'S CHAIR COMFORTABLE?

OH, WAS THIS HIS? THE TRIP OUT TO THIS ESTATE WAS GHASTLY, AND I'M AN OLD APE, ALAYA. I PICKED THE ONLY SUITABLE PIECE IN THE ROOM.

MY CONDOLENCES ON LOSING YOUR... JULIAN.

I'M SURE YOU WILL TRACK DOWN THESE TERRORISTS. I'VE HEARD THAT YOUR WHITE TROOP IS ALREADY QUESTIONING CITIZENS.

WHILE THEY'RE NOT TRAINED AS INVESTIGATORS A THE APES IN THE CITY WATCH ARE YOUR SOLDIERS AR ENTHUSIASTIC IN ENFORCING YOUR LAWS.

THAT BRINGS ME TO WHY I CALLED YOU HERE. I NEED YOUR HELP WITH THE CITY WATCH.

ANYTHING, OF COURSE.

YOUR FATHER FOUNDED THE CITY WATCH. YOU KNOW THE COMMISSIONER, HIS LIEUTENANTS.

ARE THERE ANY WHO CANNOT BE TRUSTED?

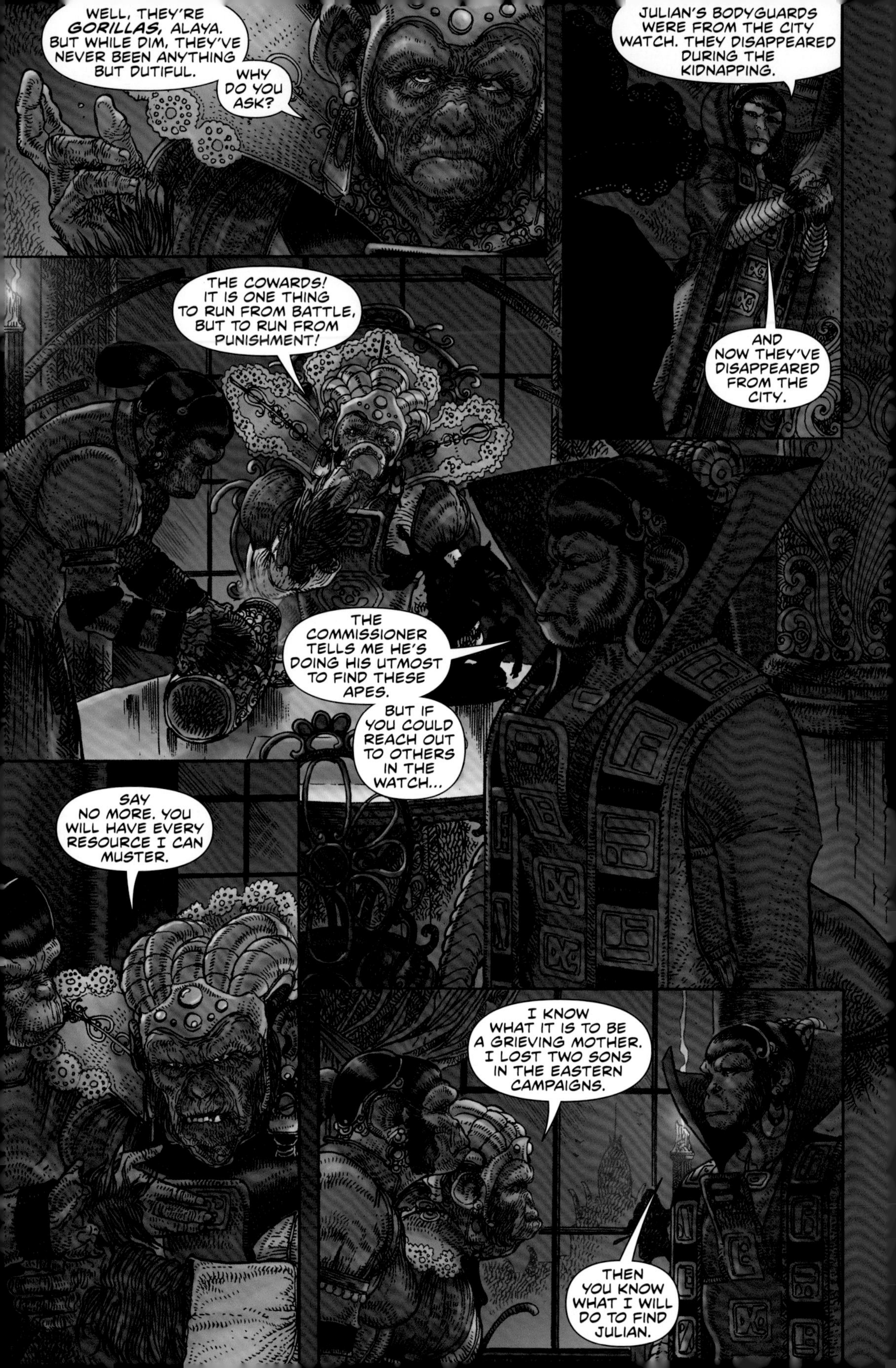
WELL, THEY'RE GORILLAS, ALAYA. BUT WHILE DIM, THEY'VE NEVER BEEN ANYTHING BUT DUTIFUL.
WHY DO YOU ASK?
JULIAN'S BODYGUARDS WERE FROM THE CITY WATCH. THEY DISAPPEARED DURING THE KIDNAPPING.
AND NOW THEY'VE DISAPPEARED FROM THE CITY.
THE COWARDS! IT IS ONE THING TO RUN FROM BATTLE, BUT TO RUN FROM PUNISHMENT!
THE COMMISSIONER TELLS ME HE'S DOING HIS UTMOST TO FIND THESE APES.
BUT IF YOU COULD REACH OUT TO OTHERS IN THE WATCH...
SAY NO MORE. YOU WILL HAVE EVERY RESOURCE I CAN MUSTER.
I KNOW WHAT IT IS TO BE A GRIEVING MOTHER. I LOST TWO SONS IN THE EASTERN CAMPAIGNS.
THEN YOU KNOW WHAT I WILL DO TO FIND JULIAN.

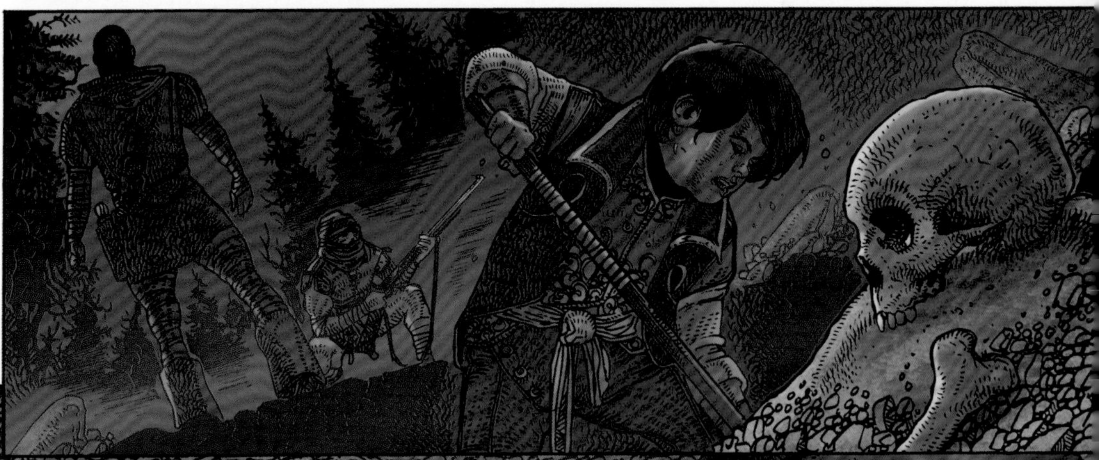

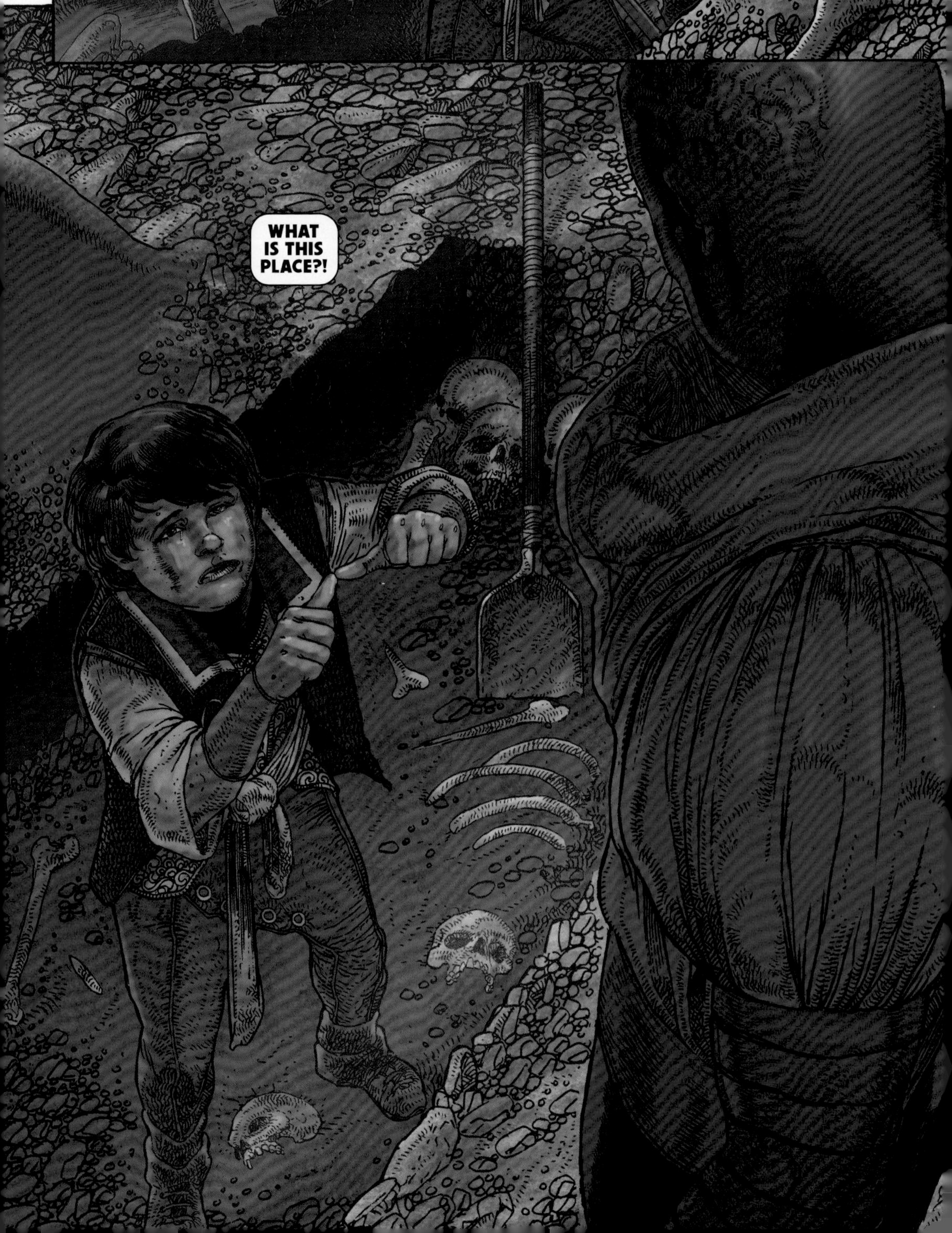
WHAT IS THIS PLACE?!

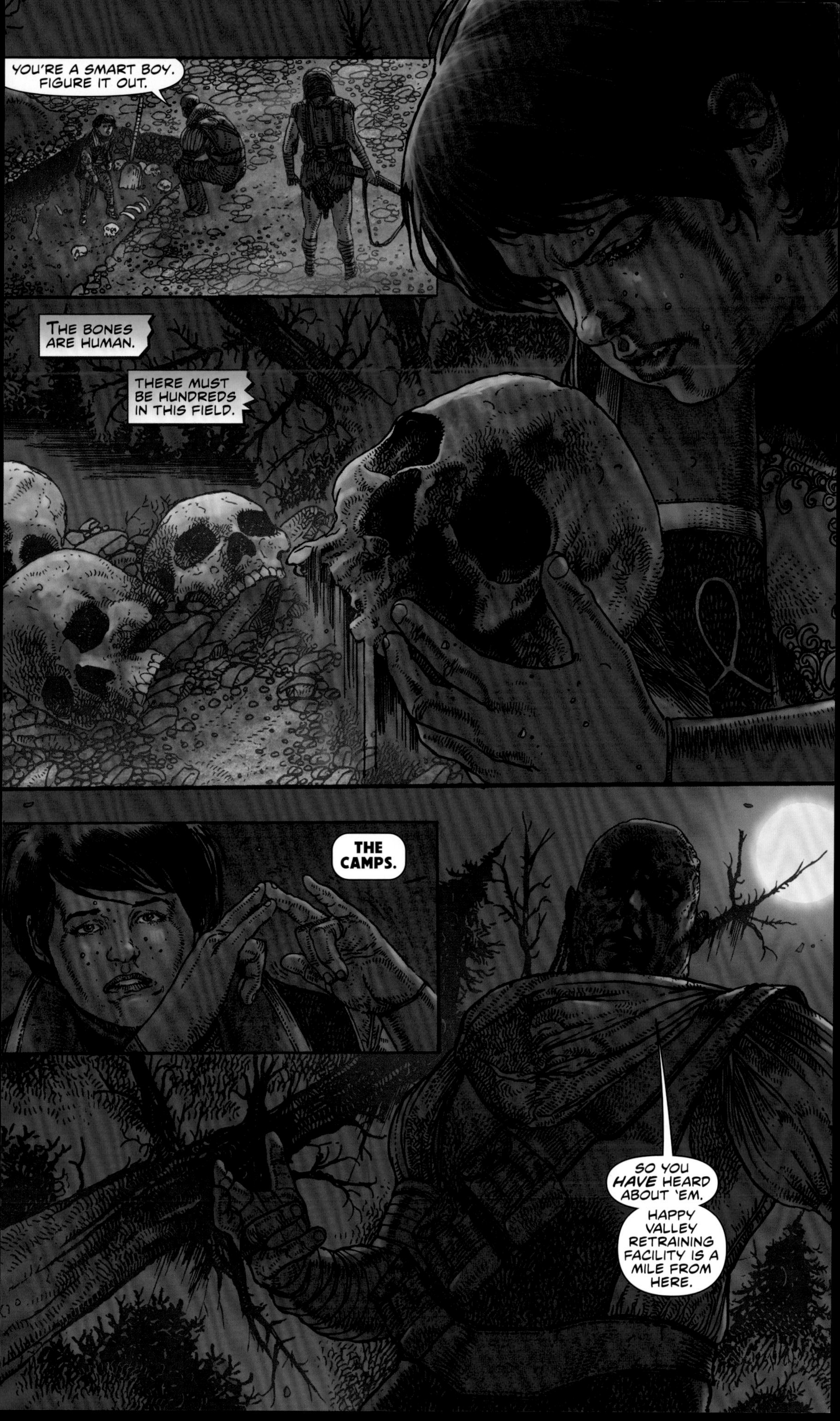
YOU'RE A SMART BOY. FIGURE IT OUT.
THE BONES ARE HUMAN.
THERE MUST BE HUNDREDS IN THIS FIELD.
THE CAMPS.
SO YOU HAVE HEARD ABOUT 'EM.
HAPPY VALLEY RETRAINING FACILITY IS A MILE FROM HERE.

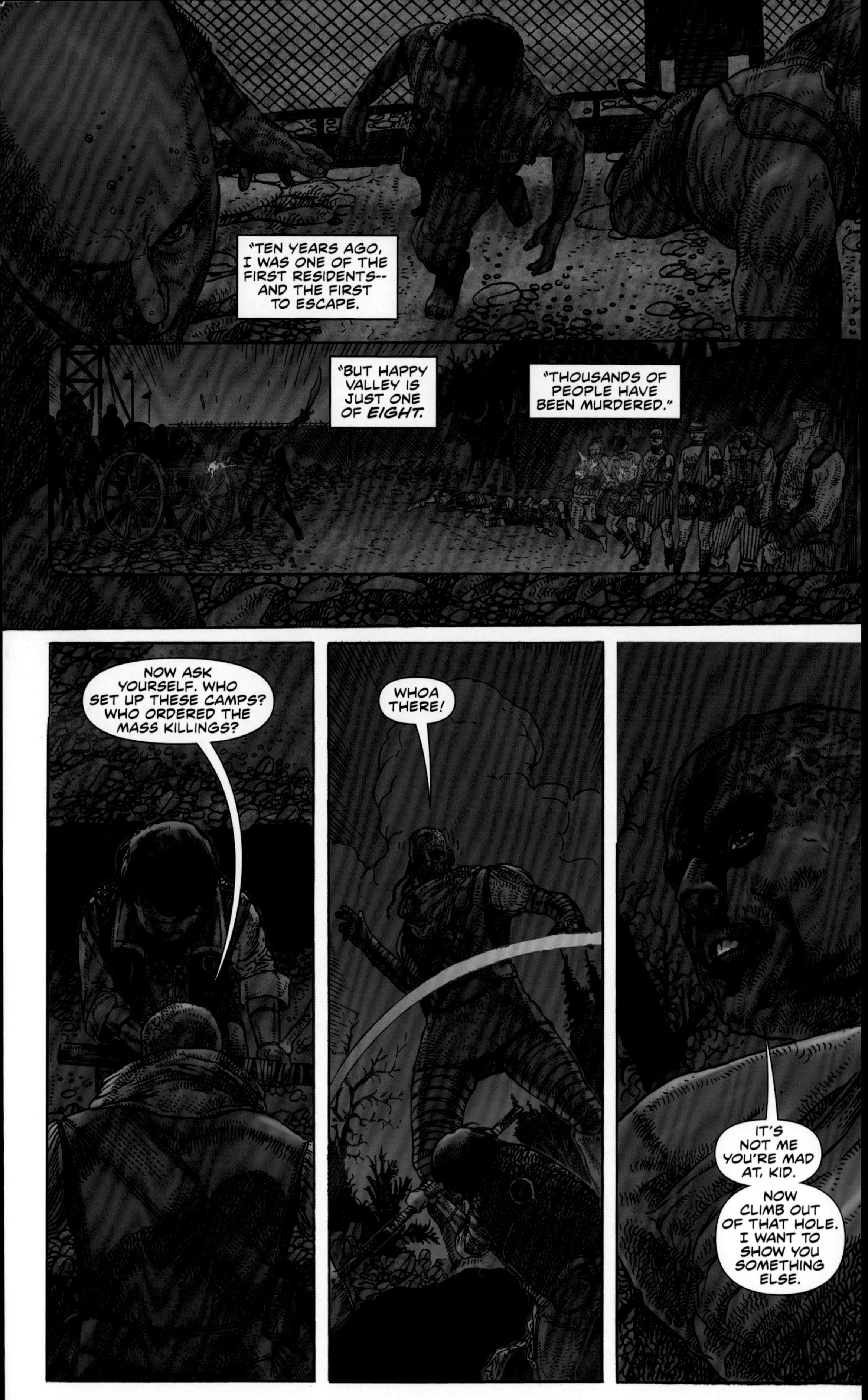
"TEN YEARS AGO, I WAS ONE OF THE FIRST RESIDENTS-- AND THE FIRST TO ESCAPE.
"BUT HAPPY VALLEY IS JUST ONE OF *EIGHT*.
"THOUSANDS OF PEOPLE HAVE BEEN MURDERED."
NOW ASK YOURSELF. WHO SET UP THESE CAMPS? WHO ORDERED THE MASS KILLINGS?
WHOA THERE!
IT'S NOT ME YOU'RE MAD AT, KID.
NOW CLIMB OUT OF THAT HOLE. I WANT TO SHOW YOU SOMETHING ELSE.

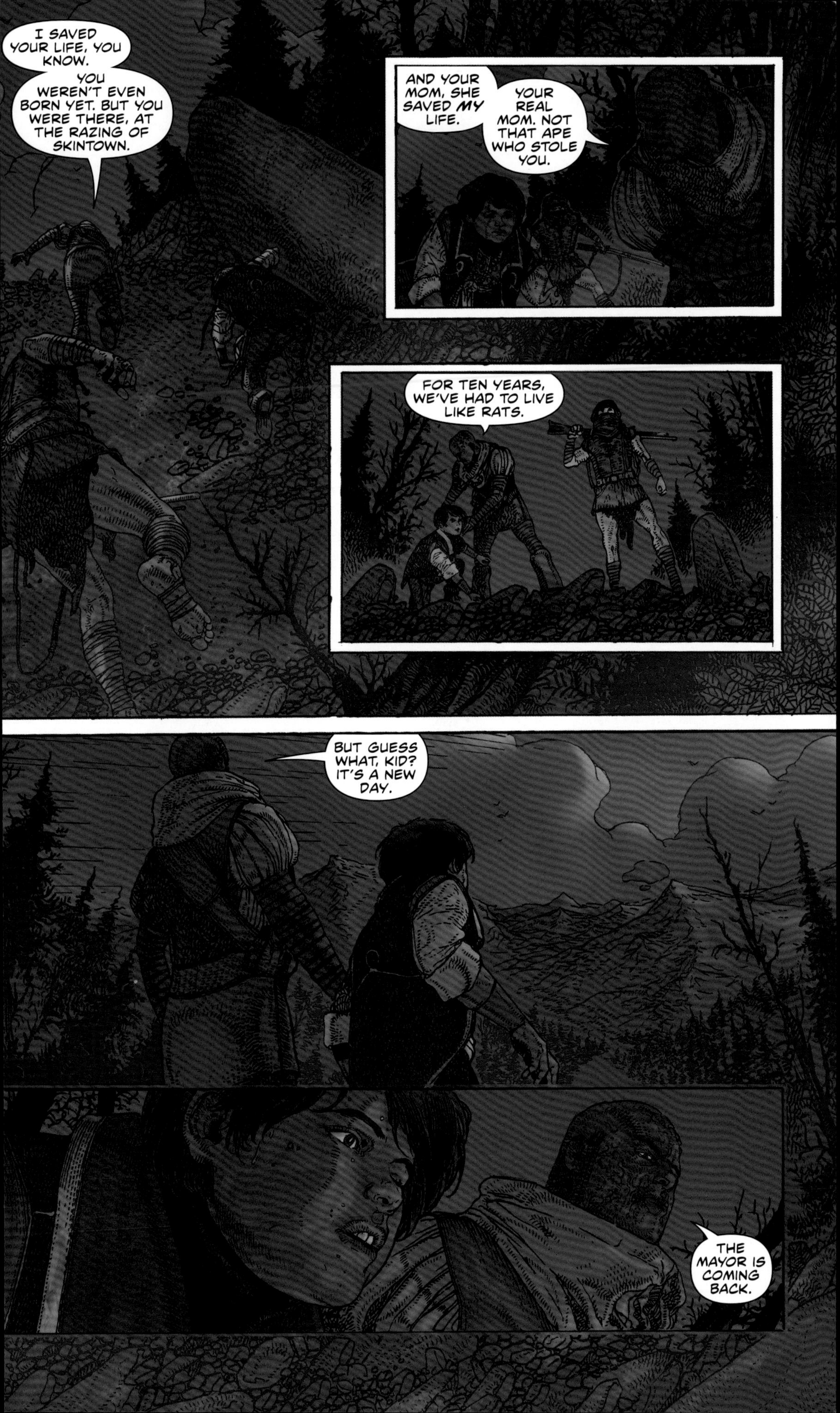
I SAVED YOUR LIFE, YOU KNOW.
YOU WEREN'T EVEN BORN YET. BUT YOU WERE THERE, AT THE RAZING OF SKINTOWN.
AND YOUR MOM, SHE SAVED MY LIFE.
YOUR REAL MOM. NOT THAT APE WHO STOLE YOU.
FOR TEN YEARS, WE'VE HAD TO LIVE LIKE RATS.
BUT GUESS WHAT, KID? IT'S A NEW DAY.
THE MAYOR IS COMING BACK.

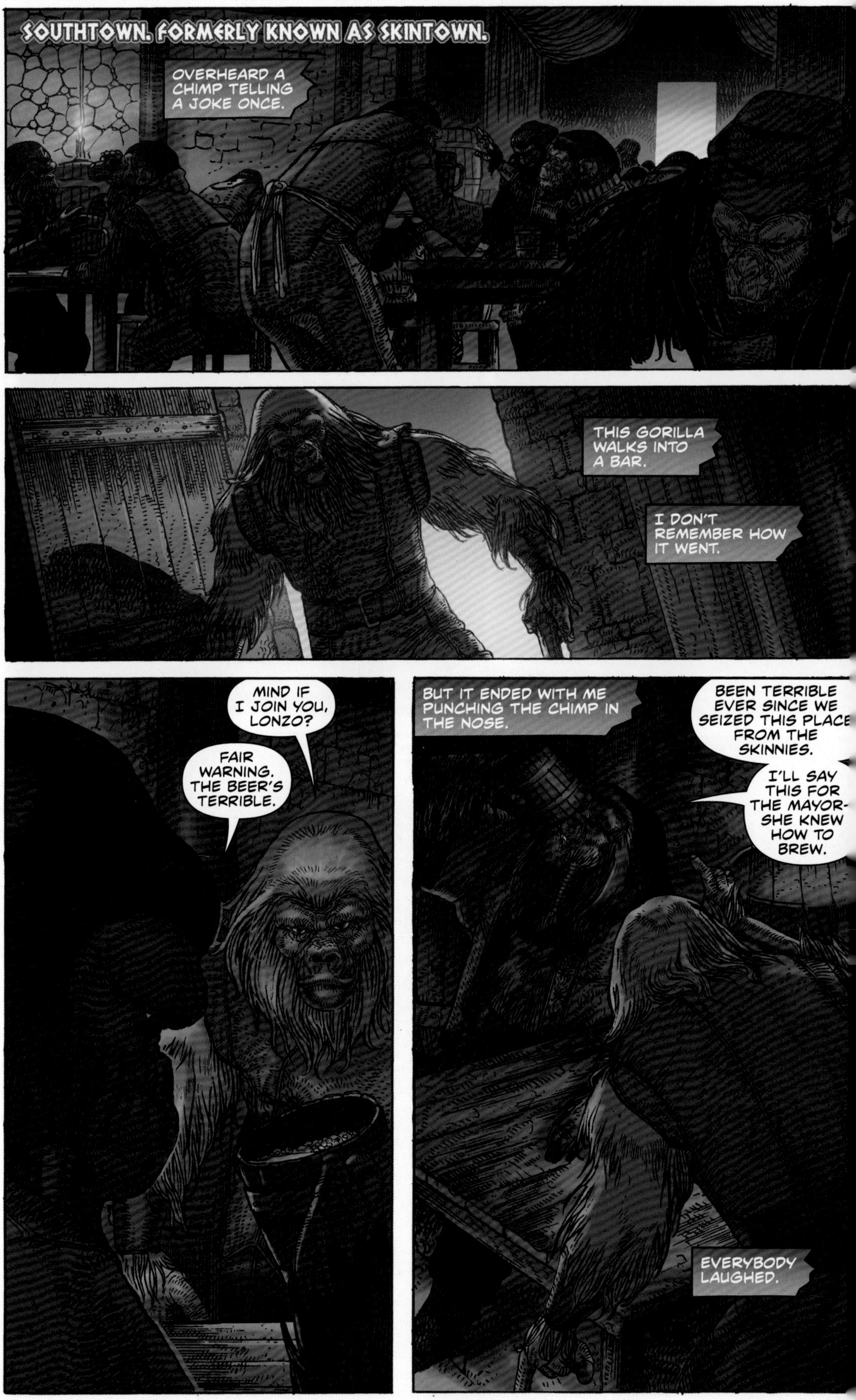
SOUTHTOWN. FORMERLY KNOWN AS SKINTOWN.
OVERHEARD A CHIMP TELLING A JOKE ONCE.
THIS GORILLA WALKS INTO A BAR.
I DON'T REMEMBER HOW IT WENT.
MIND IF I JOIN YOU, LONZO?
FAIR WARNING. THE BEER'S TERRIBLE.
BUT IT ENDED WITH ME PUNCHING THE CHIMP IN THE NOSE.
BEEN TERRIBLE EVER SINCE WE SEIZED THIS PLACE FROM THE SKINNIES.
I'LL SAY THIS FOR THE MAYOR-SHE KNEW HOW TO BREW.
EVERYBODY LAUGHED.

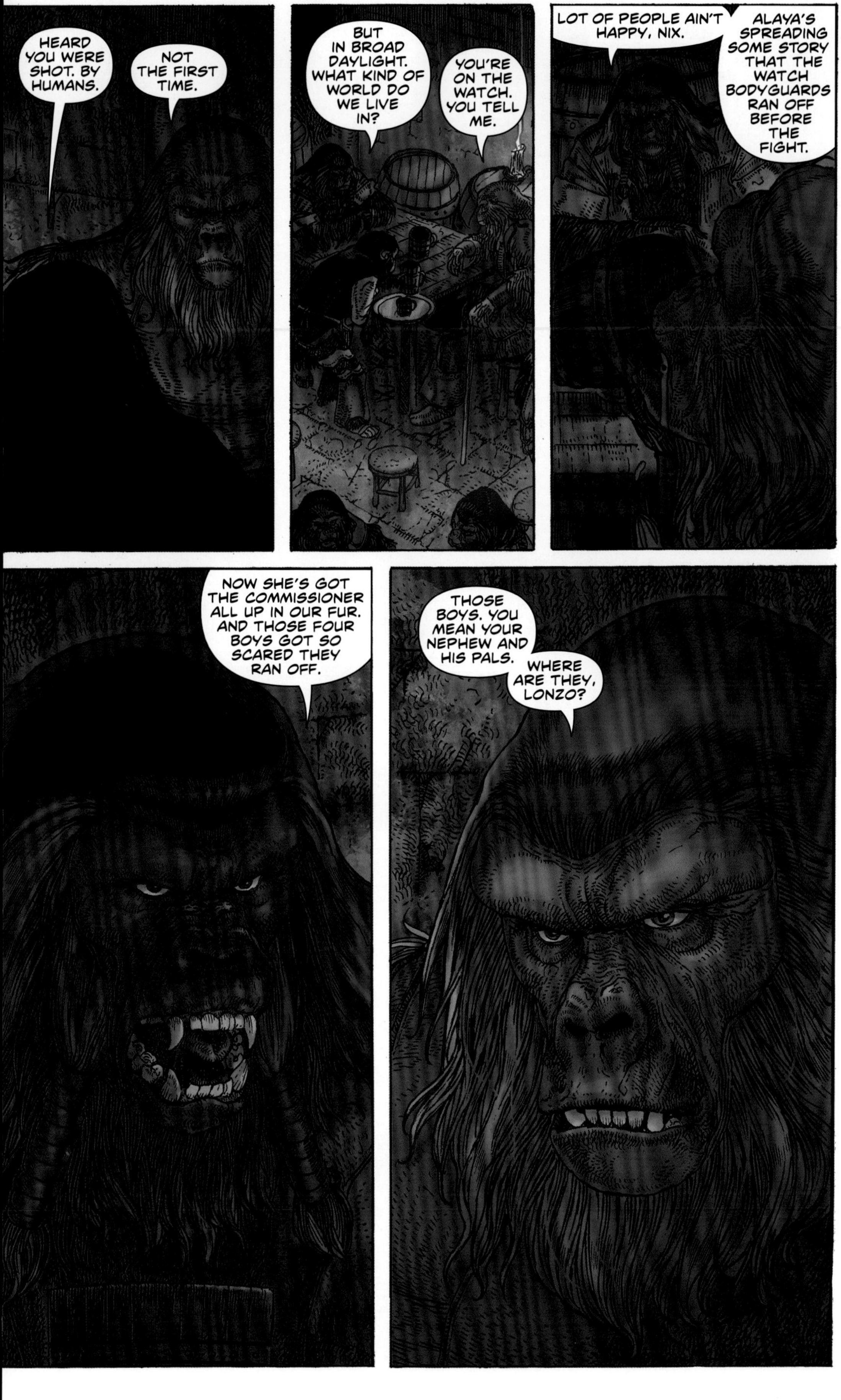
HEARD YOU WERE SHOT. BY HUMANS.
NOT THE FIRST TIME.
BUT IN BROAD DAYLIGHT. WHAT KIND OF WORLD DO WE LIVE IN?
YOU'RE ON THE WATCH. YOU TELL ME.
LOT OF PEOPLE AIN'T HAPPY, NIX.
ALAYA'S SPREADING SOME STORY THAT THE WATCH BODYGUARDS RAN OFF BEFORE THE FIGHT.
NOW SHE'S GOT THE COMMISSIONER ALL UP IN OUR FUR. AND THOSE FOUR BOYS GOT SO SCARED THEY RAN OFF.
THOSE BOYS. YOU MEAN YOUR NEPHEW AND HIS PALS.
WHERE ARE THEY, LONZO?

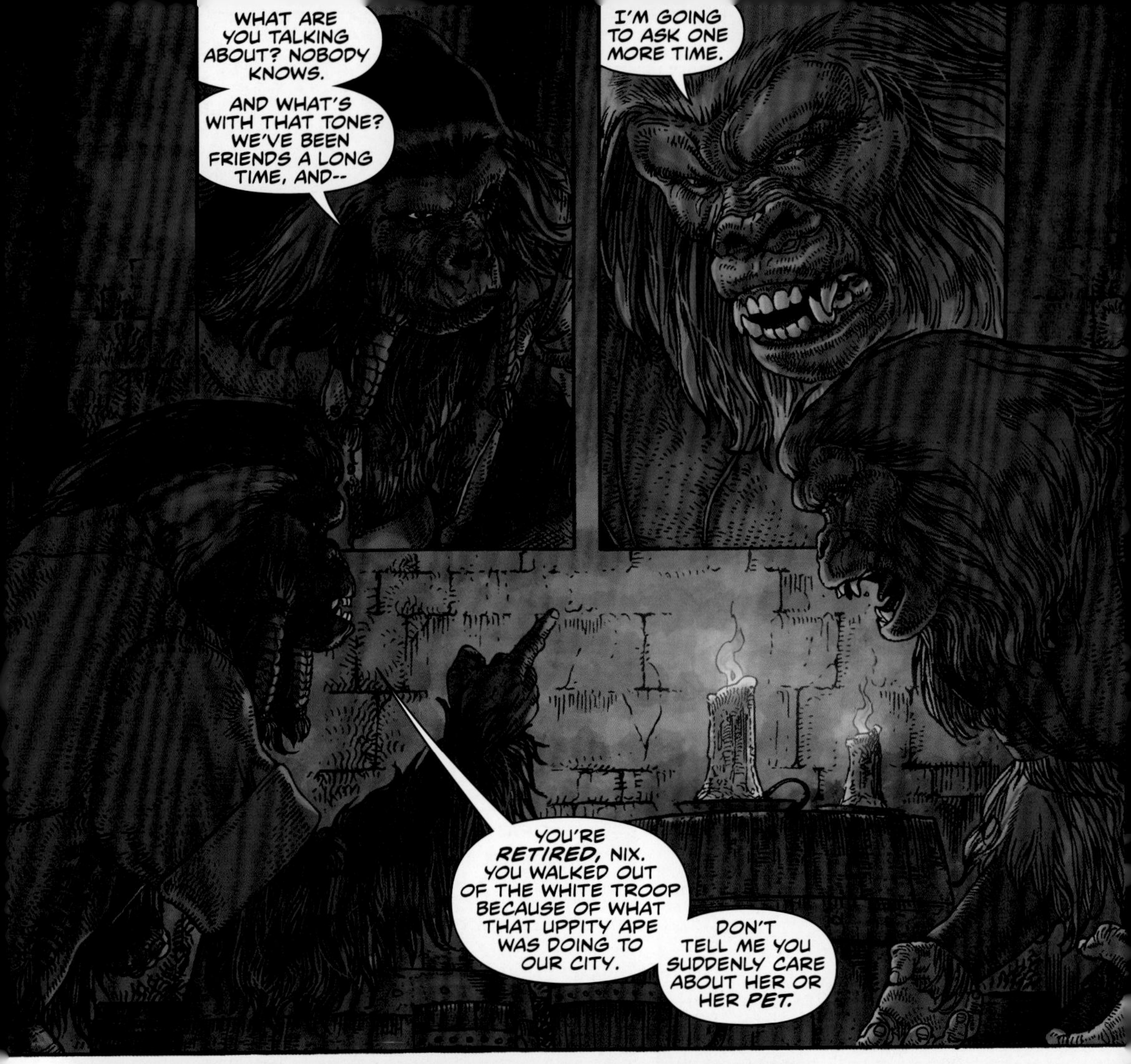
WHAT ARE YOU TALKING ABOUT? NOBODY KNOWS.
AND WHAT'S WITH THAT TONE? WE'VE BEEN FRIENDS A LONG TIME, AND--
I'M GOING TO ASK ONE MORE TIME.
YOU'RE *RETIRED,* NIX. YOU WALKED OUT OF THE WHITE TROOP BECAUSE OF WHAT THAT UPPITY APE WAS DOING TO OUR CITY.
DON'T TELL ME YOU SUDDENLY CARE ABOUT HER OR HER *PET.*

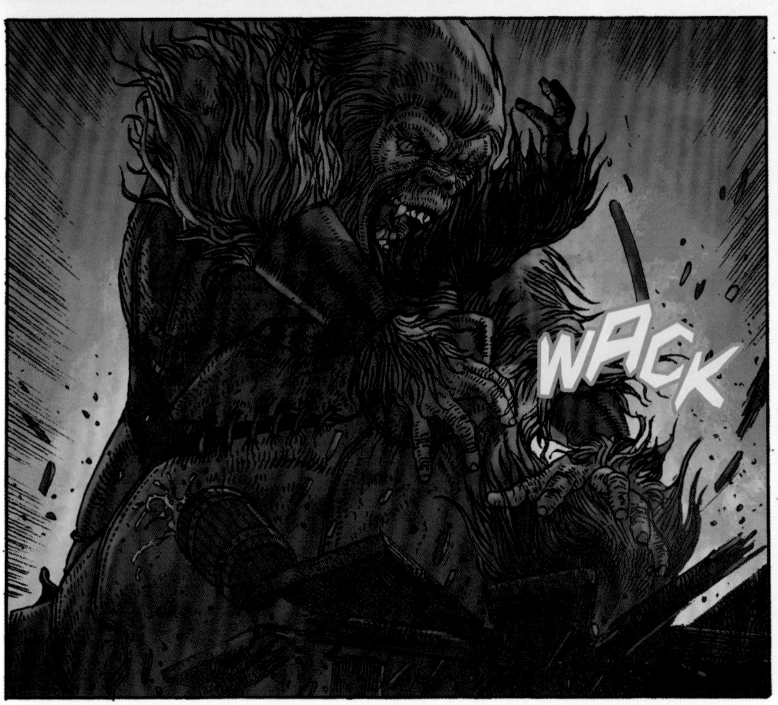
WACK

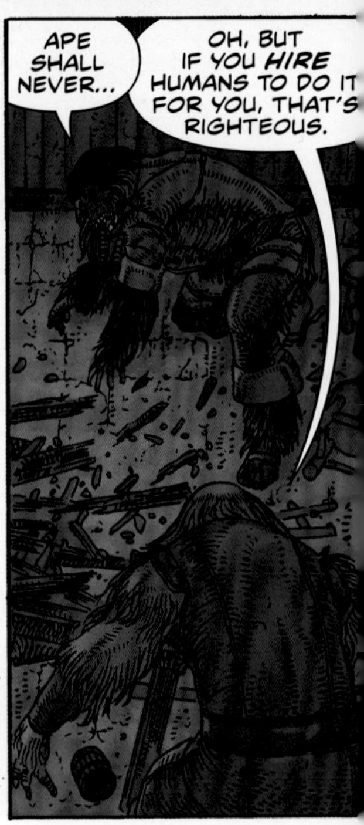
APE SHALL NEVER...
OH, BUT IF YOU *HIRE* HUMANS TO DO IT FOR YOU, THAT'S RIGHTEOUS.

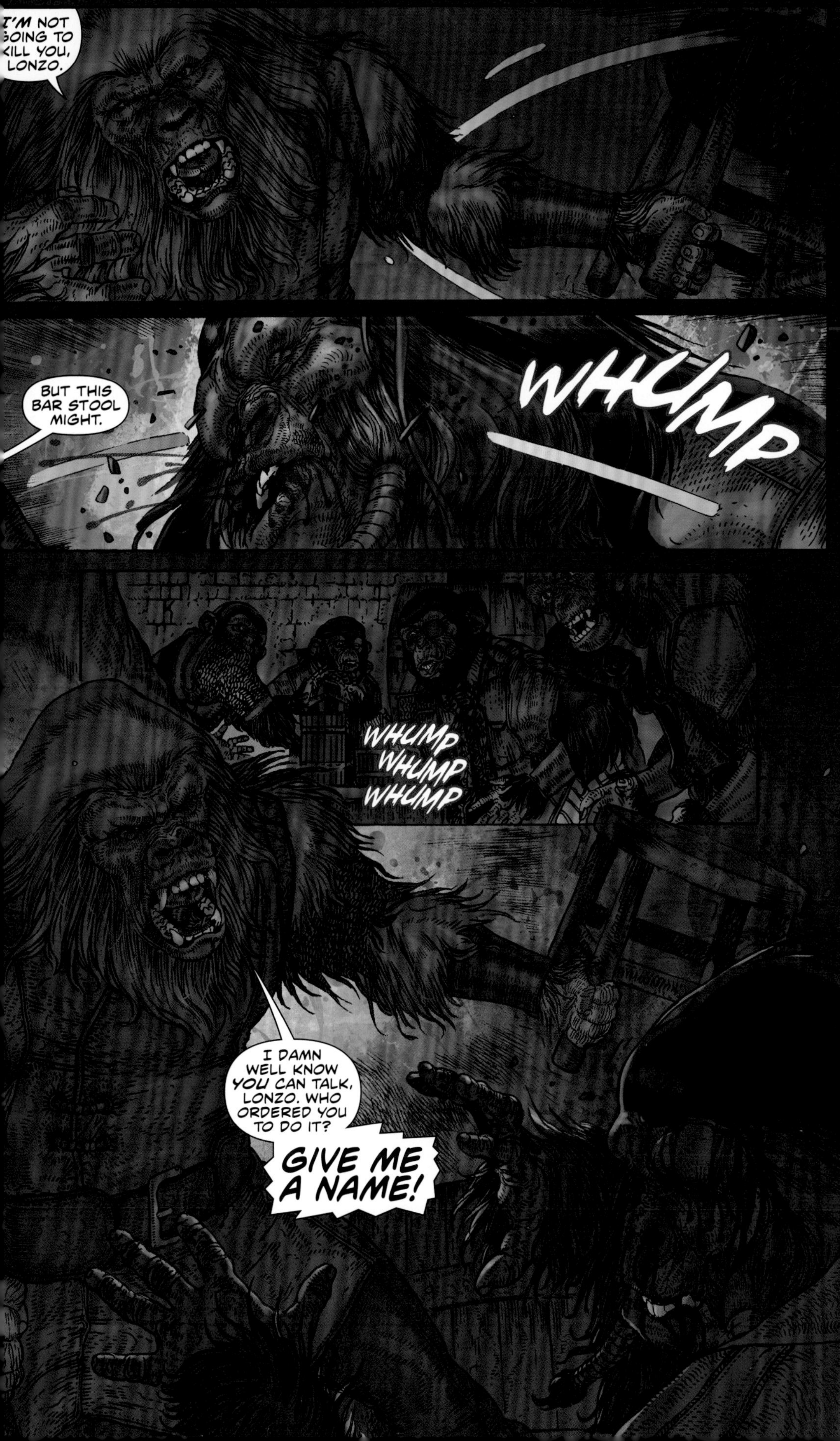
I'M NOT GOING TO KILL YOU, LONZO.
BUT THIS BAR STOOL MIGHT.
WHUMP
WHUMP WHUMP WHUMP
I DAMN WELL KNOW YOU CAN TALK, LONZO. WHO ORDERED YOU TO DO IT?
GIVE ME A NAME!

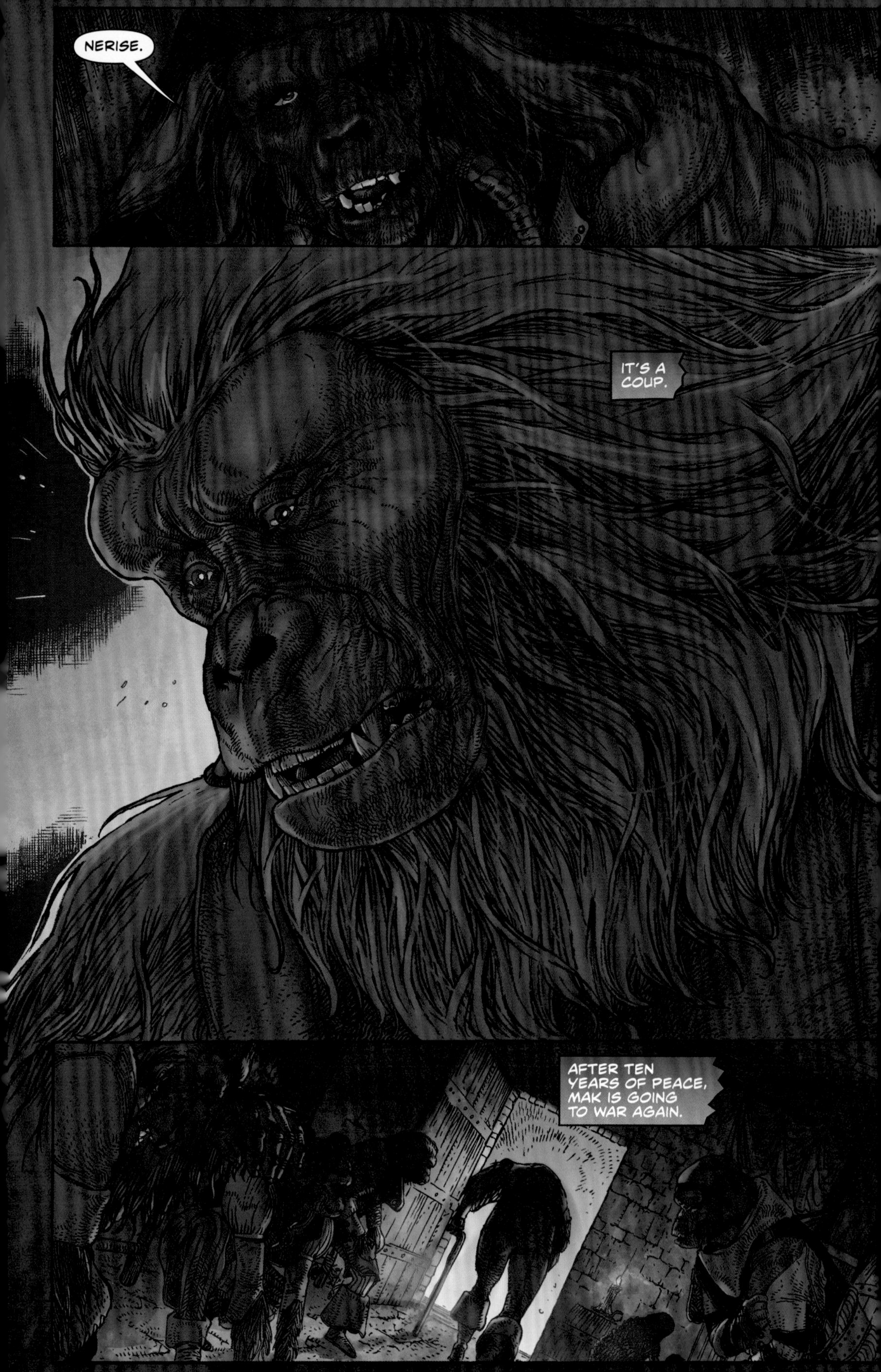
NERISE.
IT'S A COUP.
AFTER TEN YEARS OF PEACE, MAK IS GOING TO WAR AGAIN.

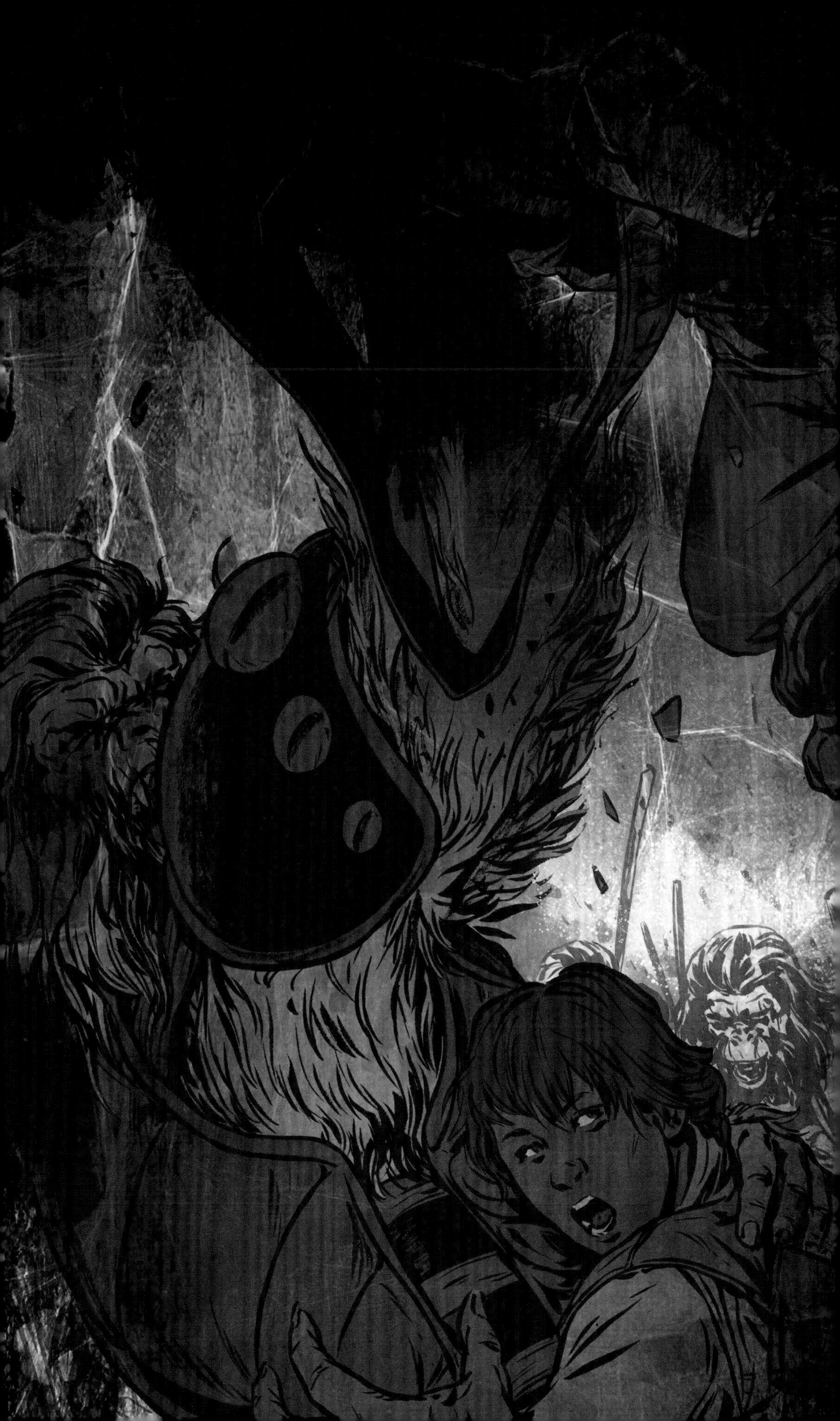

CHAPTER FIFTEEN

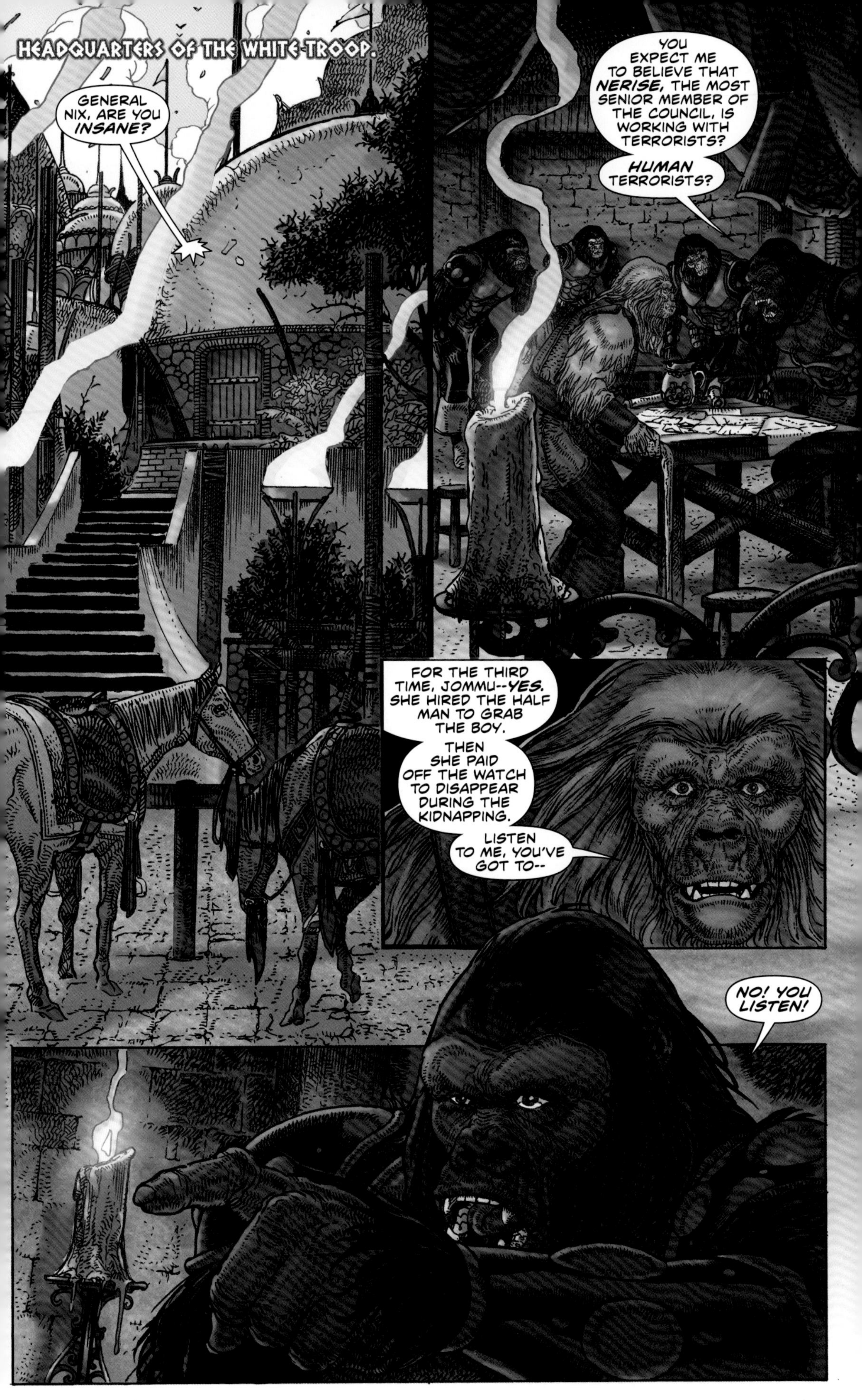
HEADQUARTERS OF THE WHITE-TROOP.
GENERAL NIX, ARE YOU *INSANE?*
YOU EXPECT ME TO BELIEVE THAT *NERISE,* THE MOST SENIOR MEMBER OF THE COUNCIL, IS WORKING WITH TERRORISTS?
HUMAN TERRORISTS?
FOR THE THIRD TIME, JOMMU--*YES.* SHE HIRED THE HALF MAN TO GRAB THE BOY.
THEN SHE PAID OFF THE WATCH TO DISAPPEAR DURING THE KIDNAPPING.
LISTEN TO ME, YOU'VE GOT TO--
NO! YOU LISTEN!

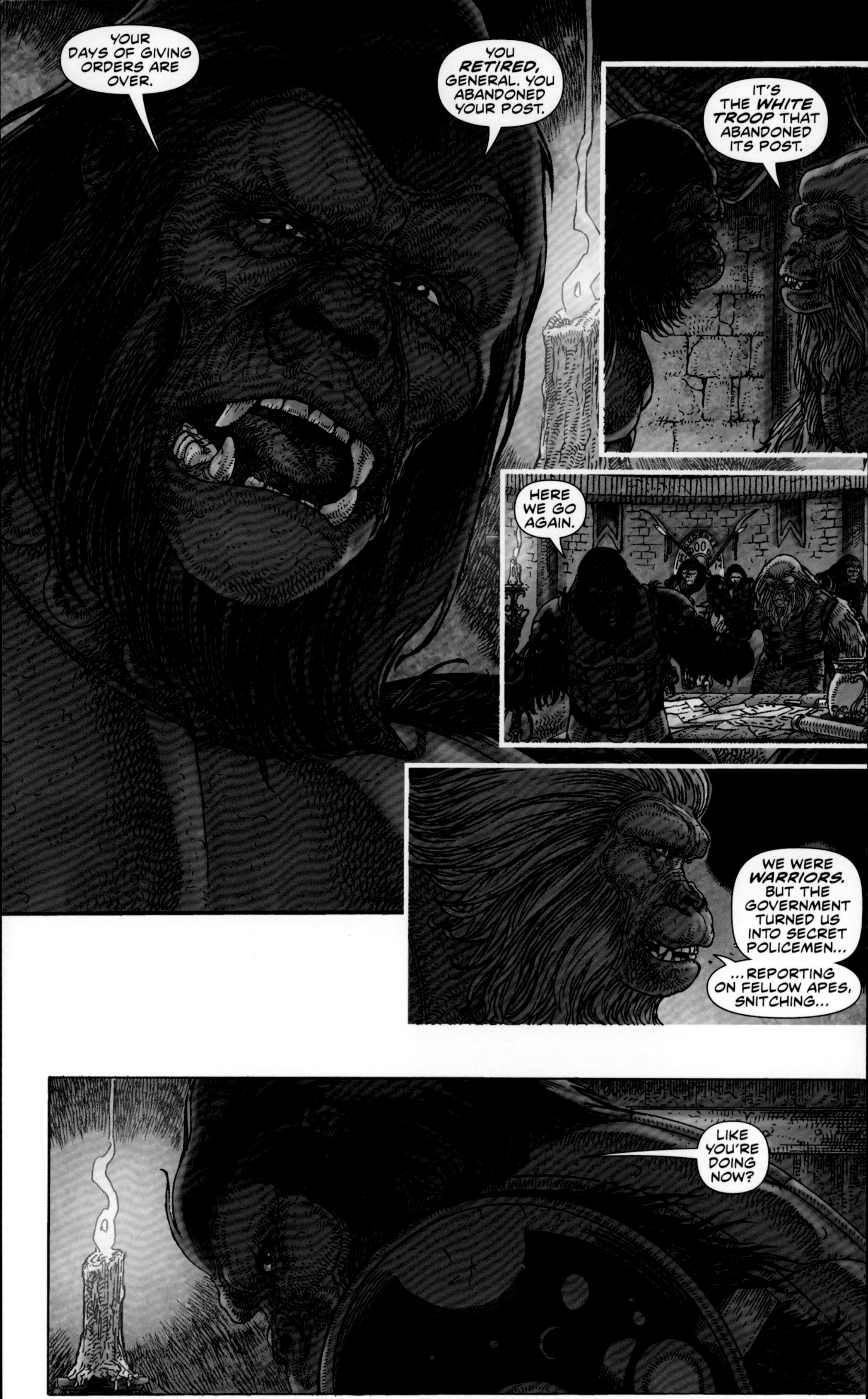

YOUR DAYS OF GIVING ORDERS ARE OVER.
YOU *RETIRED,* GENERAL. YOU ABANDONED YOUR POST.
IT'S THE *WHITE TROOP* THAT ABANDONED ITS POST.
HERE WE GO AGAIN.
WE WERE *WARRIORS.* BUT THE GOVERNMENT TURNED US INTO SECRET POLICEMEN...
...REPORTING ON FELLOW APES, SNITCHING...
LIKE YOU'RE DOING NOW?

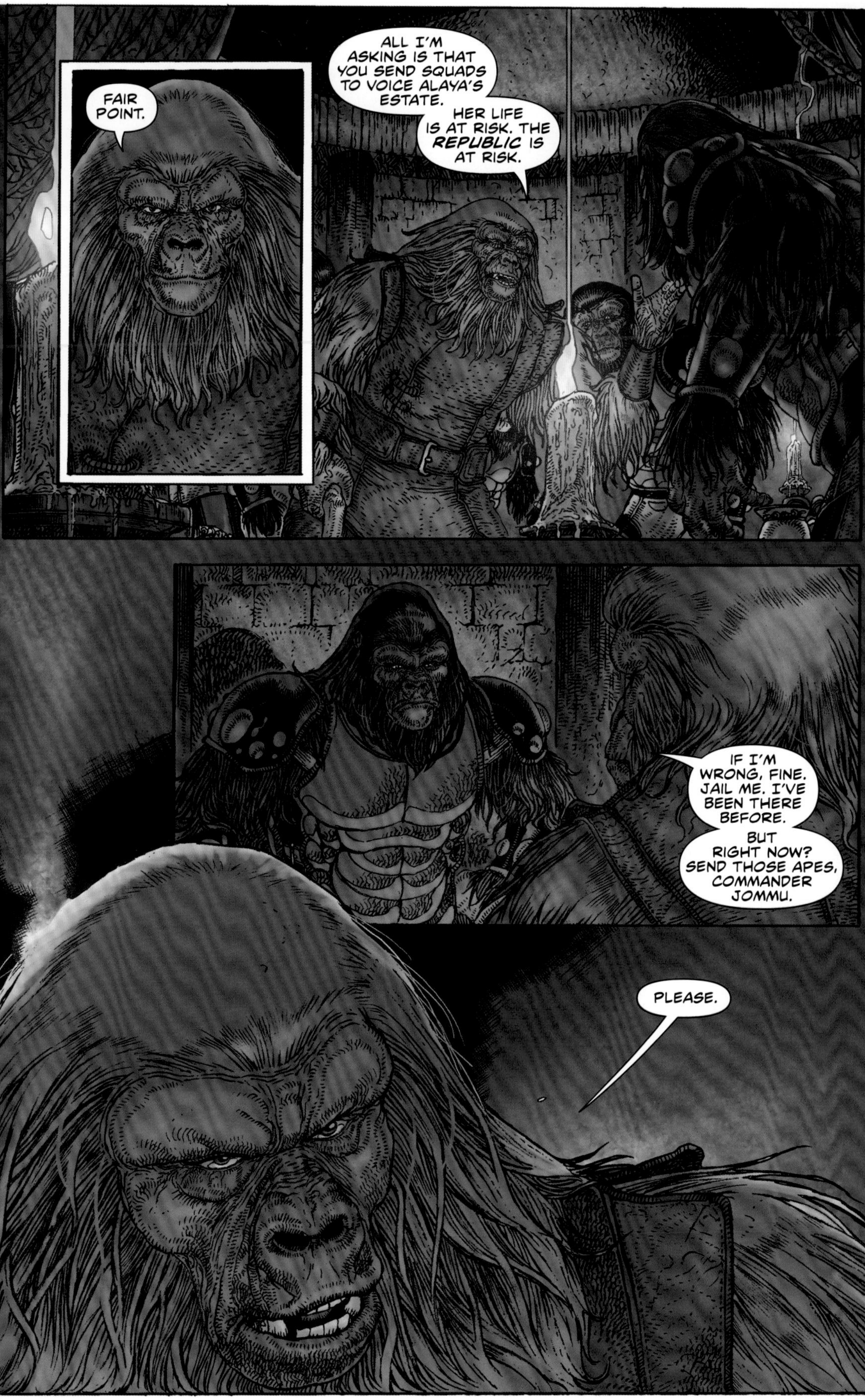

FAIR POINT.
ALL I'M ASKING IS THAT YOU SEND SQUADS TO VOICE ALAYA'S ESTATE.
HER LIFE IS AT RISK. THE *REPUBLIC* IS AT RISK.
IF I'M WRONG, FINE. JAIL ME. I'VE BEEN THERE BEFORE.
BUT RIGHT NOW? SEND THOSE APES, COMMANDER JOMMU.
PLEASE.

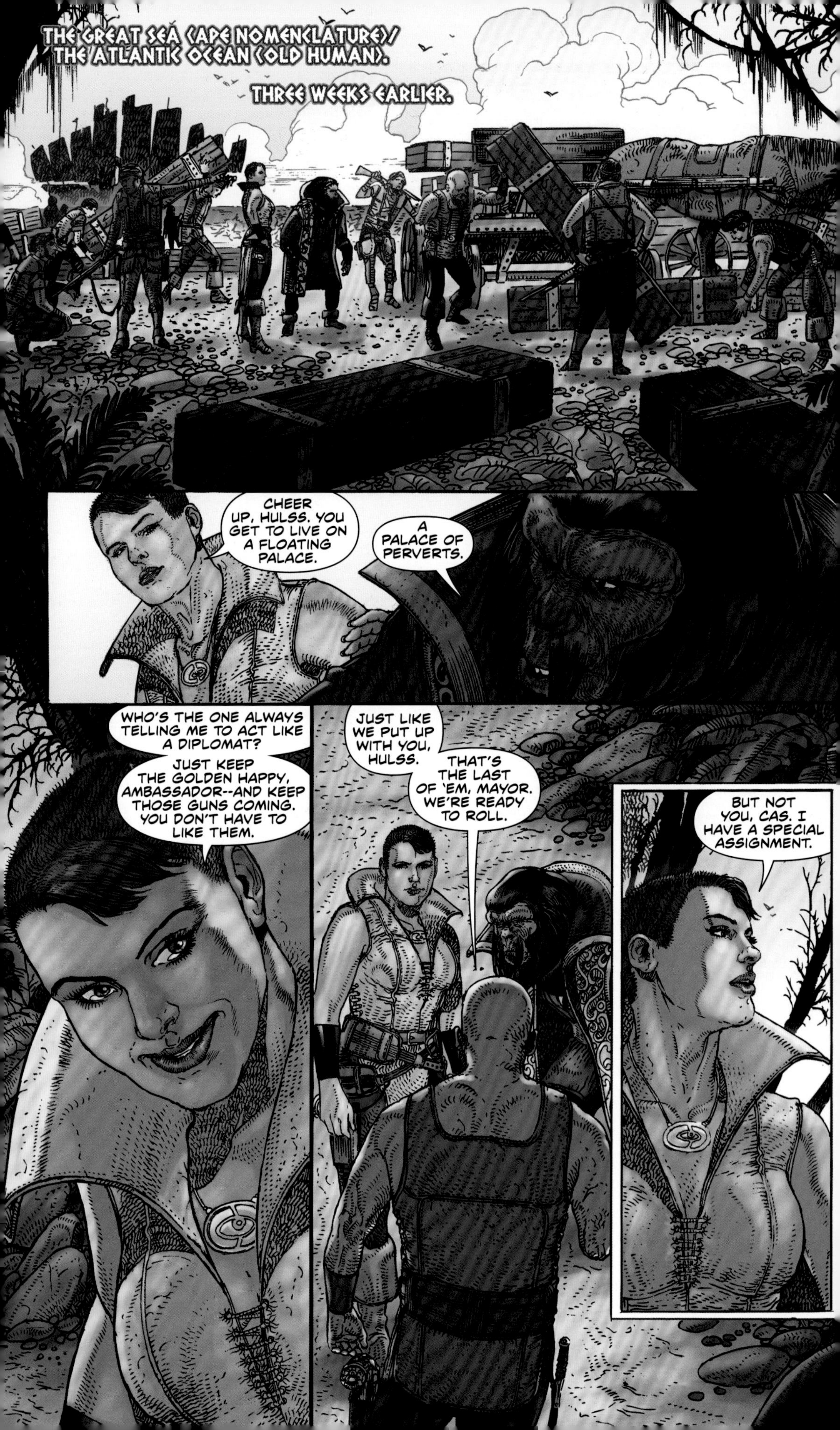
THE GREAT SEA (APE NOMENCLATURE)/ THE ATLANTIC OCEAN (OLD HUMAN).
THREE WEEKS EARLIER.
CHEER UP, HULSS. YOU GET TO LIVE ON A FLOATING PALACE.
A PALACE OF PERVERTS.
WHO'S THE ONE ALWAYS TELLING ME TO ACT LIKE A DIPLOMAT?
JUST KEEP THE GOLDEN HAPPY, AMBASSADOR--AND KEEP THOSE GUNS COMING. YOU DON'T HAVE TO LIKE THEM.
JUST LIKE WE PUT UP WITH YOU, HULSS.
THAT'S THE LAST OF 'EM, MAYOR. WE'RE READY TO ROLL.
BUT NOT YOU, CAS. I HAVE A SPECIAL ASSIGNMENT.

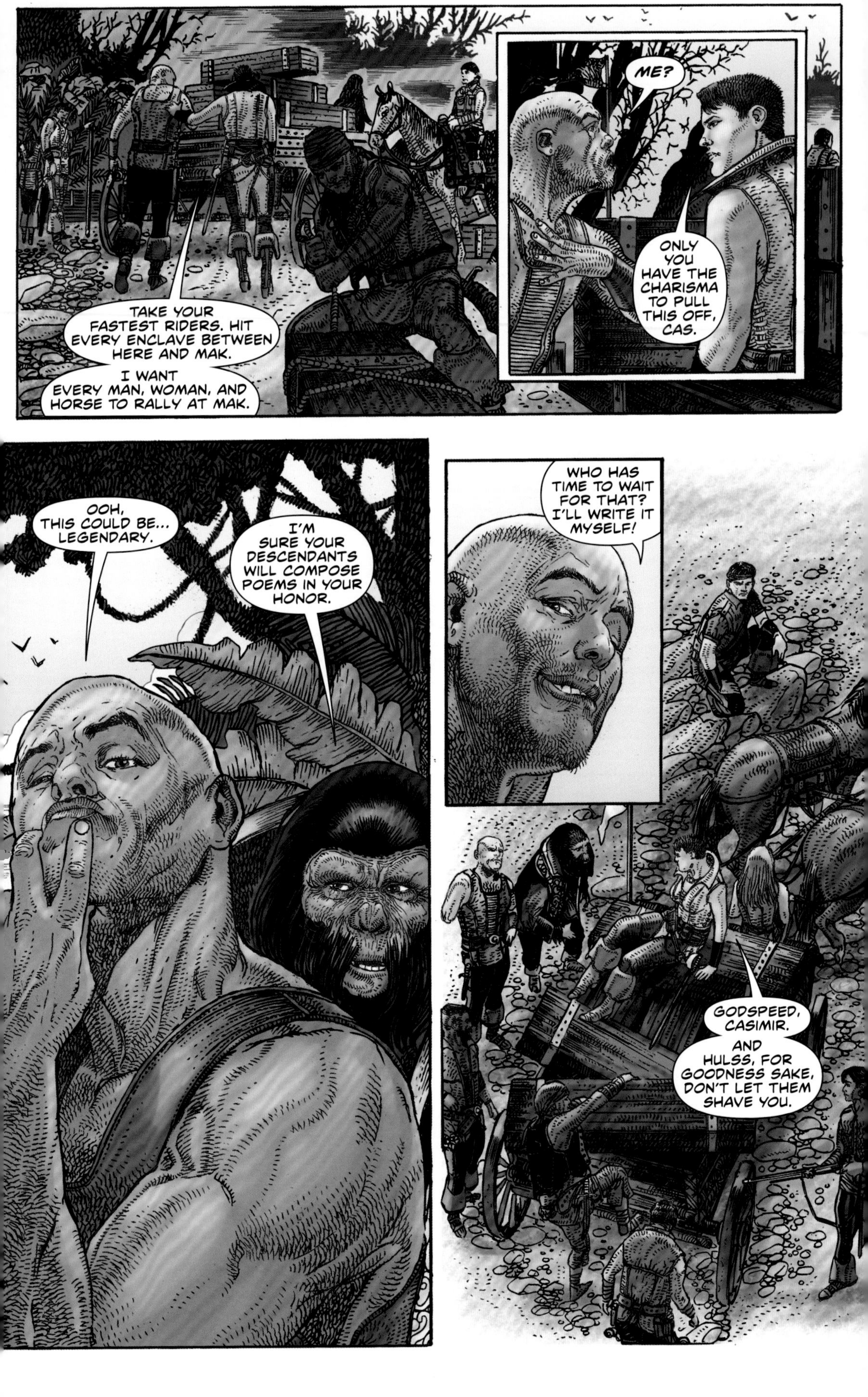
TAKE YOUR FASTEST RIDERS. HIT EVERY ENCLAVE BETWEEN HERE AND MAK.
I WANT EVERY MAN, WOMAN, AND HORSE TO RALLY AT MAK.
ME?
ONLY YOU HAVE THE CHARISMA TO PULL THIS OFF, CAS.
OOH, THIS COULD BE... LEGENDARY.
I'M SURE YOUR DESCENDANTS WILL COMPOSE POEMS IN YOUR HONOR.
WHO HAS TIME TO WAIT FOR THAT? I'LL WRITE IT MYSELF!
GODSPEED, CASIMIR.
AND HULSS, FOR GOODNESS SAKE, DON'T LET THEM SHAVE YOU.

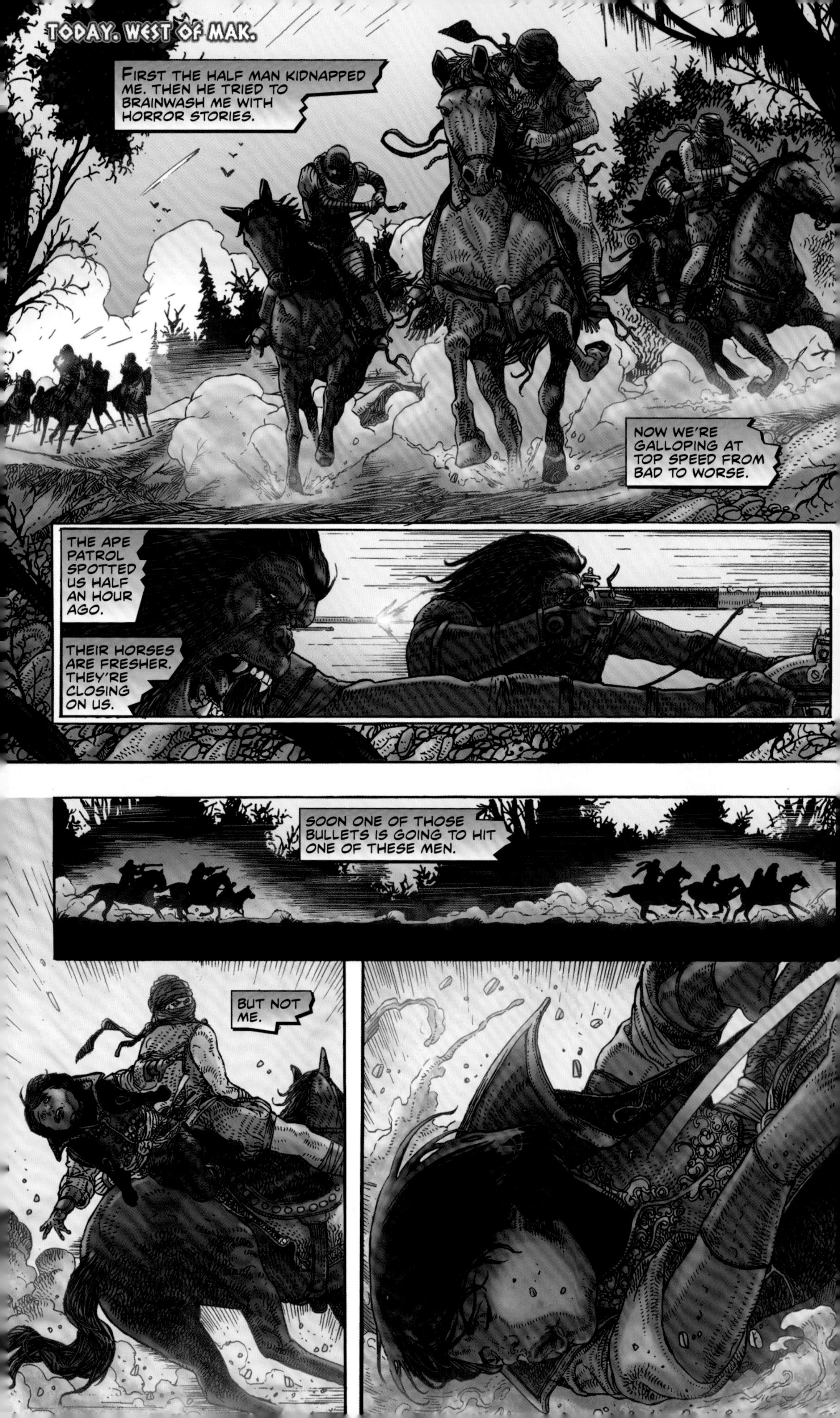
TODAY. WEST OF MAK.
FIRST THE HALF MAN KIDNAPPED ME. THEN HE TRIED TO BRAINWASH ME WITH HORROR STORIES.
NOW WE'RE GALLOPING AT TOP SPEED FROM BAD TO WORSE.
THE APE PATROL SPOTTED US HALF AN HOUR AGO.
THEIR HORSES ARE FRESHER. THEY'RE CLOSING ON US.
SOON ONE OF THOSE BULLETS IS GOING TO HIT ONE OF THESE MEN.
BUT NOT ME.

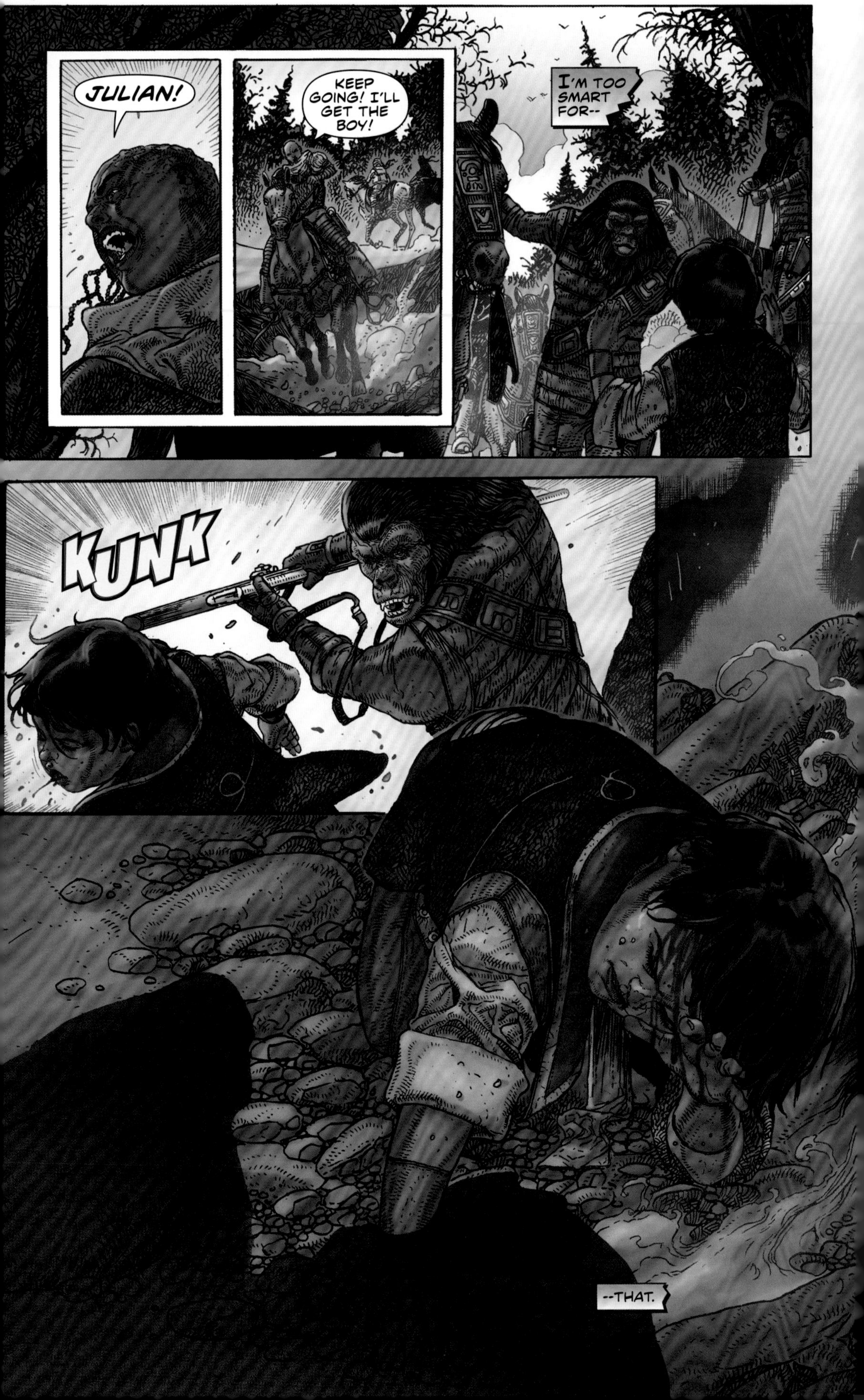

JULIAN!
KEEP GOING! I'LL GET THE BOY!
I'M TOO SMART FOR--
KUNK
--THAT.

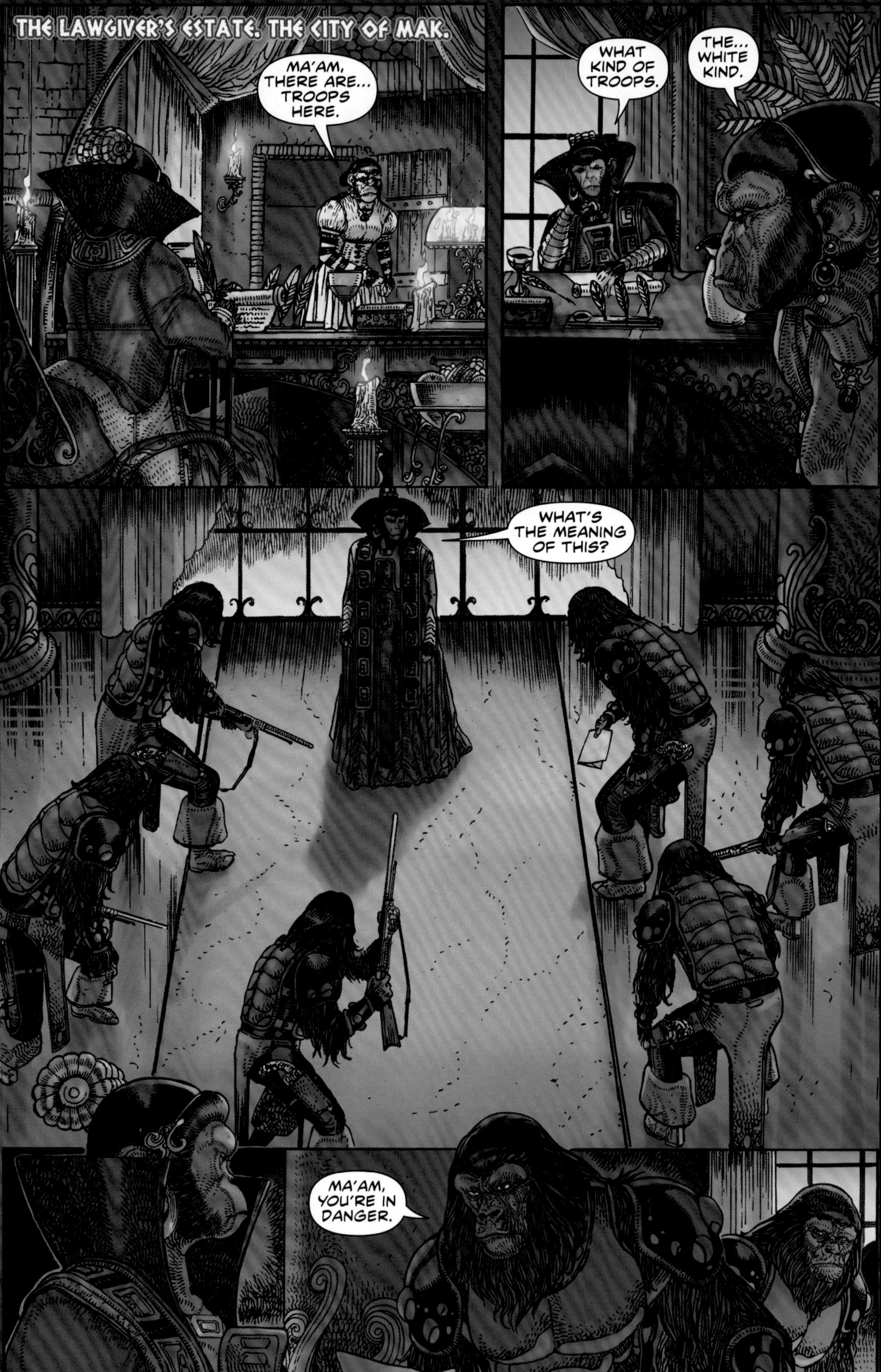
THE LAWGIVER'S ESTATE. THE CITY OF MAK.
MA'AM, THERE ARE... TROOPS HERE.
WHAT KIND OF TROOPS.
THE... WHITE KIND.
WHAT'S THE MEANING OF THIS?
MA'AM, YOU'RE IN DANGER.

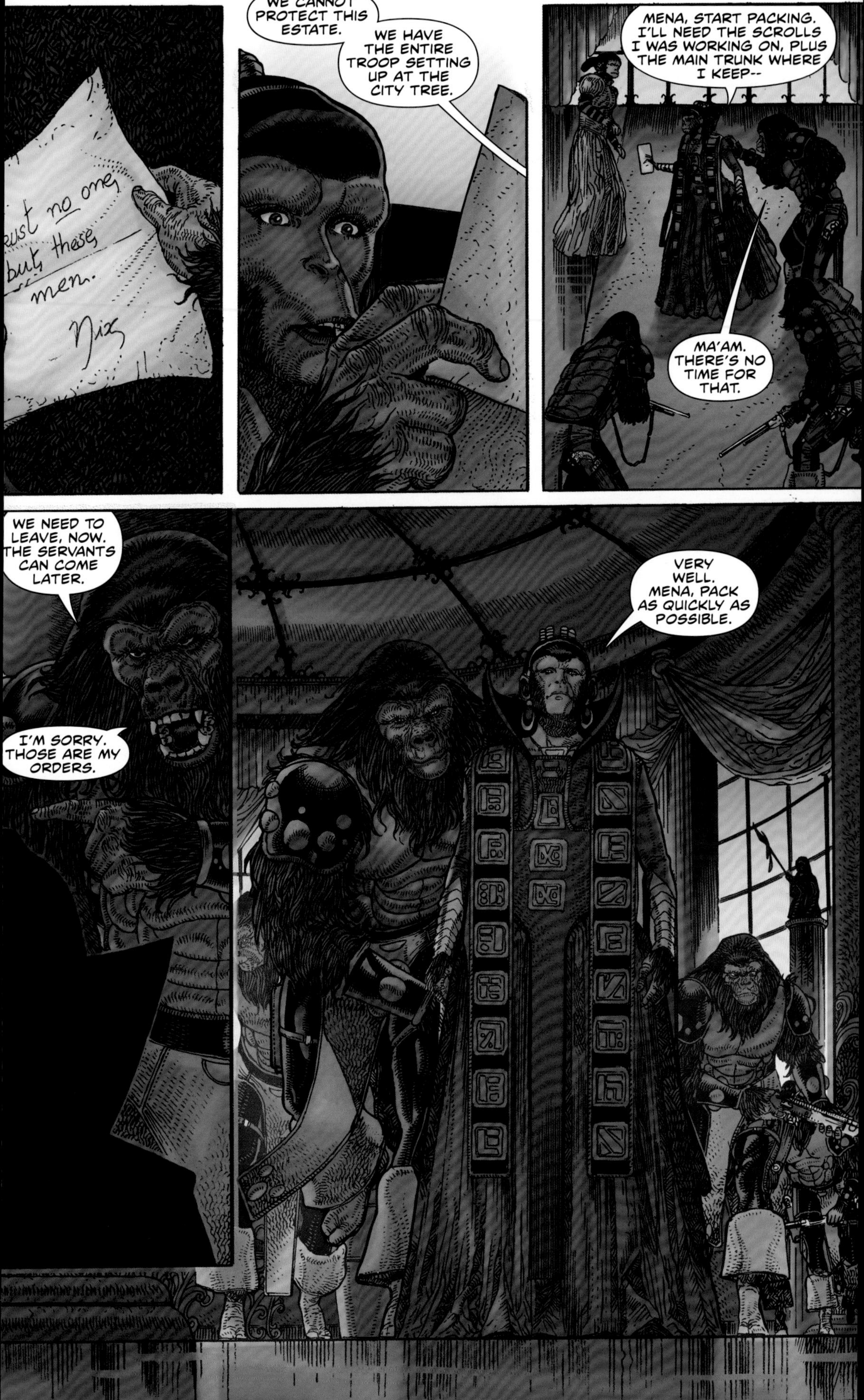
Trust no one but these men.
Nix
WE CANNOT PROTECT THIS ESTATE.
WE HAVE THE ENTIRE TROOP SETTING UP AT THE CITY TREE.
MENA, START PACKING. I'LL NEED THE SCROLLS I WAS WORKING ON, PLUS THE MAIN TRUNK WHERE I KEEP--
MA'AM. THERE'S NO TIME FOR THAT.
WE NEED TO LEAVE, NOW. THE SERVANTS CAN COME LATER.
I'M SORRY. THOSE ARE MY ORDERS.
VERY WELL. MENA, PACK AS QUICKLY AS POSSIBLE.

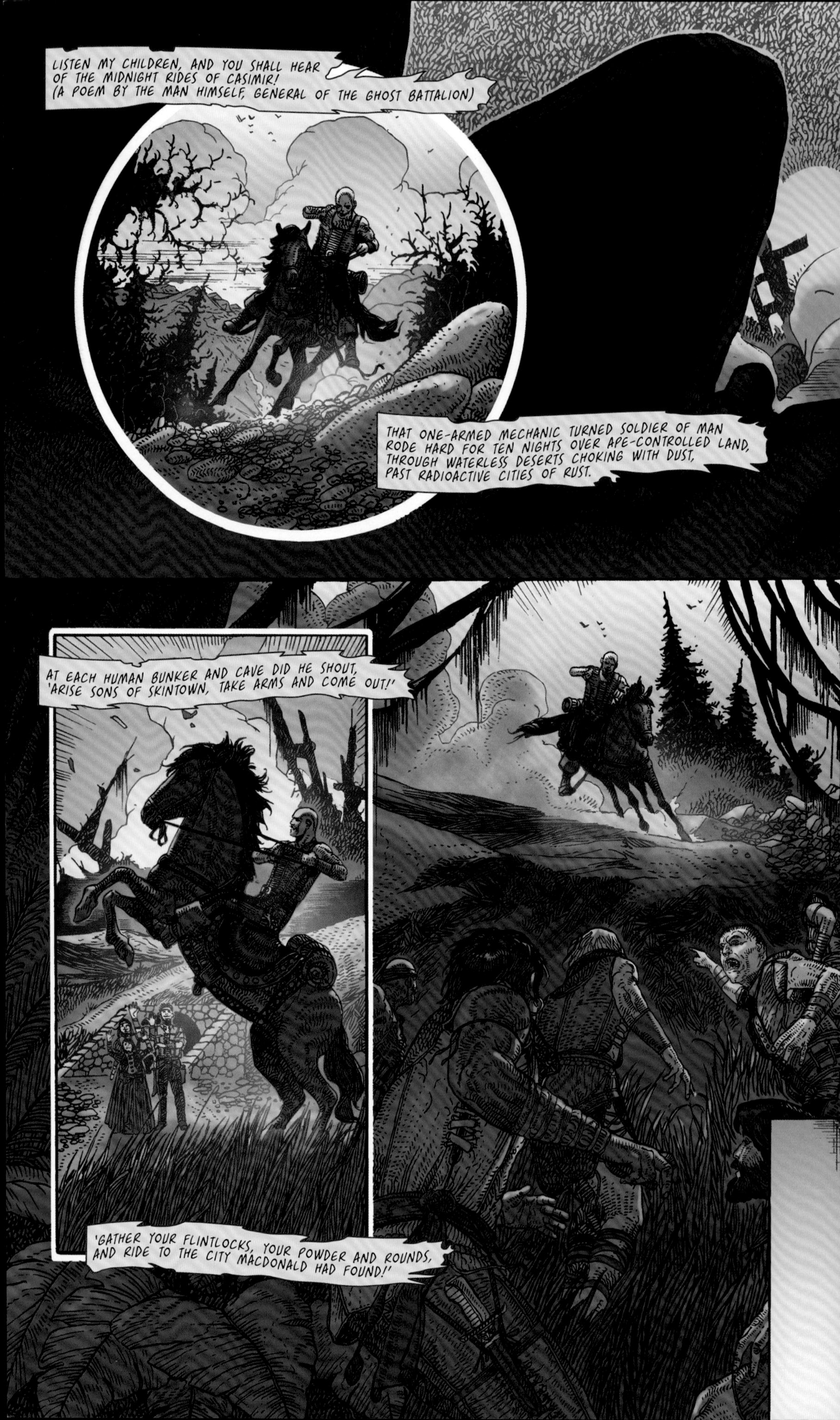
LISTEN MY CHILDREN, AND YOU SHALL HEAR OF THE MIDNIGHT RIDES OF CASIMIR! (A POEM BY THE MAN HIMSELF, GENERAL OF THE GHOST BATTALION)
THAT ONE-ARMED MECHANIC TURNED SOLDIER OF MAN RODE HARD FOR TEN NIGHTS OVER APE-CONTROLLED LAND, THROUGH WATERLESS DESERTS CHOKING WITH DUST, PAST RADIOACTIVE CITIES OF RUST.
AT EACH HUMAN BUNKER AND CAVE DID HE SHOUT, 'ARISE SONS OF SKINTOWN, TAKE ARMS AND COME OUT!'
'GATHER YOUR FLINTLOCKS, YOUR POWDER AND ROUNDS, AND RIDE TO THE CITY MACDONALD HAD FOUND!'

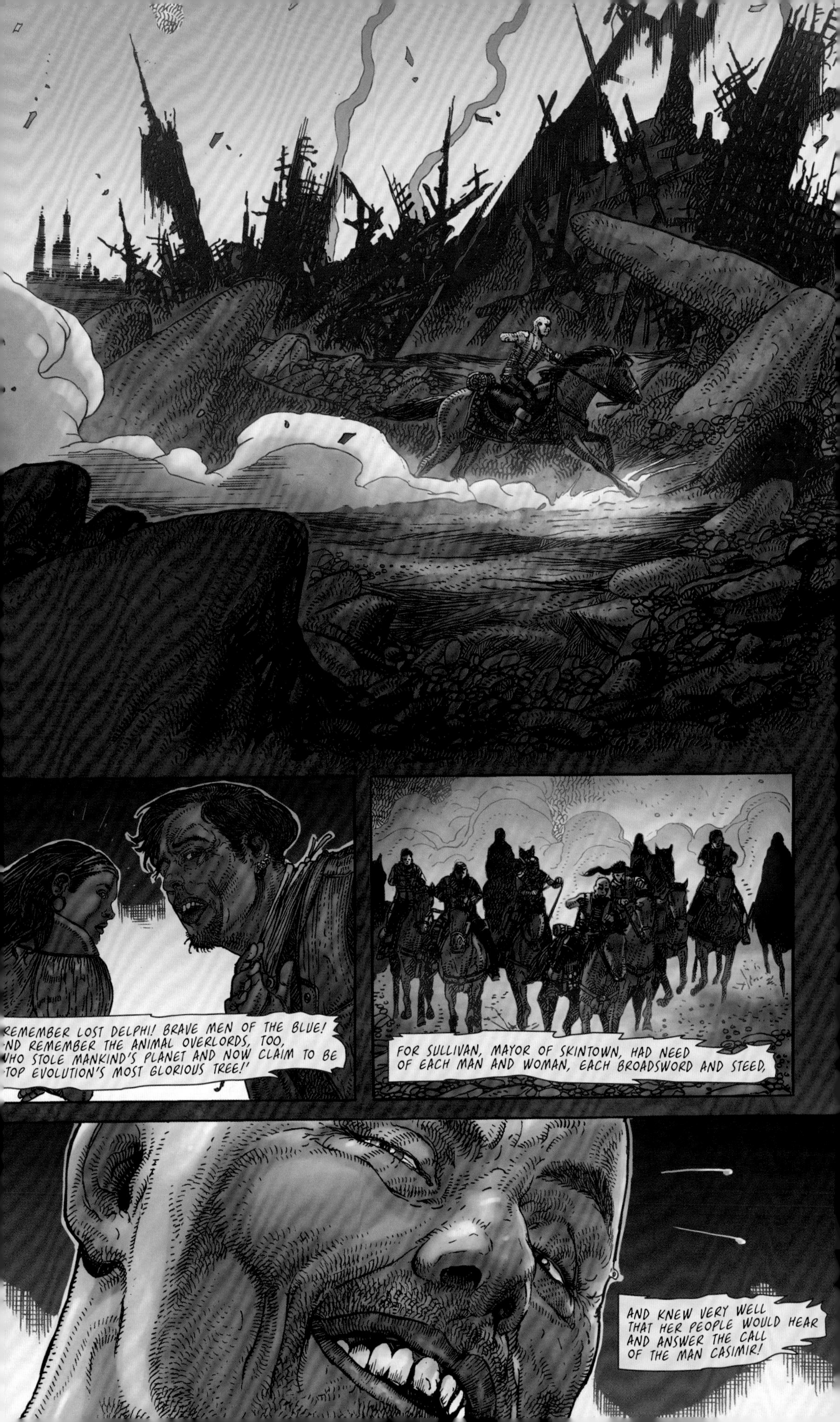
REMEMBER LOST DELPHI! BRAVE MEN OF THE BLUE!
ND REMEMBER THE ANIMAL OVERLORDS, TOO,
HO STOLE MANKIND'S PLANET AND NOW CLAIM TO BE
TOP EVOLUTION'S MOST GLORIOUS TREE!'
FOR SULLIVAN, MAYOR OF SKINTOWN, HAD NEED OF EACH MAN AND WOMAN, EACH BROADSWORD AND STEED,
AND KNEW VERY WELL THAT HER PEOPLE WOULD HEAR AND ANSWER THE CALL OF THE MAN CASIMIR!

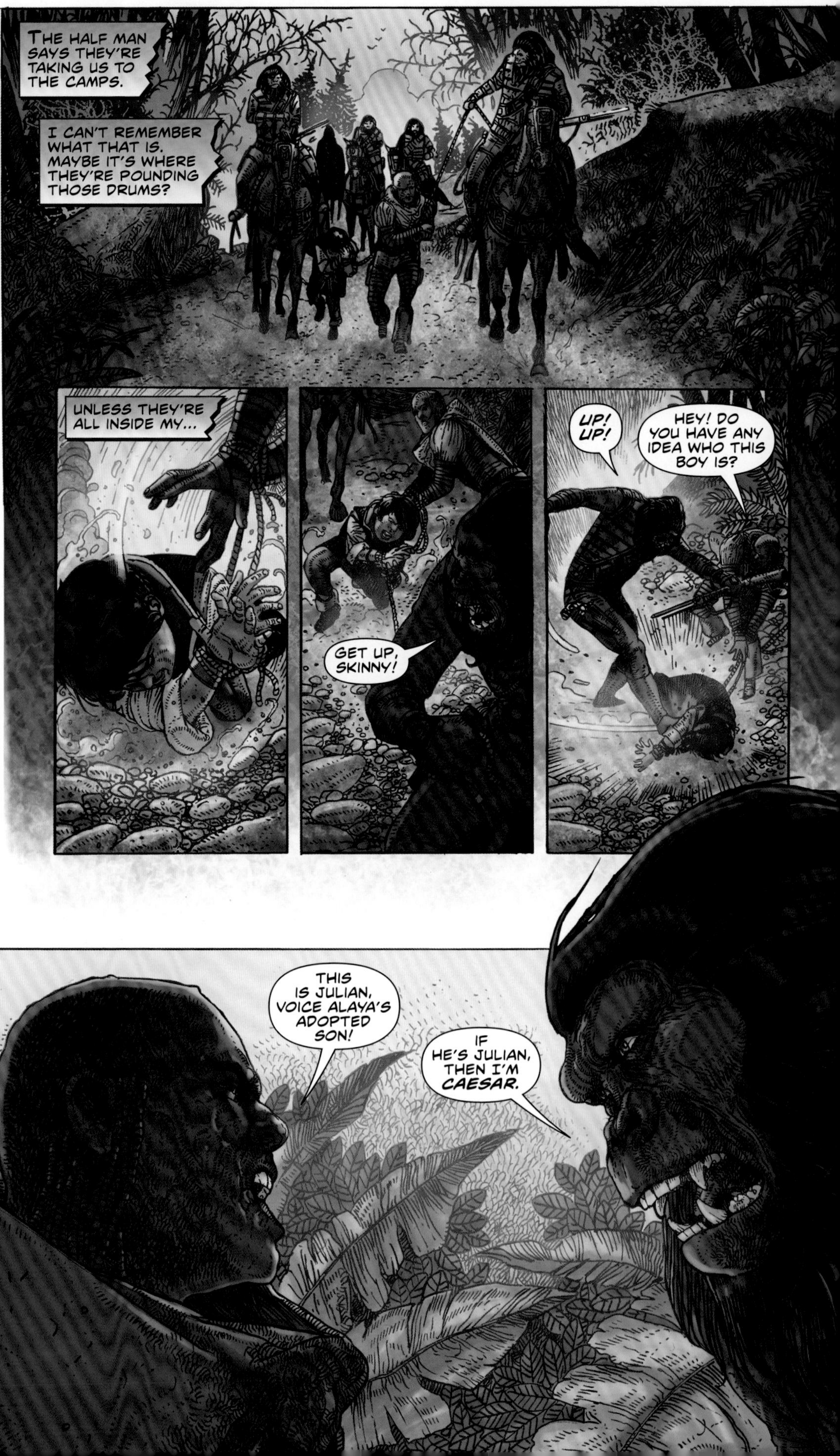

THE HALF MAN SAYS THEY'RE TAKING US TO THE CAMPS.
I CAN'T REMEMBER WHAT THAT IS. MAYBE IT'S WHERE THEY'RE POUNDING THOSE DRUMS?
UNLESS THEY'RE ALL INSIDE MY...
GET UP, SKINNY!
UP! UP!
HEY! DO YOU HAVE ANY IDEA WHO THIS BOY IS?
THIS IS JULIAN, VOICE ALAYA'S ADOPTED SON!
IF HE'S JULIAN, THEN I'M CAESAR.

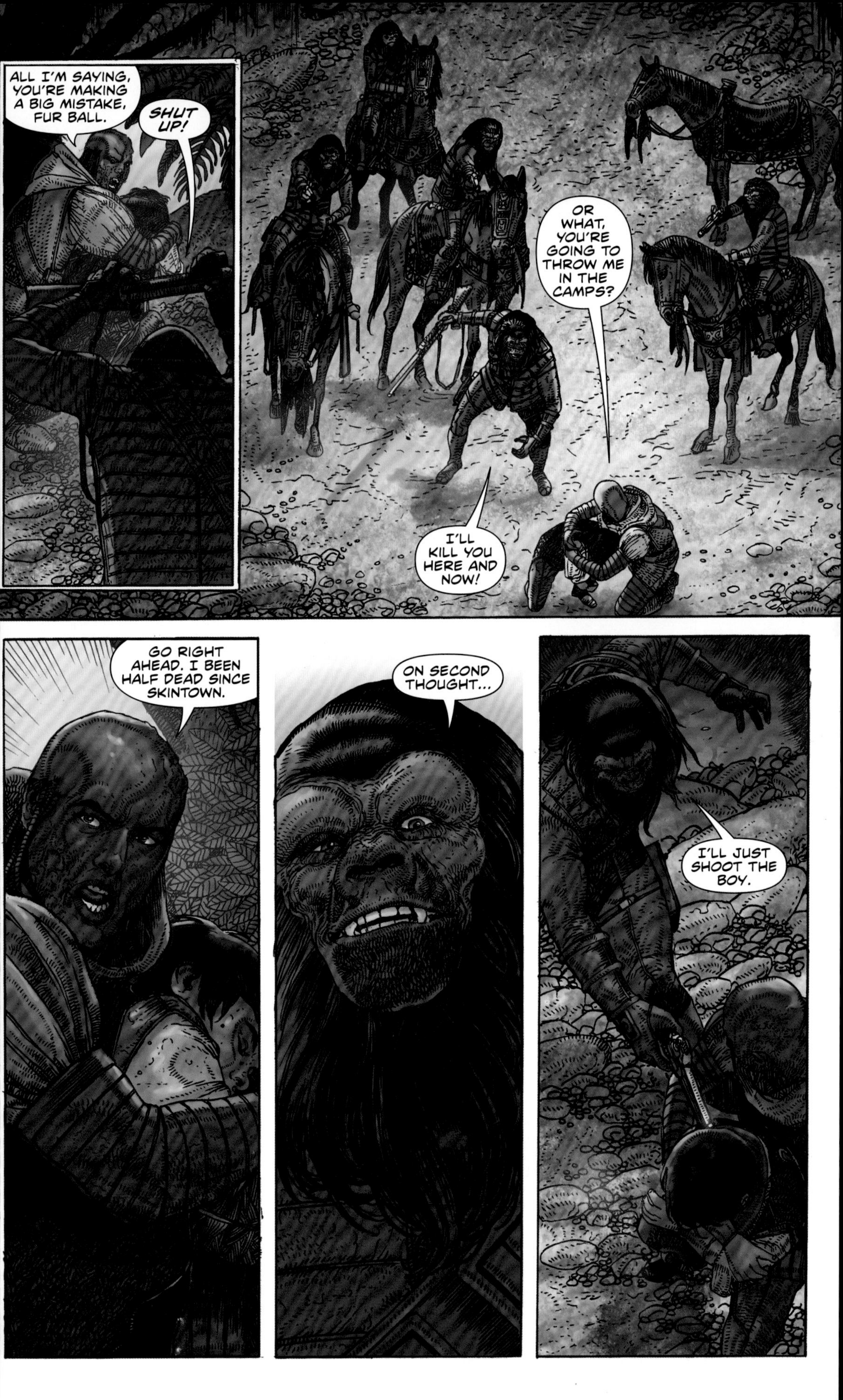
ALL I'M SAYING, YOU'RE MAKING A BIG MISTAKE, FUR BALL.
SHUT UP!
OR WHAT, YOU'RE GOING TO THROW ME IN THE CAMPS?
I'LL KILL YOU HERE AND NOW!
GO RIGHT AHEAD. I BEEN HALF DEAD SINCE SKINTOWN.
ON SECOND THOUGHT...
I'LL JUST SHOOT THE BOY.

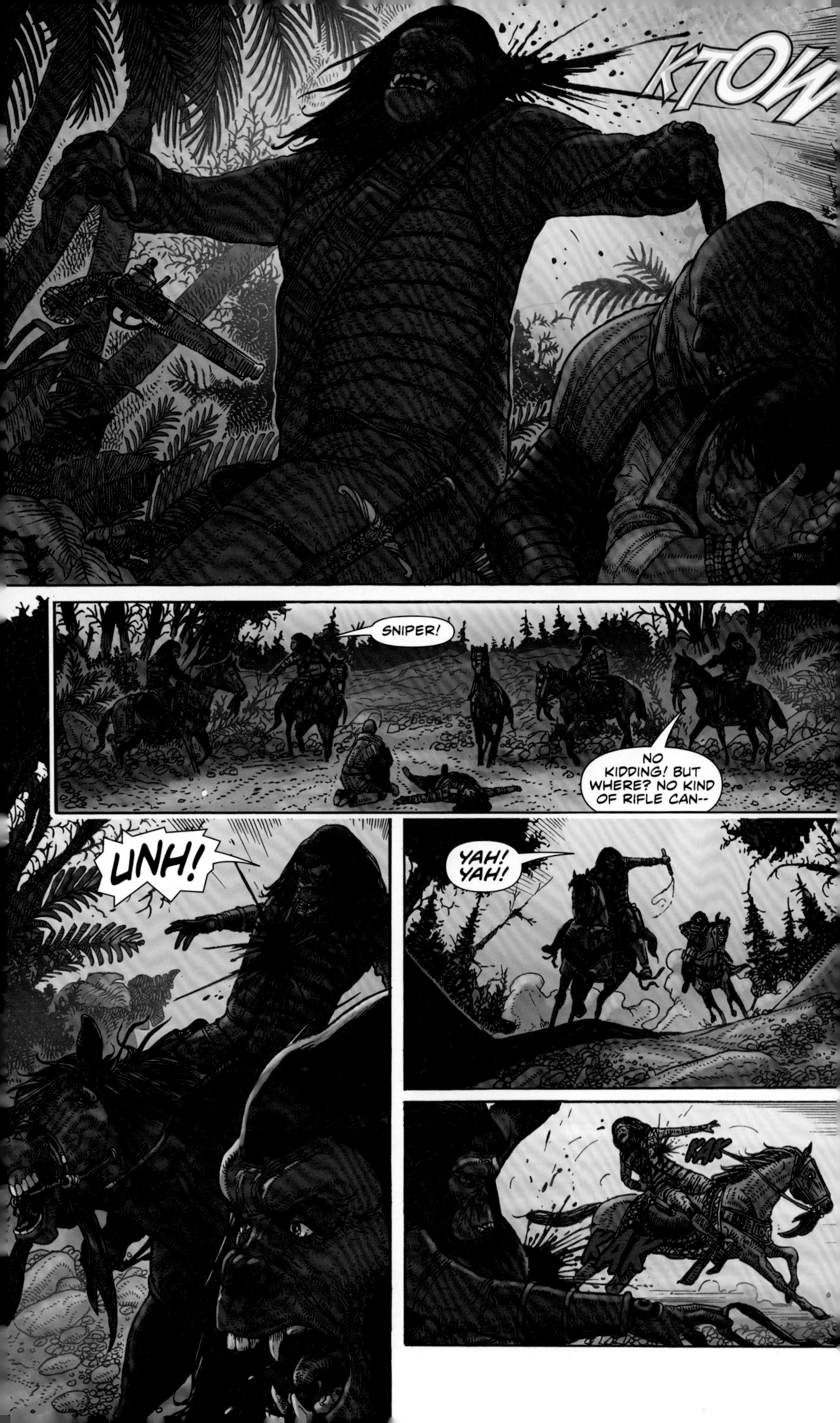
KTOW
SNIPER!
NO KIDDING! BUT WHERE? NO KIND OF RIFLE CAN--
UNH!
YAH! YAH!
KAK

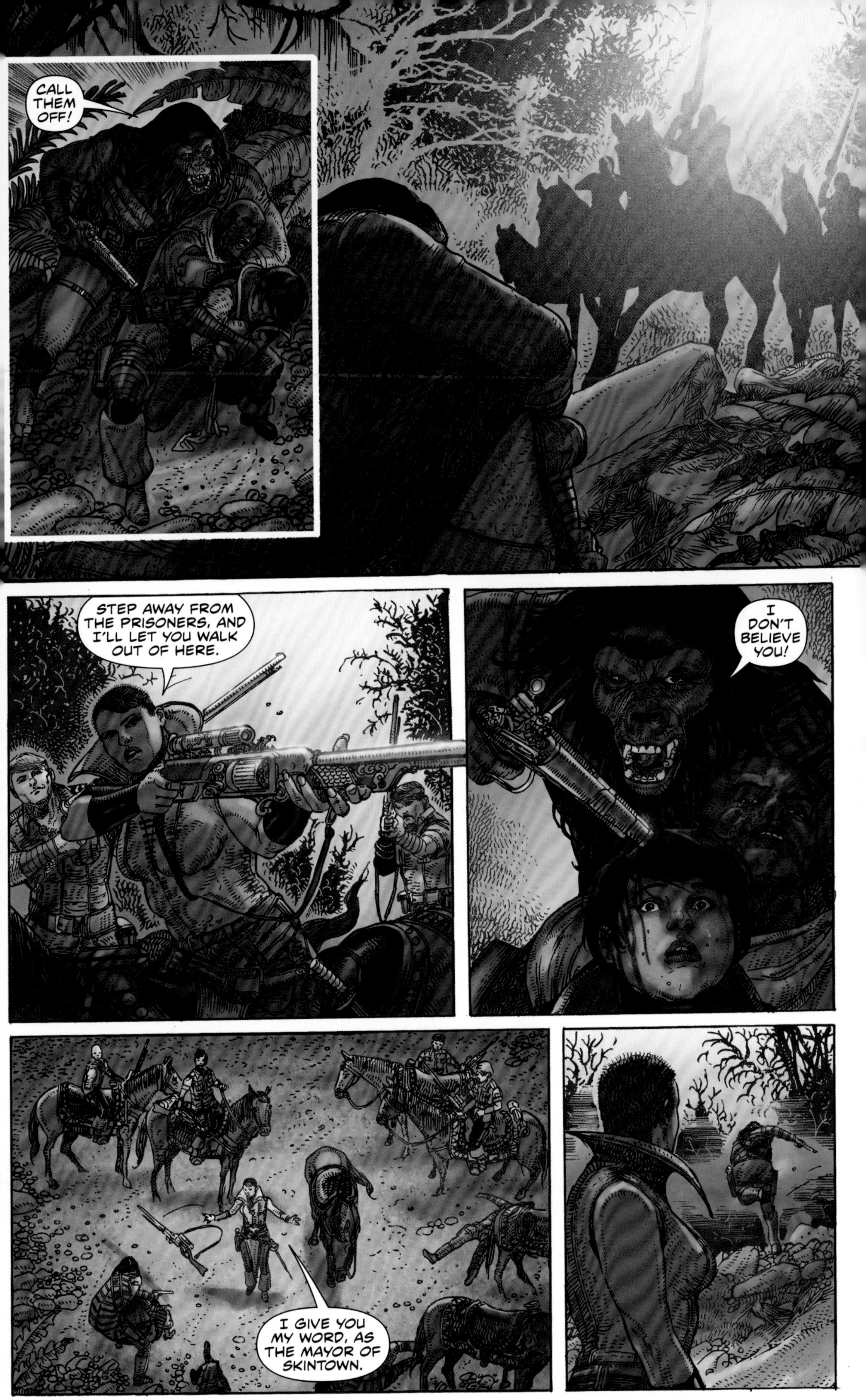
CALL THEM OFF!
STEP AWAY FROM THE PRISONERS, AND I'LL LET YOU WALK OUT OF HERE.
I DON'T BELIEVE YOU!
I GIVE YOU MY WORD, AS THE MAYOR OF SKINTOWN.

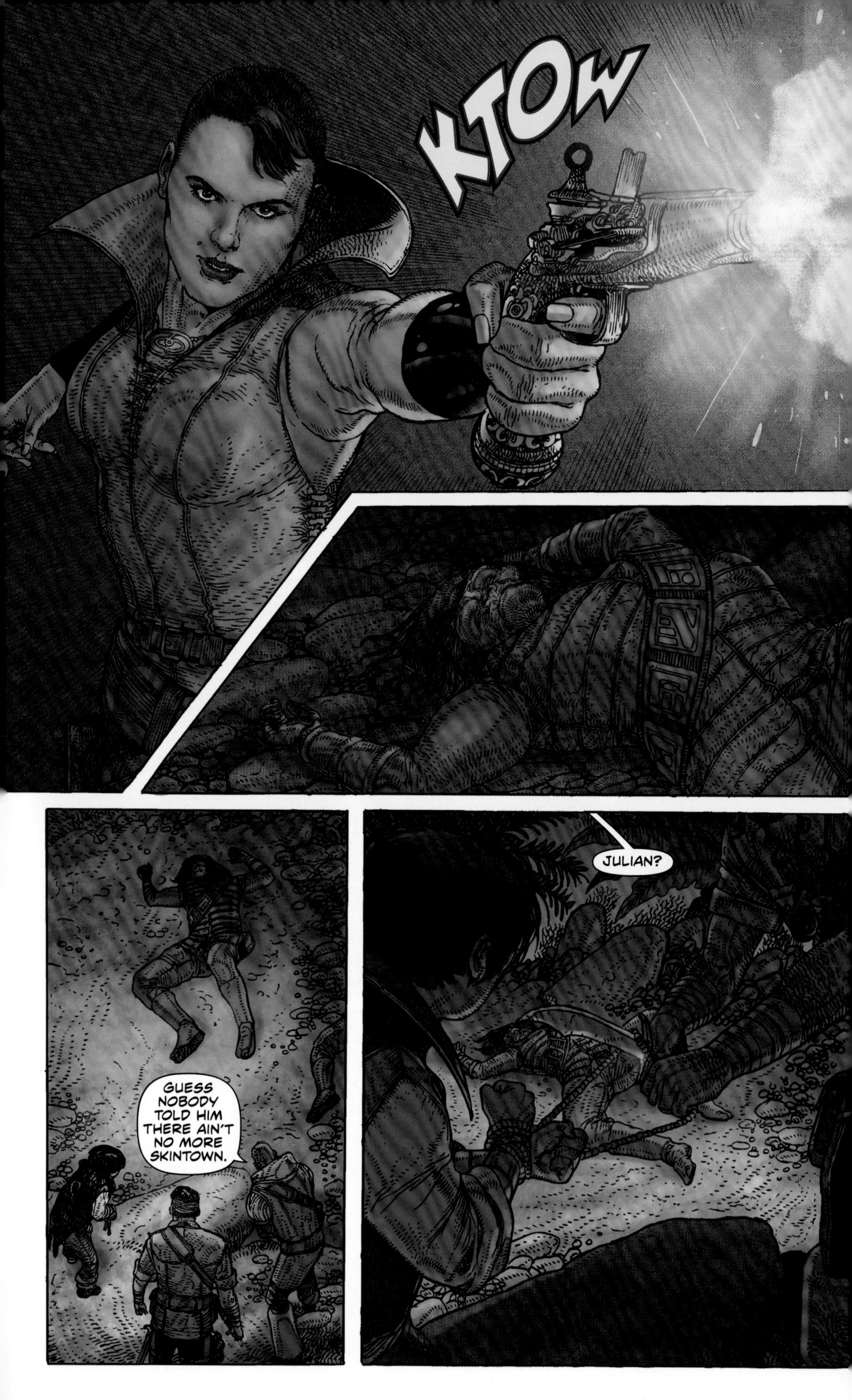
KTOW
GUESS NOBODY TOLD HIM THERE AIN'T NO MORE SKINTOWN.
JULIAN?

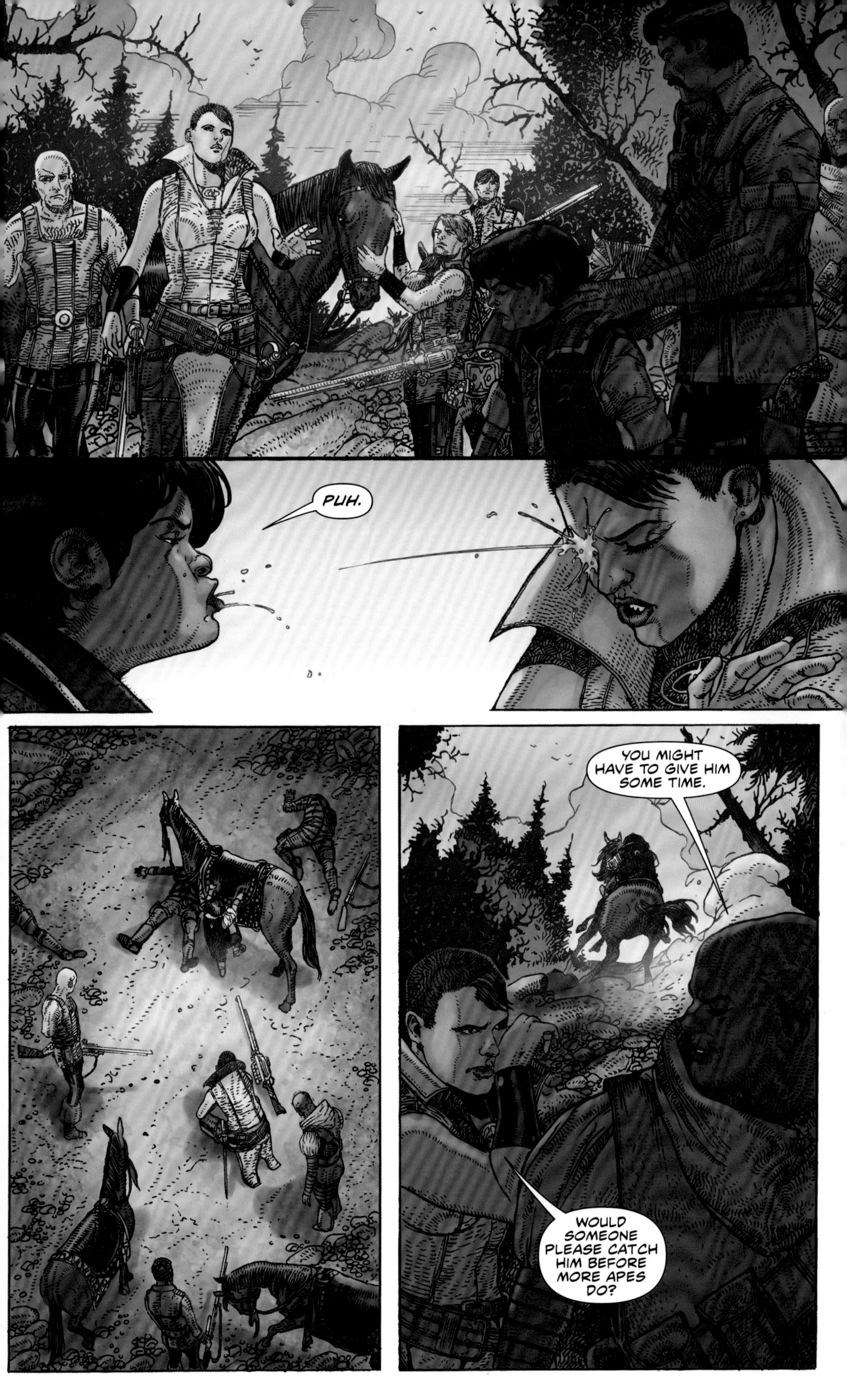
PUH.
YOU MIGHT HAVE TO GIVE HIM SOME TIME.
WOULD SOMEONE PLEASE CATCH HIM BEFORE MORE APES DO?

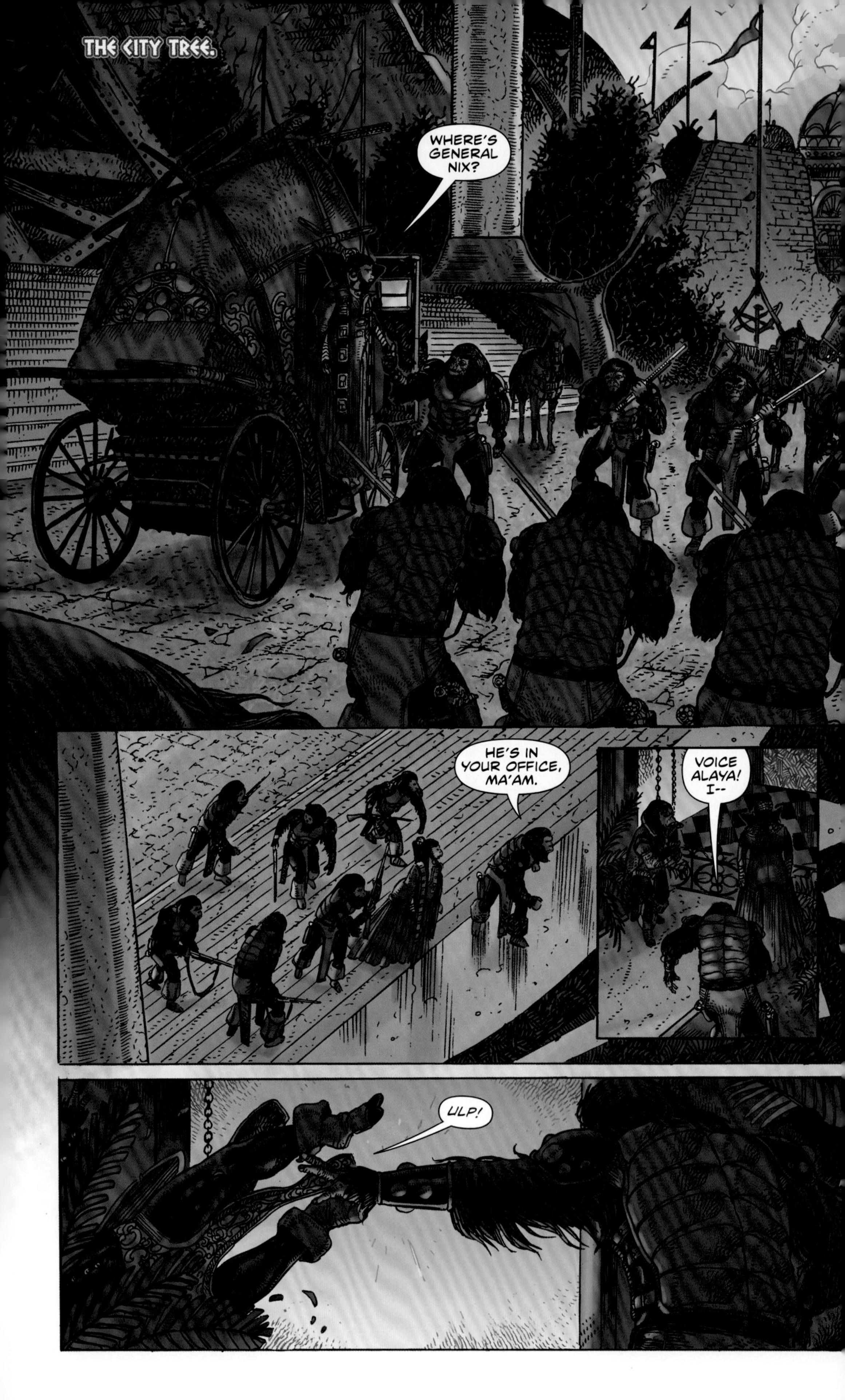
THE CITY TREE.
WHERE'S GENERAL NIX?
HE'S IN YOUR OFFICE, MA'AM.
VOICE ALAYA! I--
ULP!

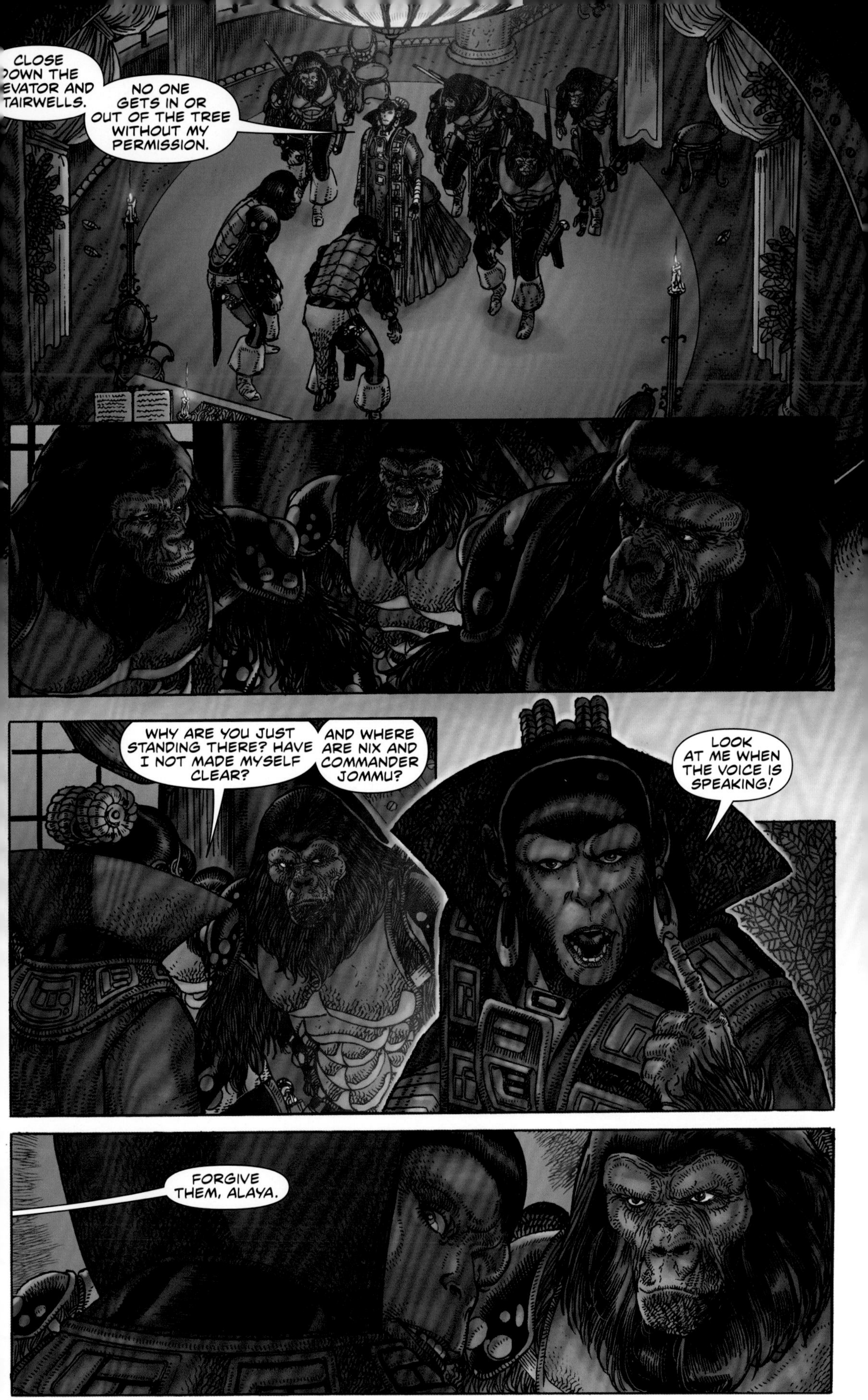
CLOSE
DOWN THE
EVATOR AND
TAIRWELLS.
NO ONE GETS IN OR OUT OF THE TREE WITHOUT MY PERMISSION.
WHY ARE YOU JUST STANDING THERE? HAVE I NOT MADE MYSELF CLEAR?
AND WHERE ARE NIX AND COMMANDER JOMMU?
LOOK AT ME WHEN THE VOICE IS SPEAKING!
FORGIVE THEM, ALAYA.

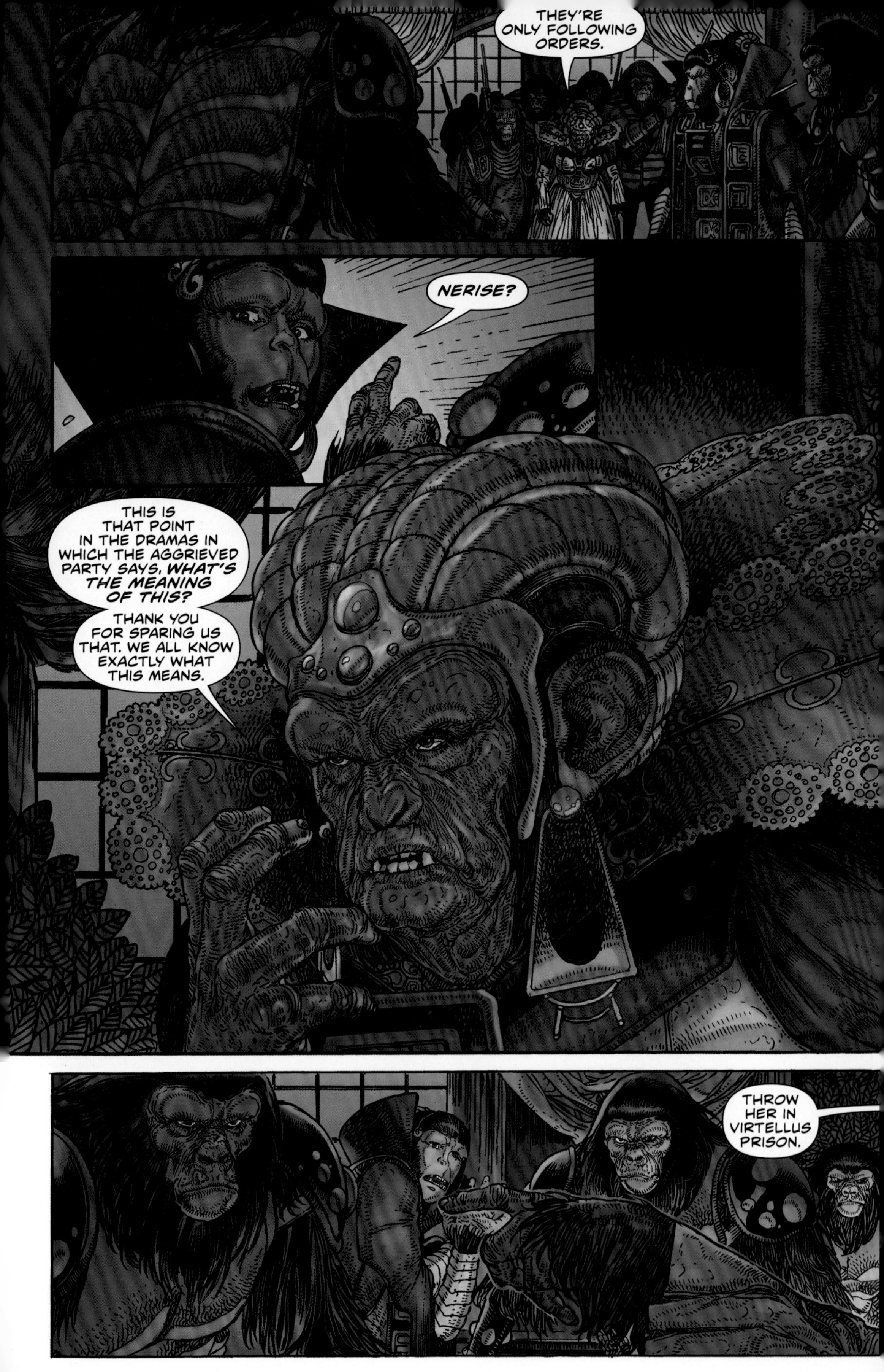
THEY'RE ONLY FOLLOWING ORDERS.
NERISE?
THIS IS THAT POINT IN THE DRAMAS IN WHICH THE AGGRIEVED PARTY SAYS, *WHAT'S THE MEANING OF THIS?*
THANK YOU FOR SPARING US THAT. WE ALL KNOW EXACTLY WHAT THIS MEANS.
THROW HER IN VIRTELLUS PRISON.

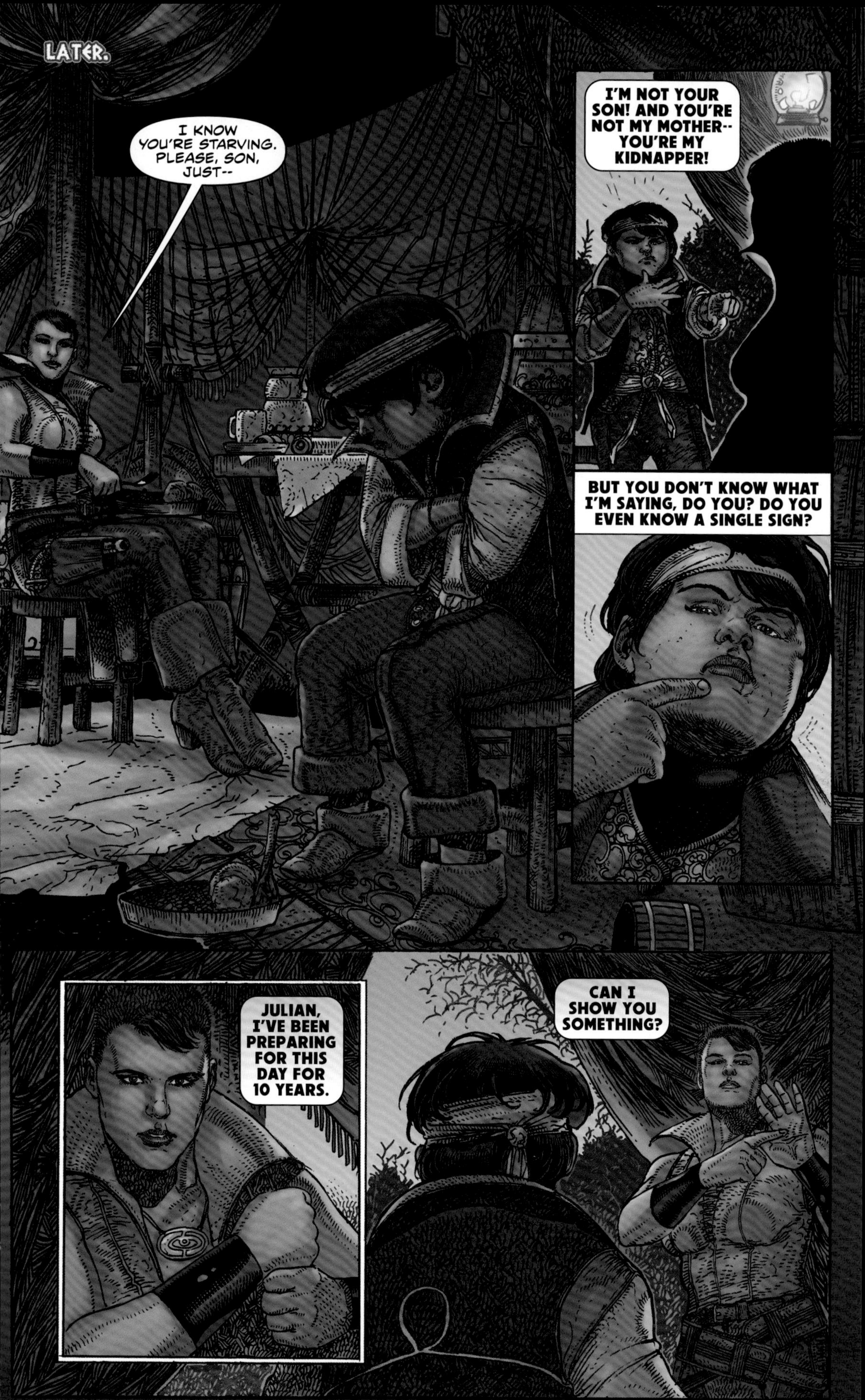
LATER.
I KNOW YOU'RE STARVING. PLEASE, SON, JUST--
I'M NOT YOUR SON! AND YOU'RE NOT MY MOTHER-- YOU'RE MY KIDNAPPER!
BUT YOU DON'T KNOW WHAT I'M SAYING, DO YOU? DO YOU EVEN KNOW A SINGLE SIGN?
JULIAN, I'VE BEEN PREPARING FOR THIS DAY FOR 10 YEARS.
CAN I SHOW YOU SOMETHING?

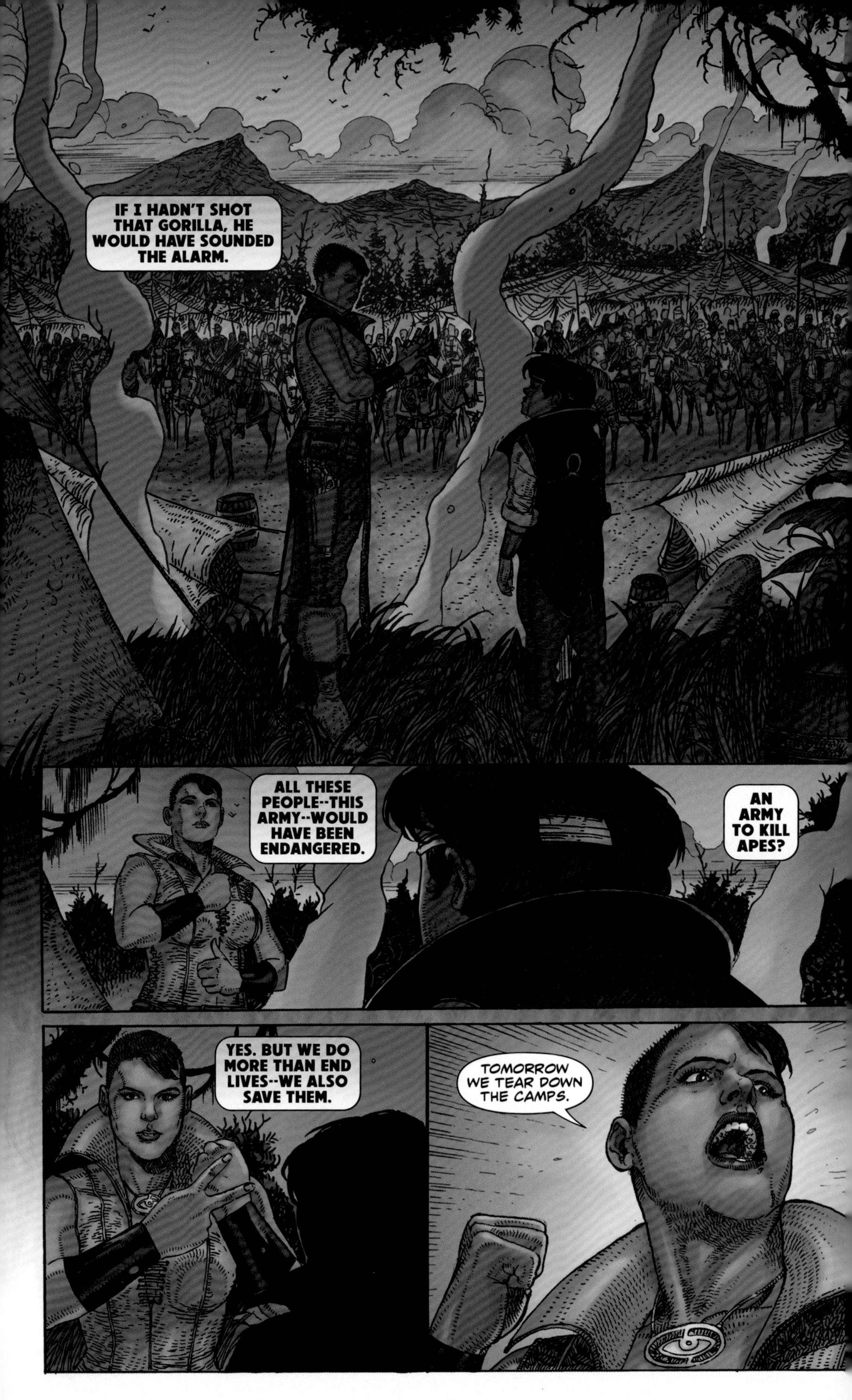
IF I HADN'T SHOT THAT GORILLA, HE WOULD HAVE SOUNDED THE ALARM.
ALL THESE PEOPLE--THIS ARMY--WOULD HAVE BEEN ENDANGERED.
AN ARMY TO KILL APES?
YES. BUT WE DO MORE THAN END LIVES--WE ALSO SAVE THEM.
TOMORROW WE TEAR DOWN THE CAMPS.

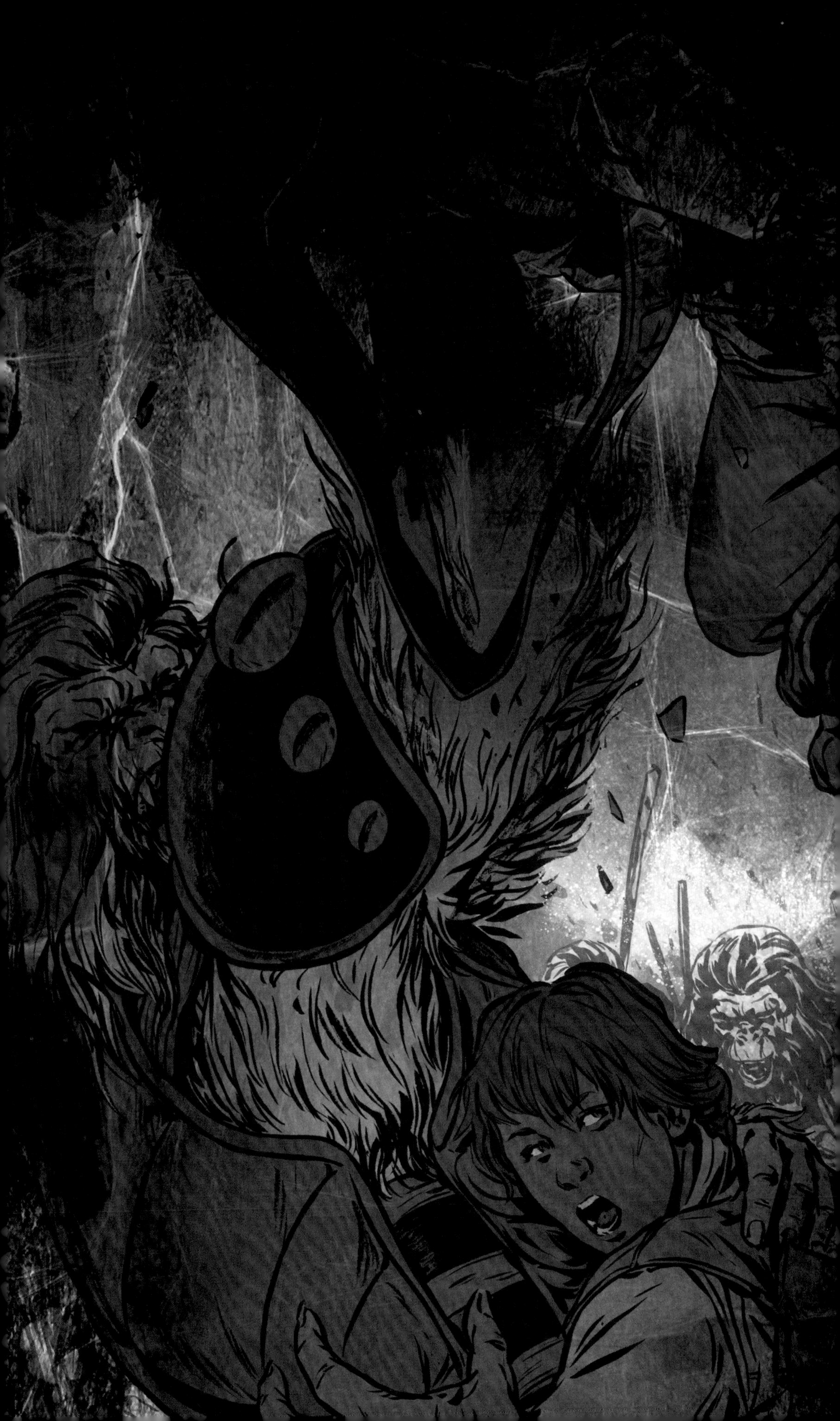

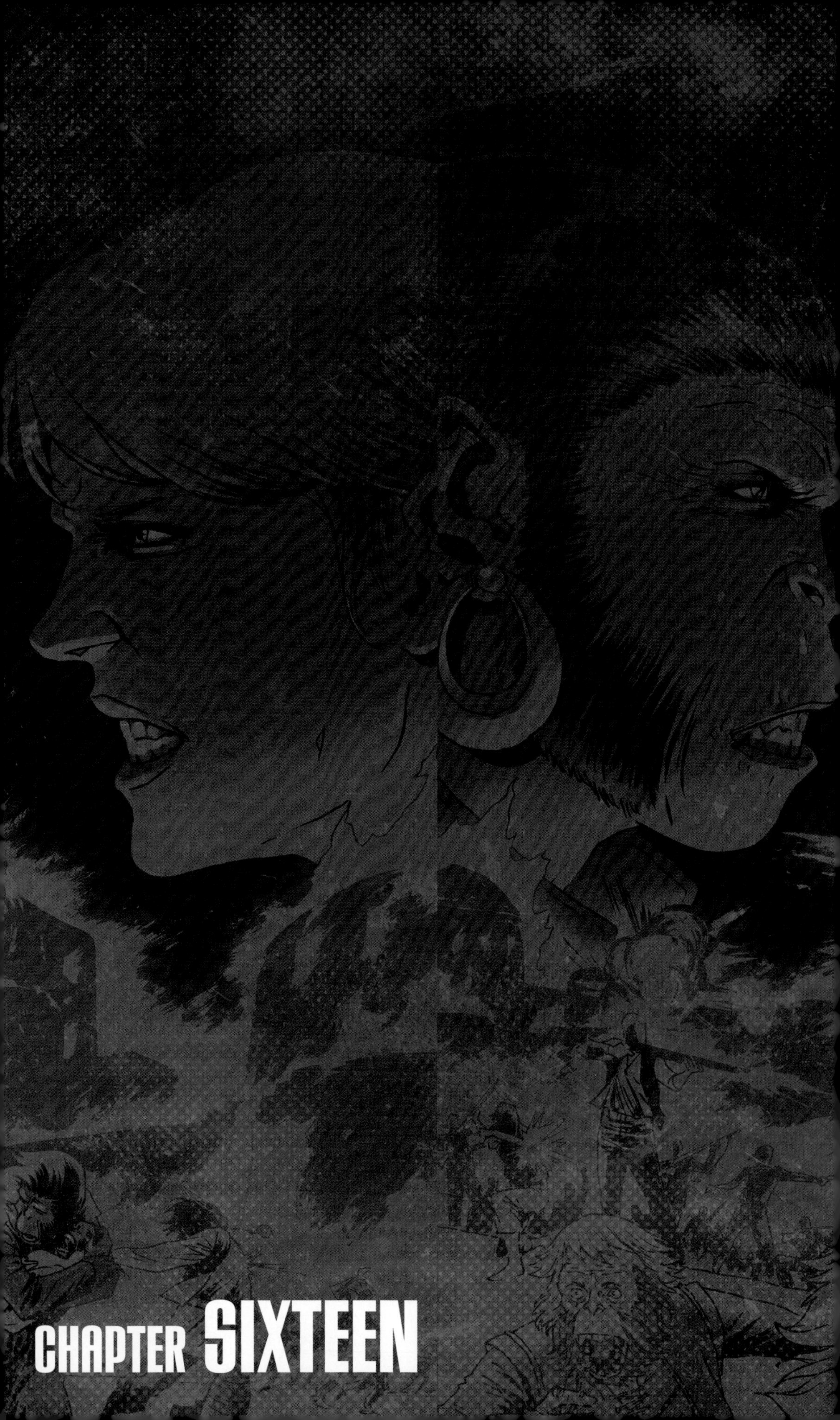
CHAPTER SIXTEEN

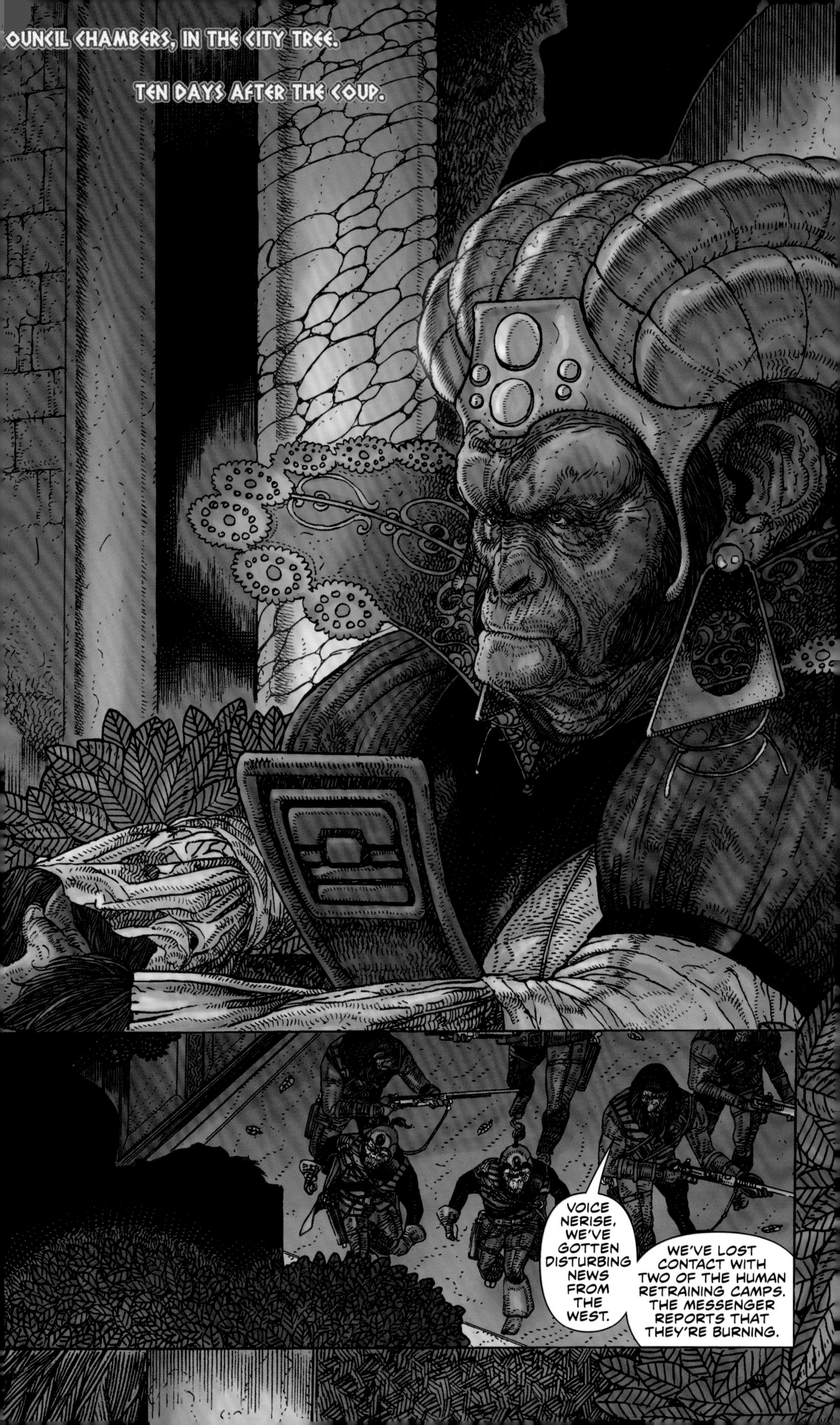
OUNCIL CHAMBERS, IN THE CITY TREE.
TEN DAYS AFTER THE COUP.
VOICE NERISE, WE'VE GOTTEN DISTURBING NEWS FROM THE WEST.
WE'VE LOST CONTACT WITH TWO OF THE HUMAN RETRAINING CAMPS. THE MESSENGER REPORTS THAT THEY'RE BURNING.

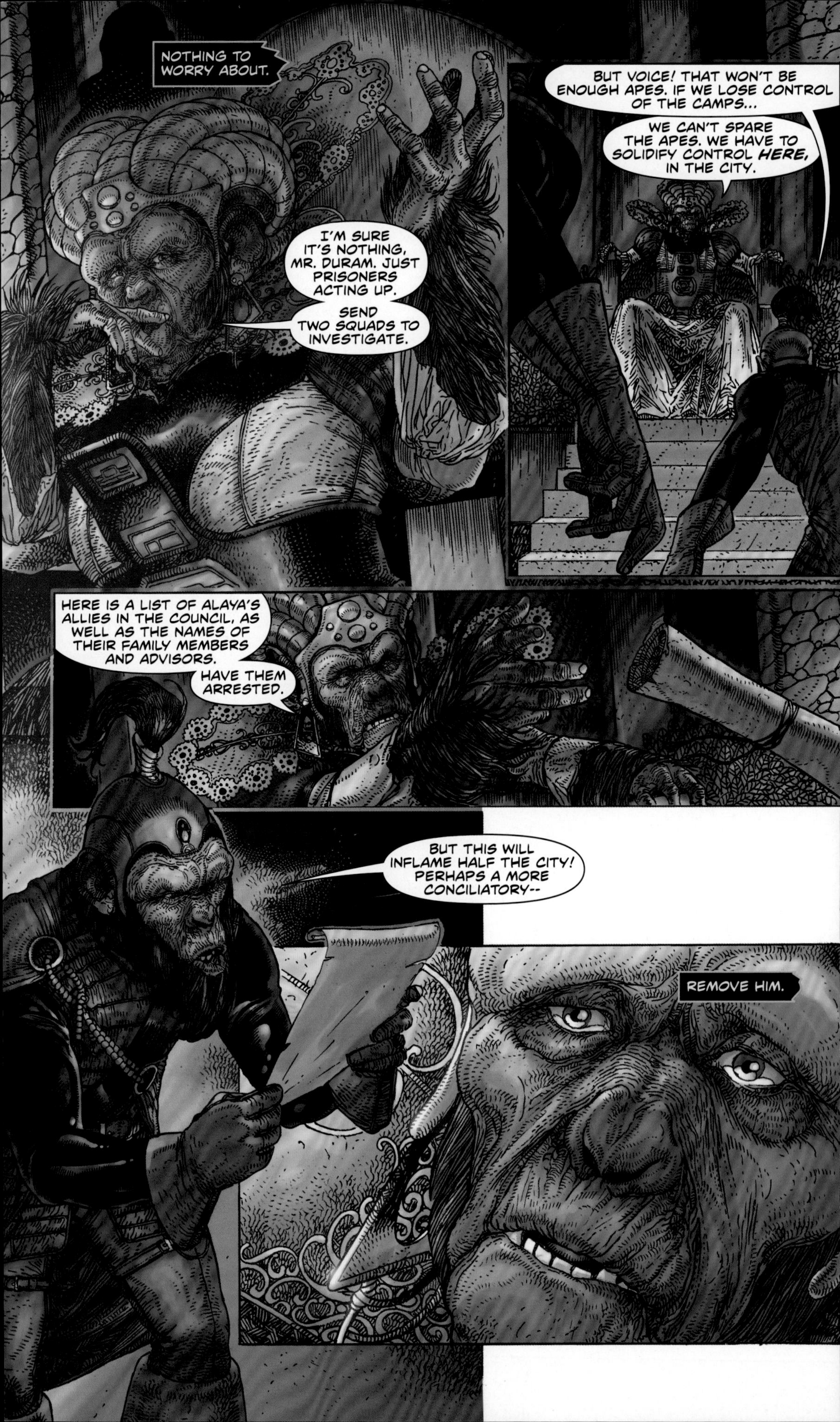
NOTHING TO WORRY ABOUT.
BUT VOICE! THAT WON'T BE ENOUGH APES. IF WE LOSE CONTROL OF THE CAMPS...
WE CAN'T SPARE THE APES. WE HAVE TO SOLIDIFY CONTROL HERE, IN THE CITY.
I'M SURE IT'S NOTHING, MR. DURAM. JUST PRISONERS ACTING UP.
SEND TWO SQUADS TO INVESTIGATE.
HERE IS A LIST OF ALAYA'S ALLIES IN THE COUNCIL, AS WELL AS THE NAMES OF THEIR FAMILY MEMBERS AND ADVISORS.
HAVE THEM ARRESTED.
BUT THIS WILL INFLAME HALF THE CITY! PERHAPS A MORE CONCILIATORY--
REMOVE HIM.

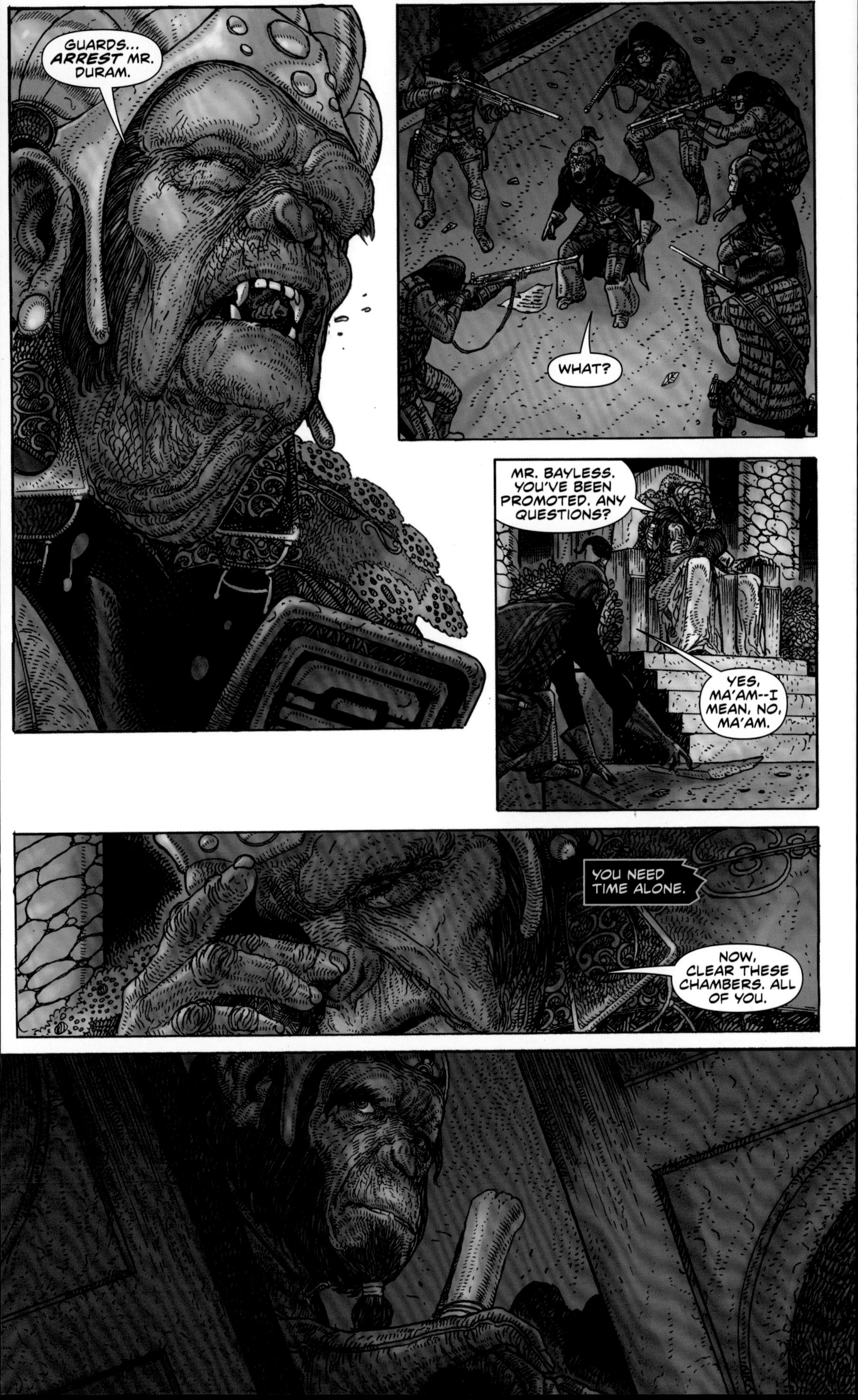
GUARDS... *ARREST* MR. DURAM.
WHAT?
MR. BAYLESS. YOU'VE BEEN PROMOTED. ANY QUESTIONS?
YES, MA'AM--I MEAN, NO, MA'AM.
YOU NEED TIME ALONE.
NOW, CLEAR THESE CHAMBERS. ALL OF YOU.

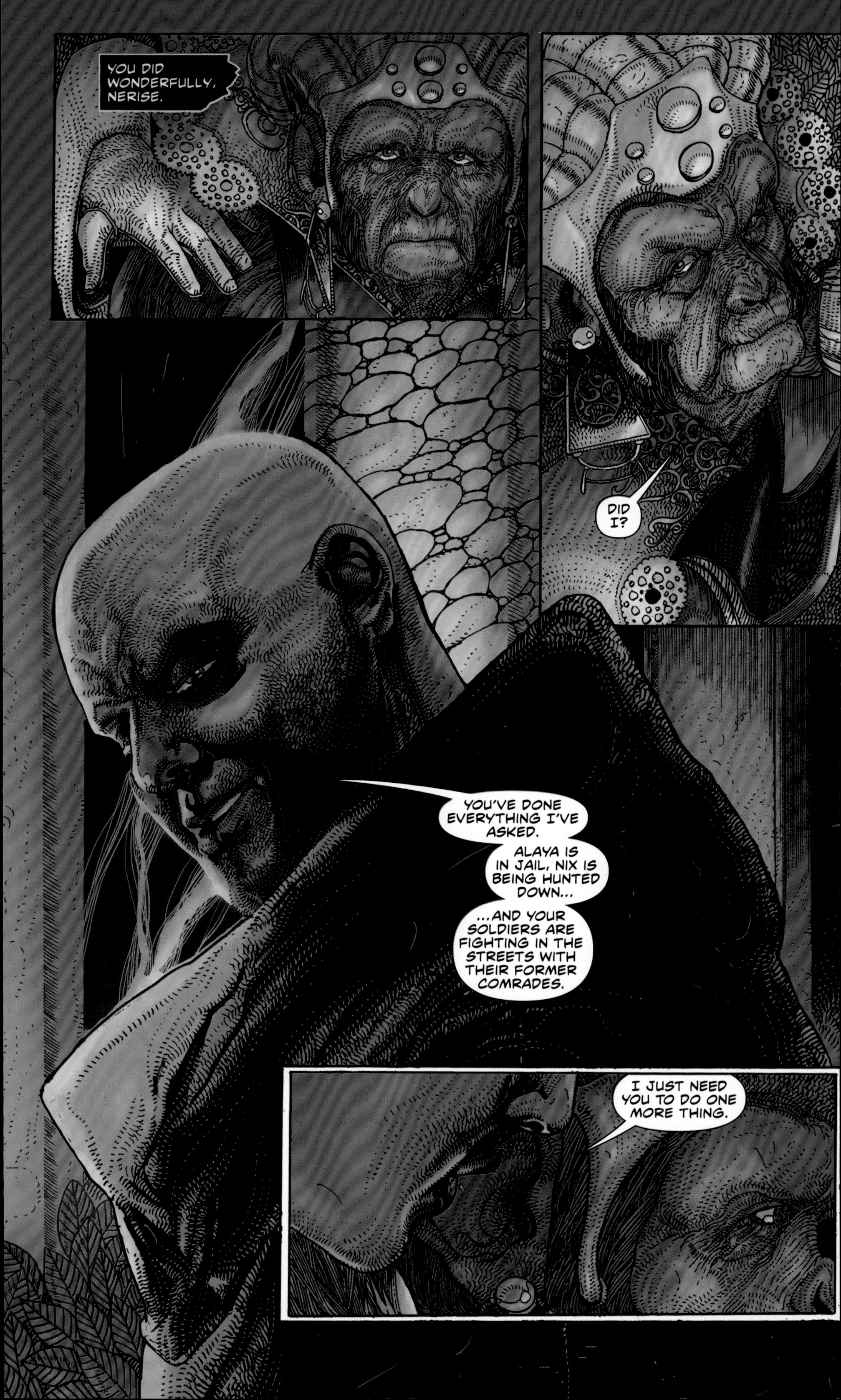
YOU DID WONDERFULLY, NERISE.
DID I?
YOU'VE DONE EVERYTHING I'VE ASKED.
ALAYA IS IN JAIL, NIX IS BEING HUNTED DOWN...
...AND YOUR SOLDIERS ARE FIGHTING IN THE STREETS WITH THEIR FORMER COMRADES.
I JUST NEED YOU TO DO ONE MORE THING.

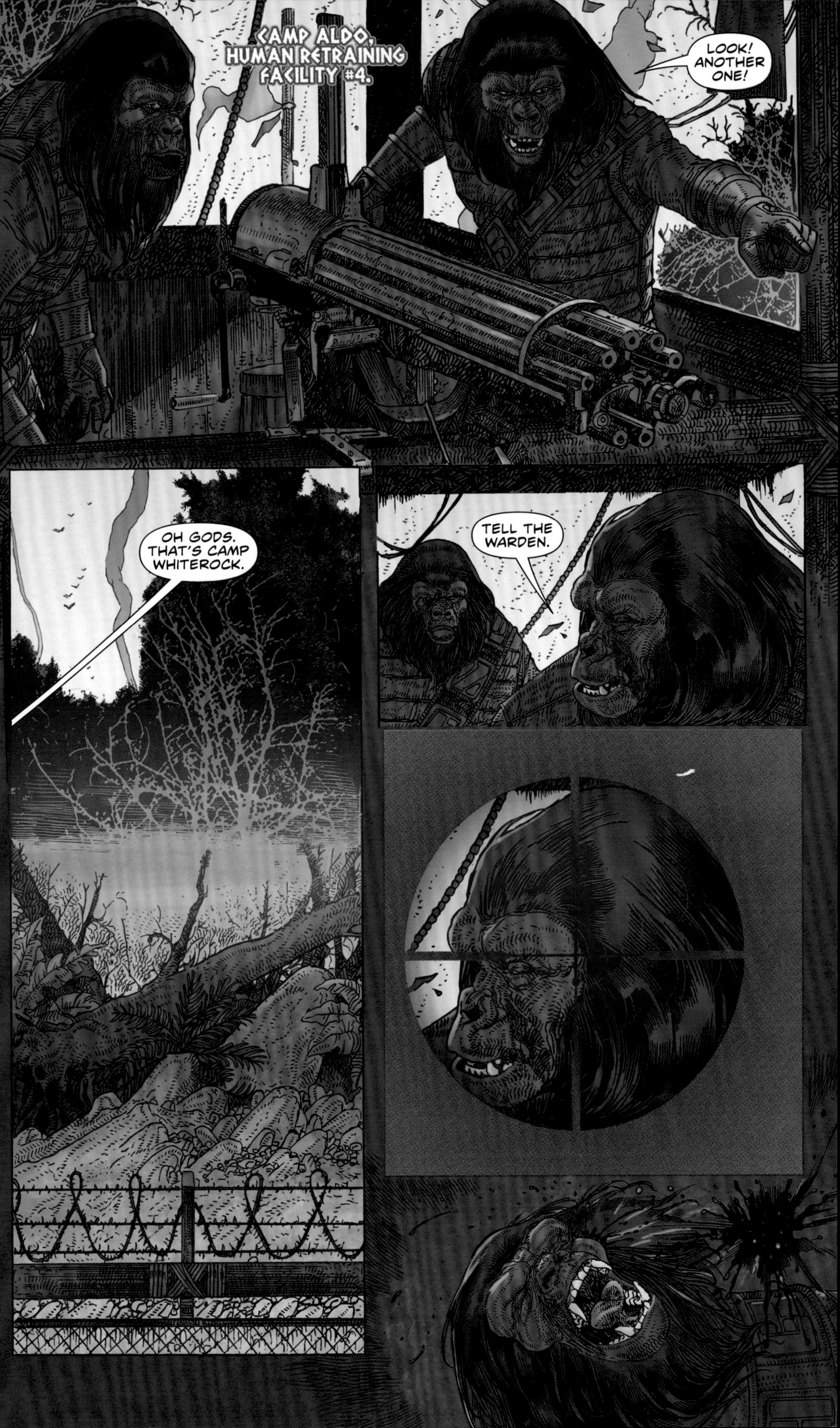
CAMP ALDO, HUMAN RETRAINING FACILITY #4.
LOOK! ANOTHER ONE!
OH GODS. THAT'S CAMP WHITEROCK.
TELL THE WARDEN.

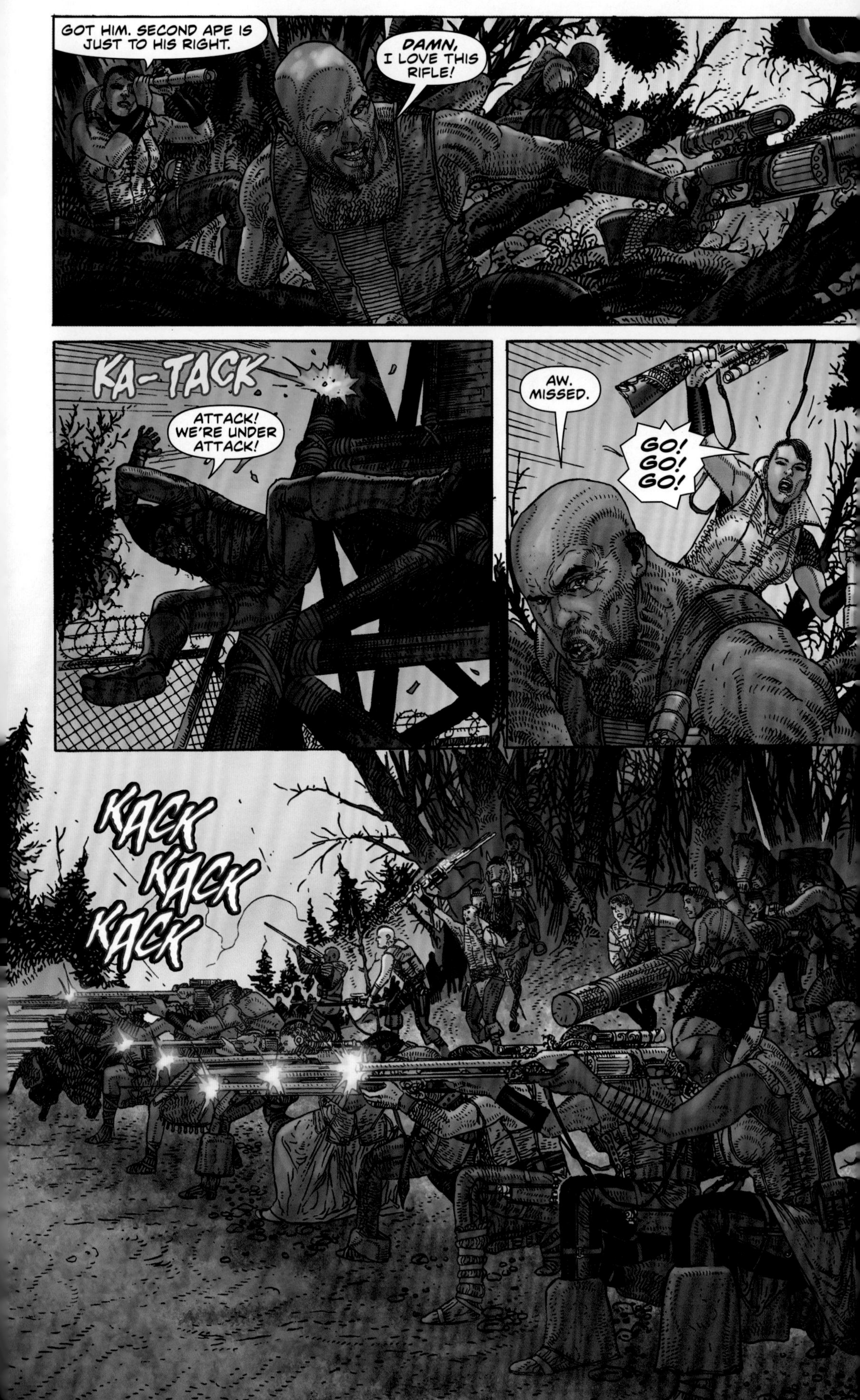
GOT HIM. SECOND APE IS JUST TO HIS RIGHT.
DAMN, I LOVE THIS RIFLE!
KA-TACK
ATTACK! WE'RE UNDER ATTACK!
AW. MISSED.
GO! GO! GO!
KACK KACK KACK

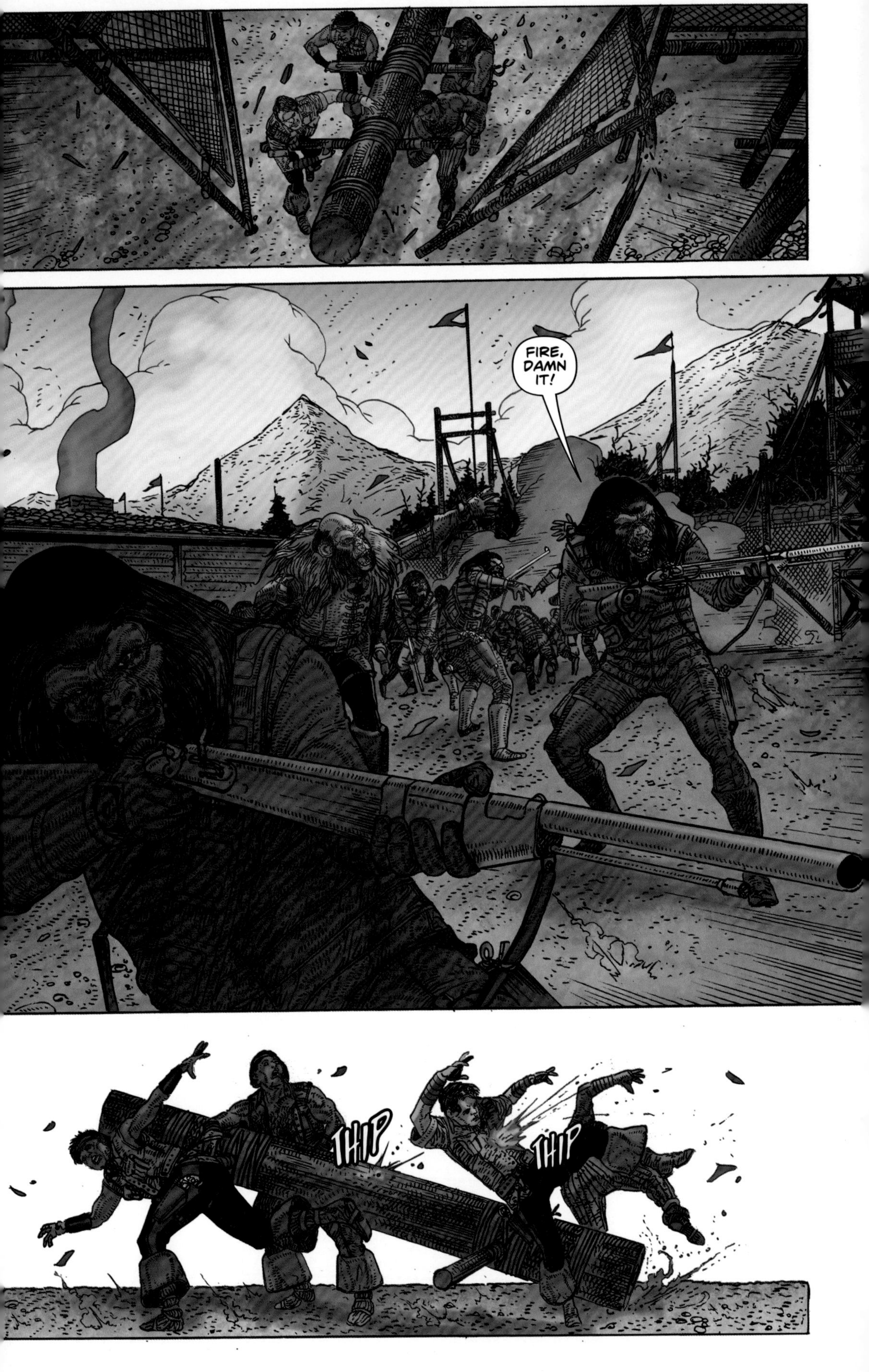
FIRE, DAMN IT!
THIP
THIP

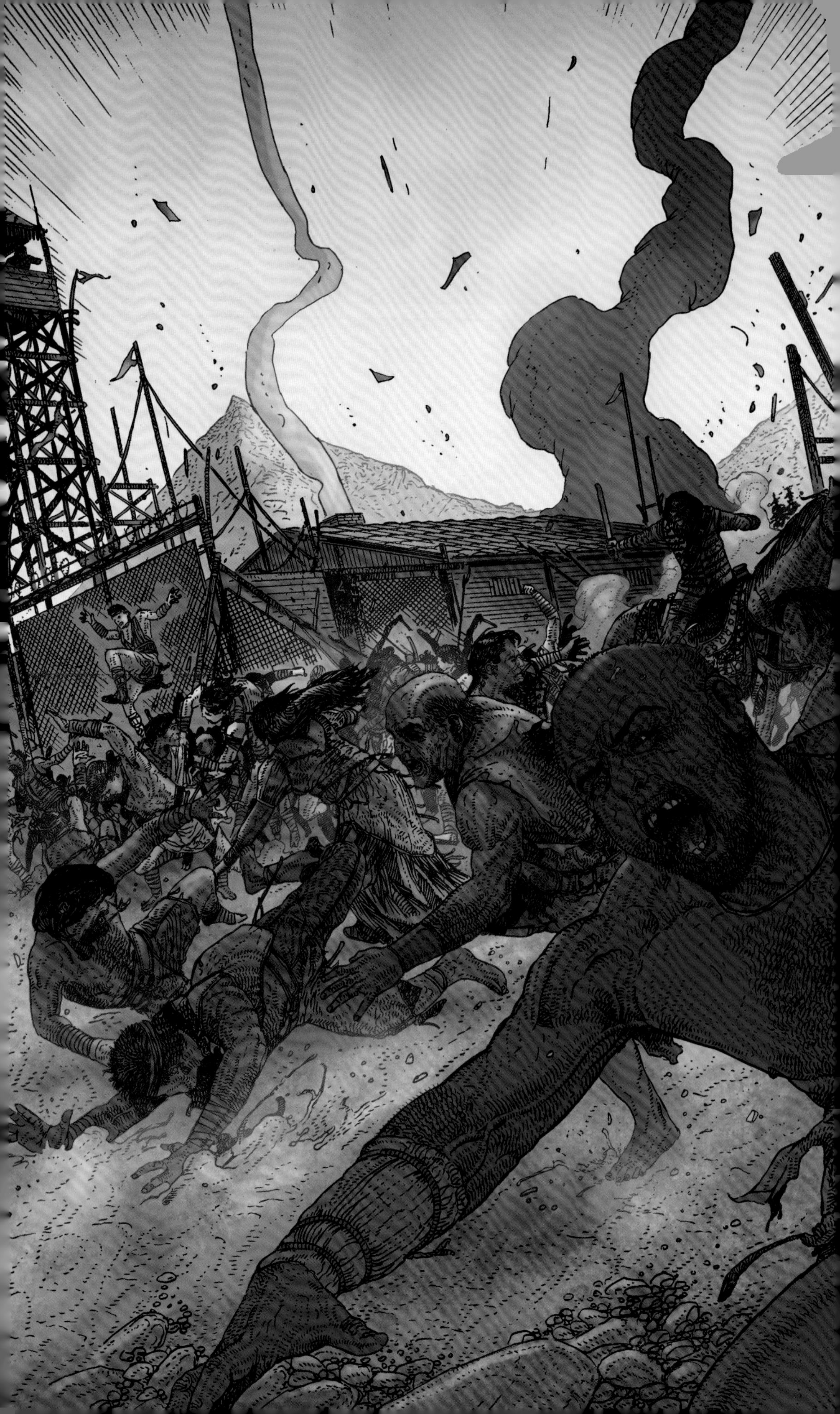

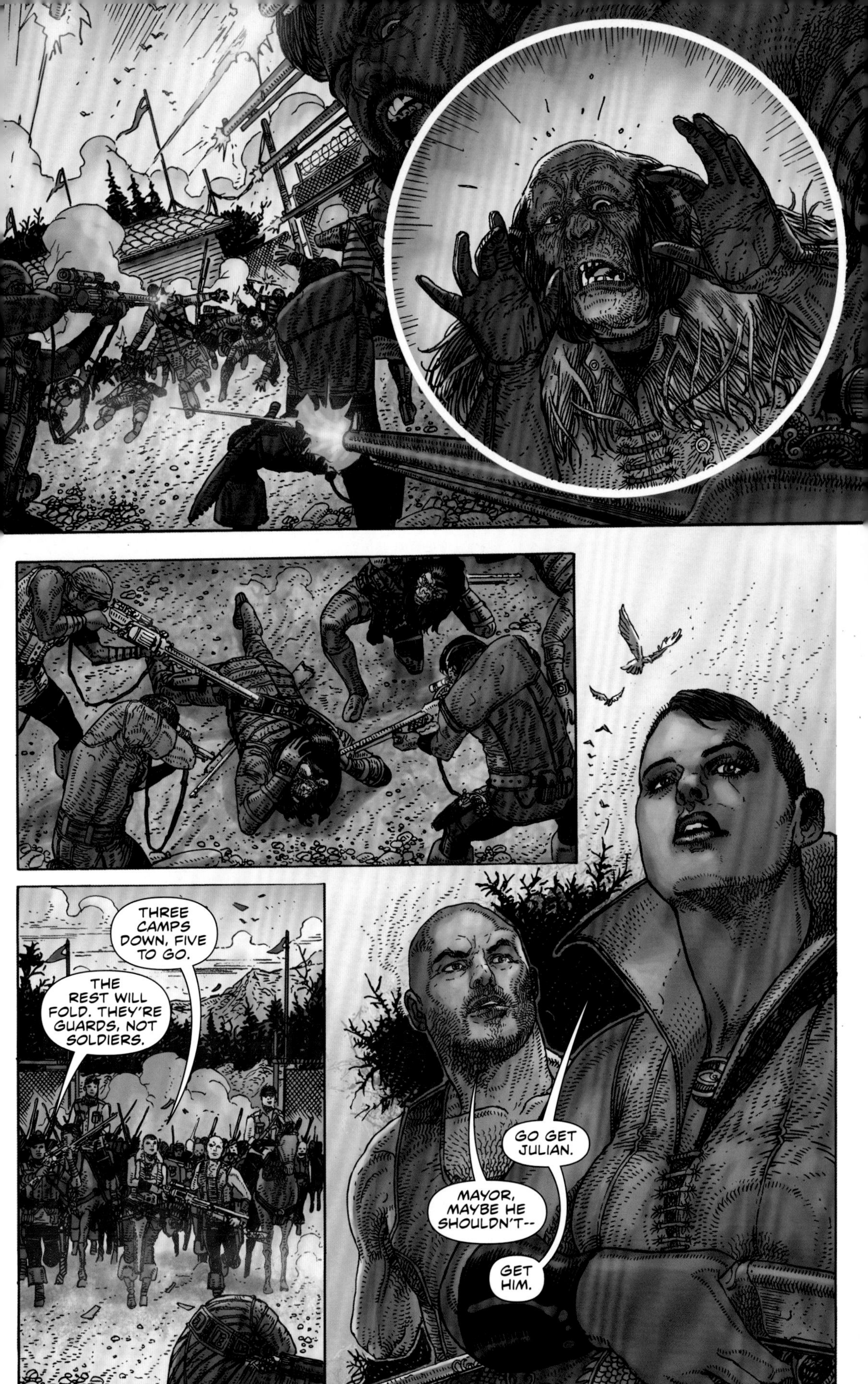
THREE CAMPS DOWN, FIVE TO GO.
THE REST WILL FOLD. THEY'RE GUARDS, NOT SOLDIERS.
GO GET JULIAN.
MAYOR, MAYBE HE SHOULDN'T--
GET HIM.

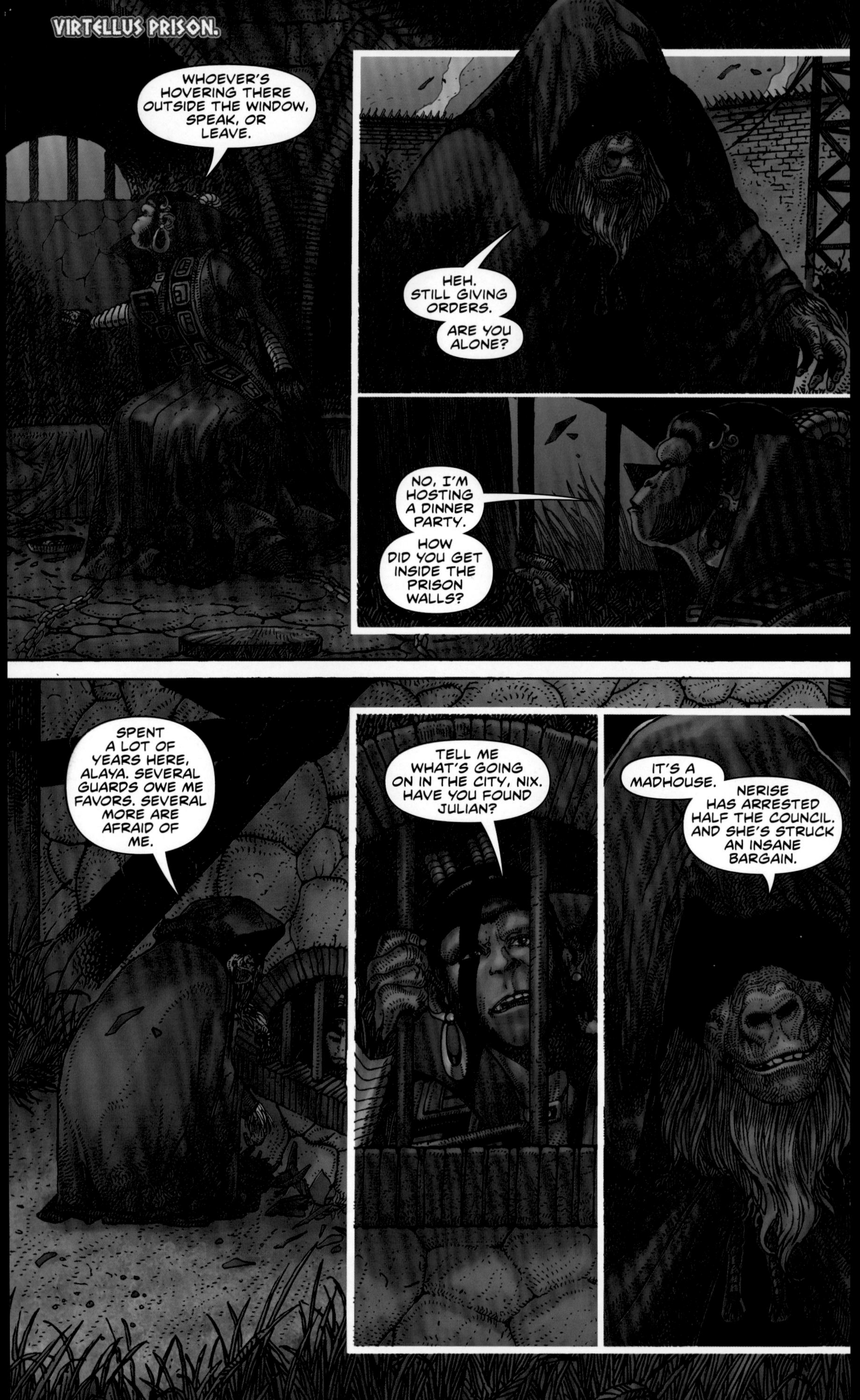
VIRTELLUS PRISON.
WHOEVER'S HOVERING THERE OUTSIDE THE WINDOW, SPEAK, OR LEAVE.
HEH. STILL GIVING ORDERS.
ARE YOU ALONE?
NO, I'M HOSTING A DINNER PARTY.
HOW DID YOU GET INSIDE THE PRISON WALLS?
SPENT A LOT OF YEARS HERE, ALAYA. SEVERAL GUARDS OWE ME FAVORS. SEVERAL MORE ARE AFRAID OF ME.
TELL ME WHAT'S GOING ON IN THE CITY, NIX. HAVE YOU FOUND JULIAN?
IT'S A MADHOUSE.
NERISE HAS ARRESTED HALF THE COUNCIL. AND SHE'S STRUCK AN INSANE BARGAIN.

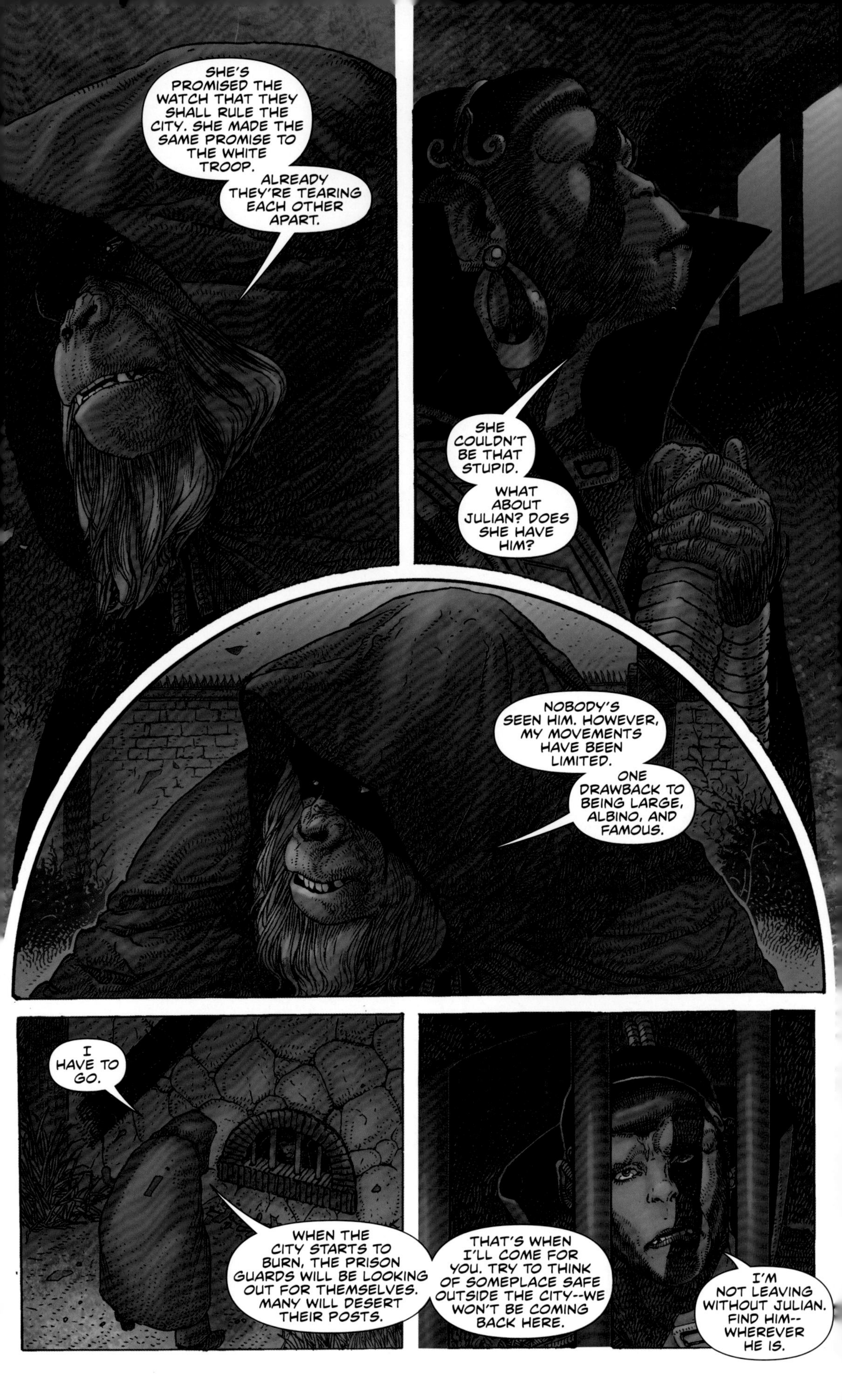
SHE'S PROMISED THE WATCH THAT THEY SHALL RULE THE CITY. SHE MADE THE SAME PROMISE TO THE WHITE TROOP.
ALREADY THEY'RE TEARING EACH OTHER APART.
SHE COULDN'T BE THAT STUPID.
WHAT ABOUT JULIAN? DOES SHE HAVE HIM?
NOBODY'S SEEN HIM. HOWEVER, MY MOVEMENTS HAVE BEEN LIMITED.
ONE DRAWBACK TO BEING LARGE, ALBINO, AND FAMOUS.
I HAVE TO GO.
WHEN THE CITY STARTS TO BURN, THE PRISON GUARDS WILL BE LOOKING OUT FOR THEMSELVES. MANY WILL DESERT THEIR POSTS.
THAT'S WHEN I'LL COME FOR YOU. TRY TO THINK OF SOMEPLACE SAFE OUTSIDE THE CITY--WE WON'T BE COMING BACK HERE.
I'M NOT LEAVING WITHOUT JULIAN. FIND HIM--WHEREVER HE IS.

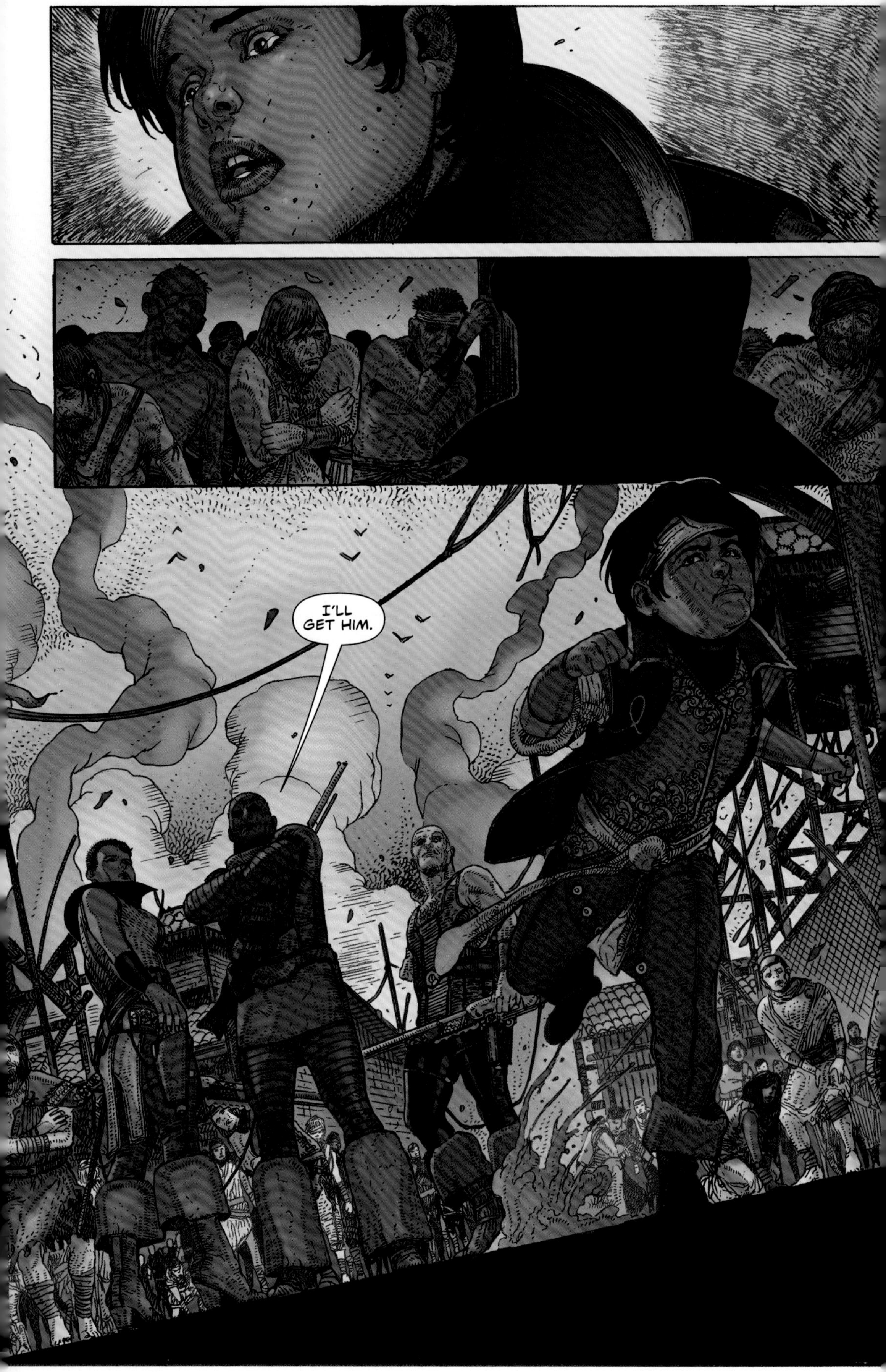
I'LL GET HIM.

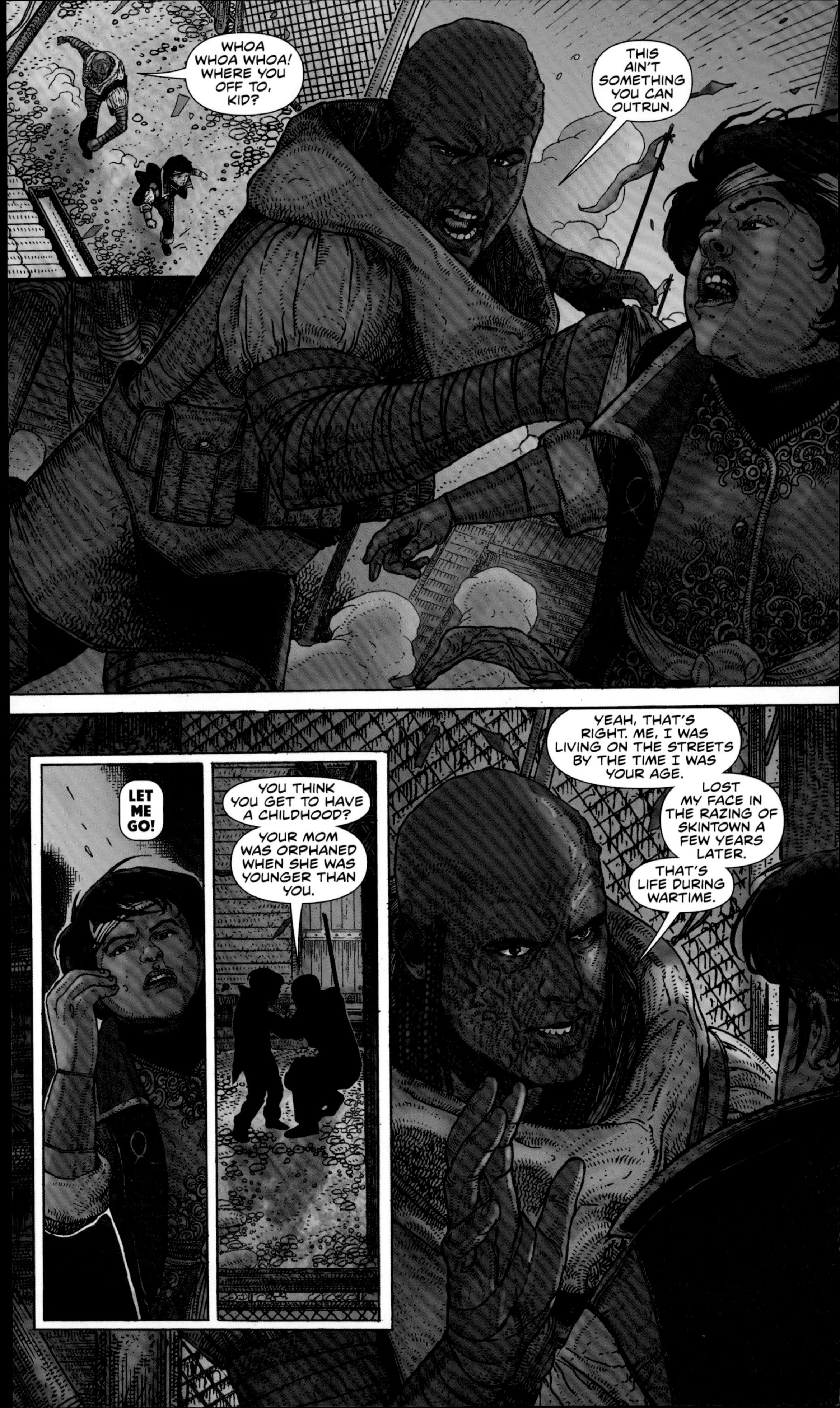
WHOA WHOA WHOA! WHERE YOU OFF TO, KID?
THIS AIN'T SOMETHING YOU CAN OUTRUN.
LET ME GO!
YOU THINK YOU GET TO HAVE A CHILDHOOD?
YOUR MOM WAS ORPHANED WHEN SHE WAS YOUNGER THAN YOU.
YEAH, THAT'S RIGHT. ME, I WAS LIVING ON THE STREETS BY THE TIME I WAS YOUR AGE.
LOST MY FACE IN THE RAZING OF SKINTOWN A FEW YEARS LATER.
THAT'S LIFE DURING WARTIME.

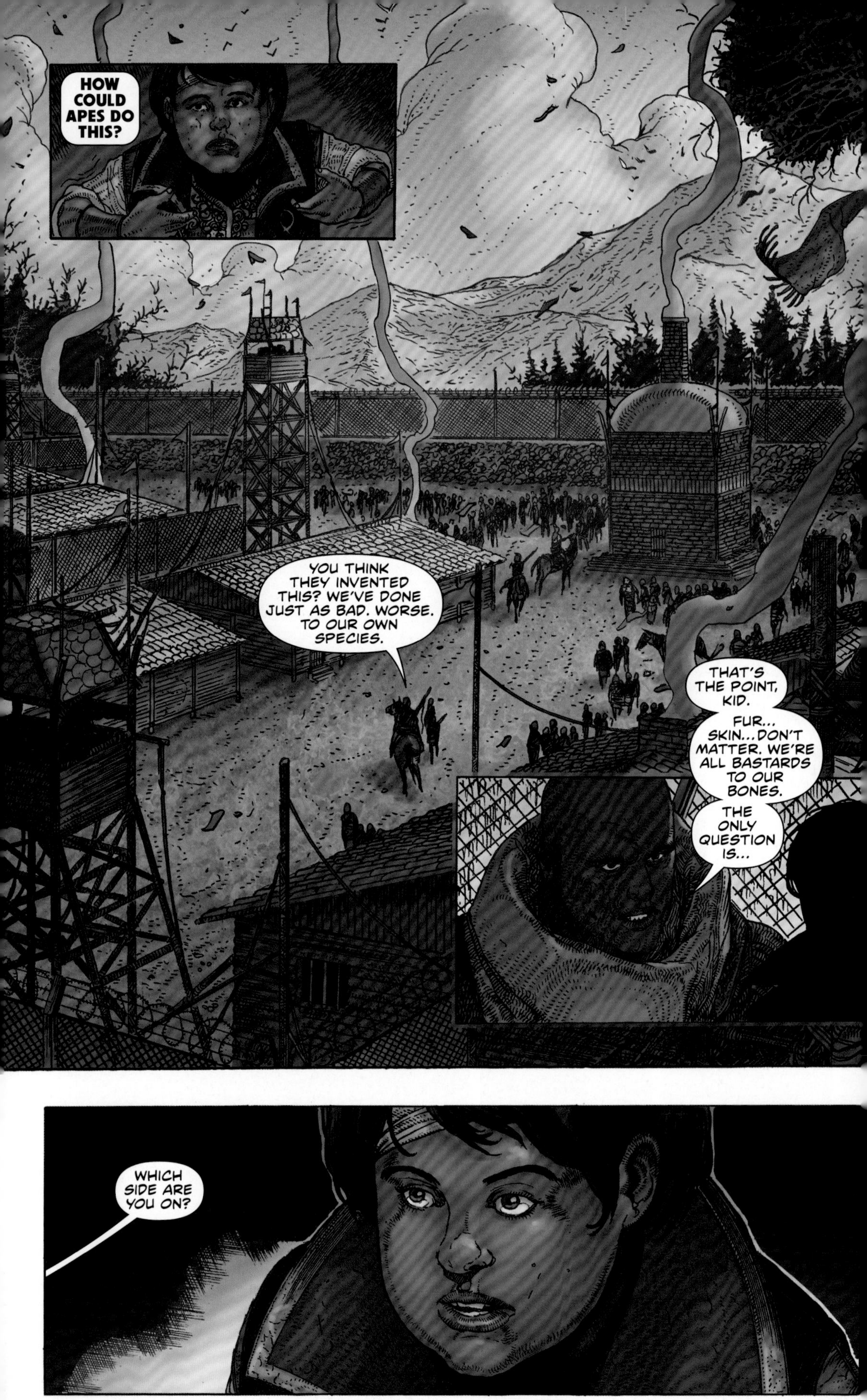
HOW COULD APES DO THIS?
YOU THINK THEY INVENTED THIS? WE'VE DONE JUST AS BAD. WORSE. TO OUR OWN SPECIES.
THAT'S THE POINT, KID.
FUR... SKIN...DON'T MATTER. WE'RE ALL BASTARDS TO OUR BONES.
THE ONLY QUESTION IS...
WHICH SIDE ARE YOU ON?

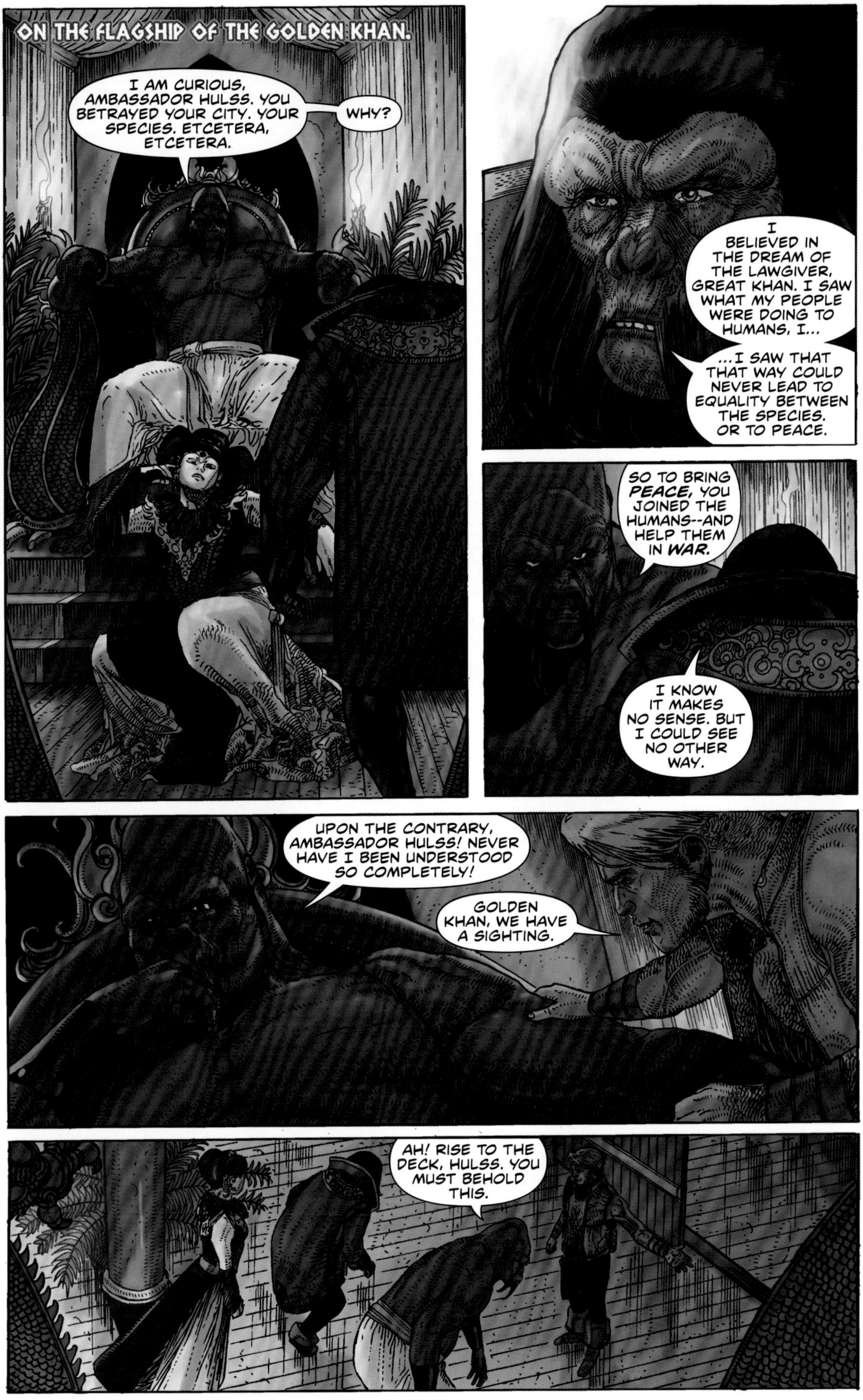
ON THE FLAGSHIP OF THE GOLDEN KHAN.
I AM CURIOUS, AMBASSADOR HULSS. YOU BETRAYED YOUR CITY. YOUR SPECIES. ETCETERA, ETCETERA.
WHY?
I BELIEVED IN THE DREAM OF THE LAWGIVER, GREAT KHAN. I SAW WHAT MY PEOPLE WERE DOING TO HUMANS, I...
...I SAW THAT THAT WAY COULD NEVER LEAD TO EQUALITY BETWEEN THE SPECIES. OR TO PEACE.
SO TO BRING *PEACE*, YOU JOINED THE HUMANS--AND HELP THEM IN *WAR.*
I KNOW IT MAKES NO SENSE. BUT I COULD SEE NO OTHER WAY.
UPON THE CONTRARY, AMBASSADOR HULSS! NEVER HAVE I BEEN UNDERSTOOD SO COMPLETELY!
GOLDEN KHAN, WE HAVE A SIGHTING.
AH! RISE TO THE DECK, HULSS. YOU MUST BEHOLD THIS.

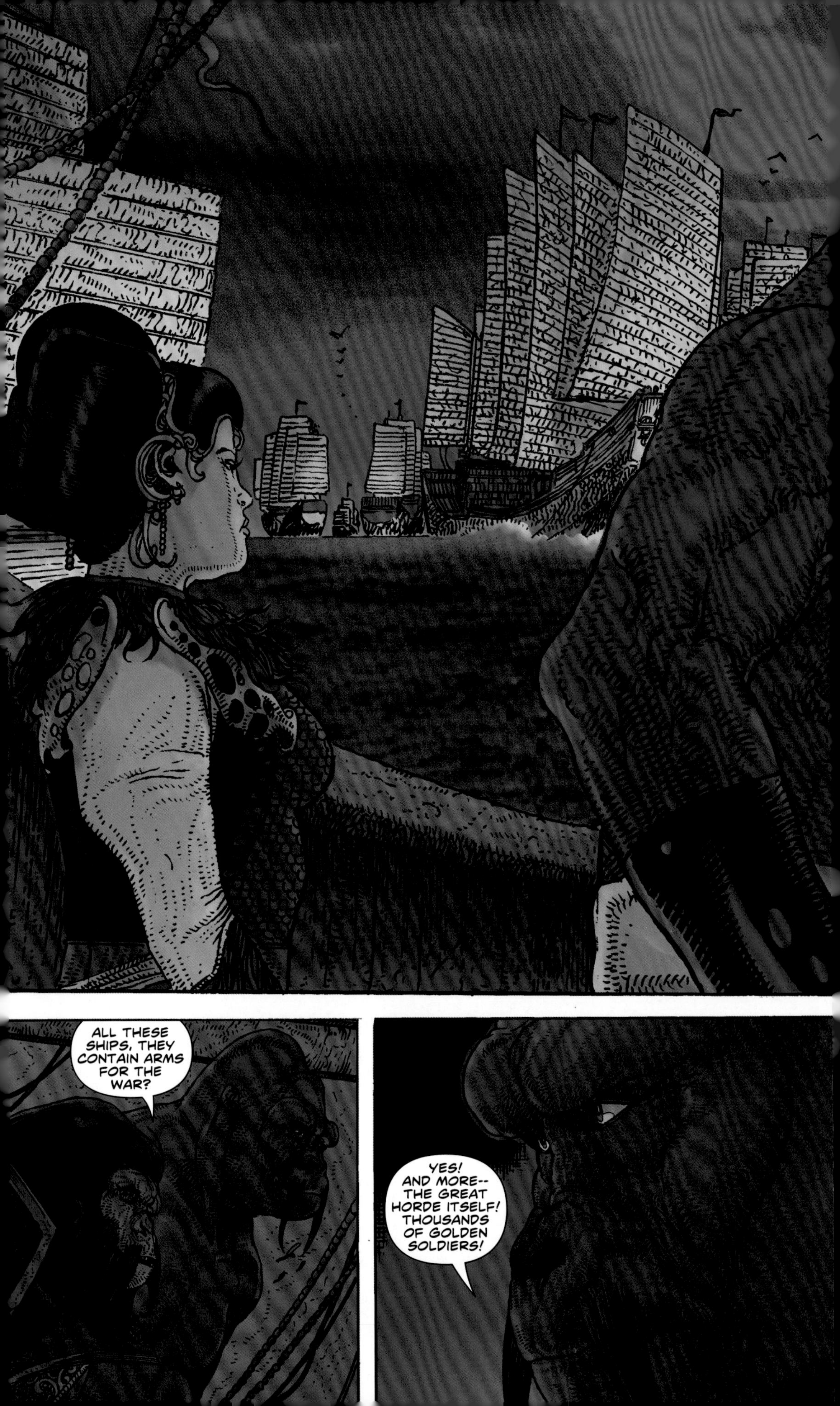
ALL THESE SHIPS, THEY CONTAIN ARMS FOR THE WAR?
YES! AND MORE-- THE GREAT HORDE ITSELF! THOUSANDS OF GOLDEN SOLDIERS!

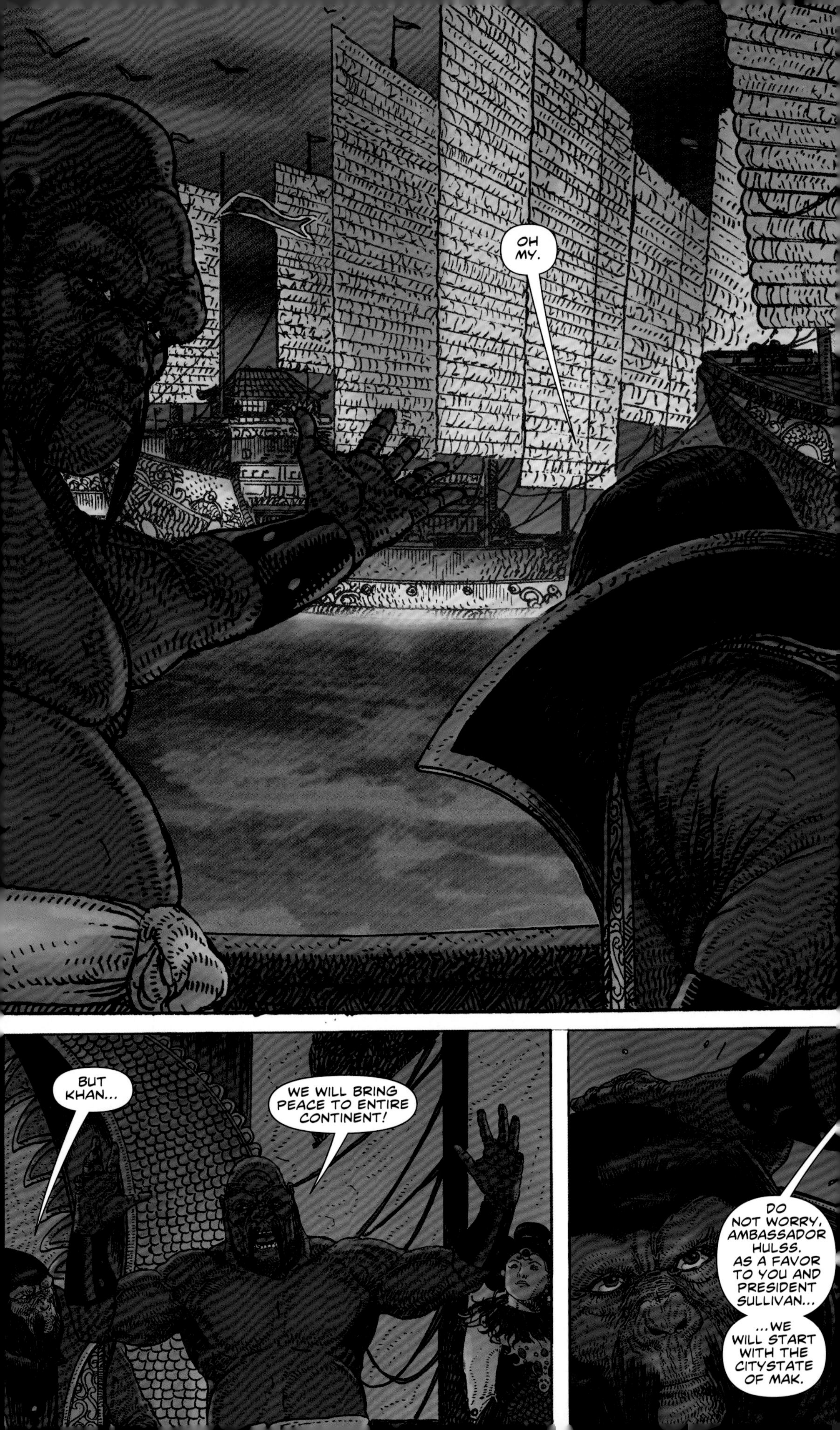
OH MY.
BUT KHAN...
WE WILL BRING PEACE TO ENTIRE CONTINENT!
DO NOT WORRY, AMBASSADOR HULSS. AS A FAVOR TO YOU AND PRESIDENT SULLIVAN...
...WE WILL START WITH THE CITYSTATE OF MAK.

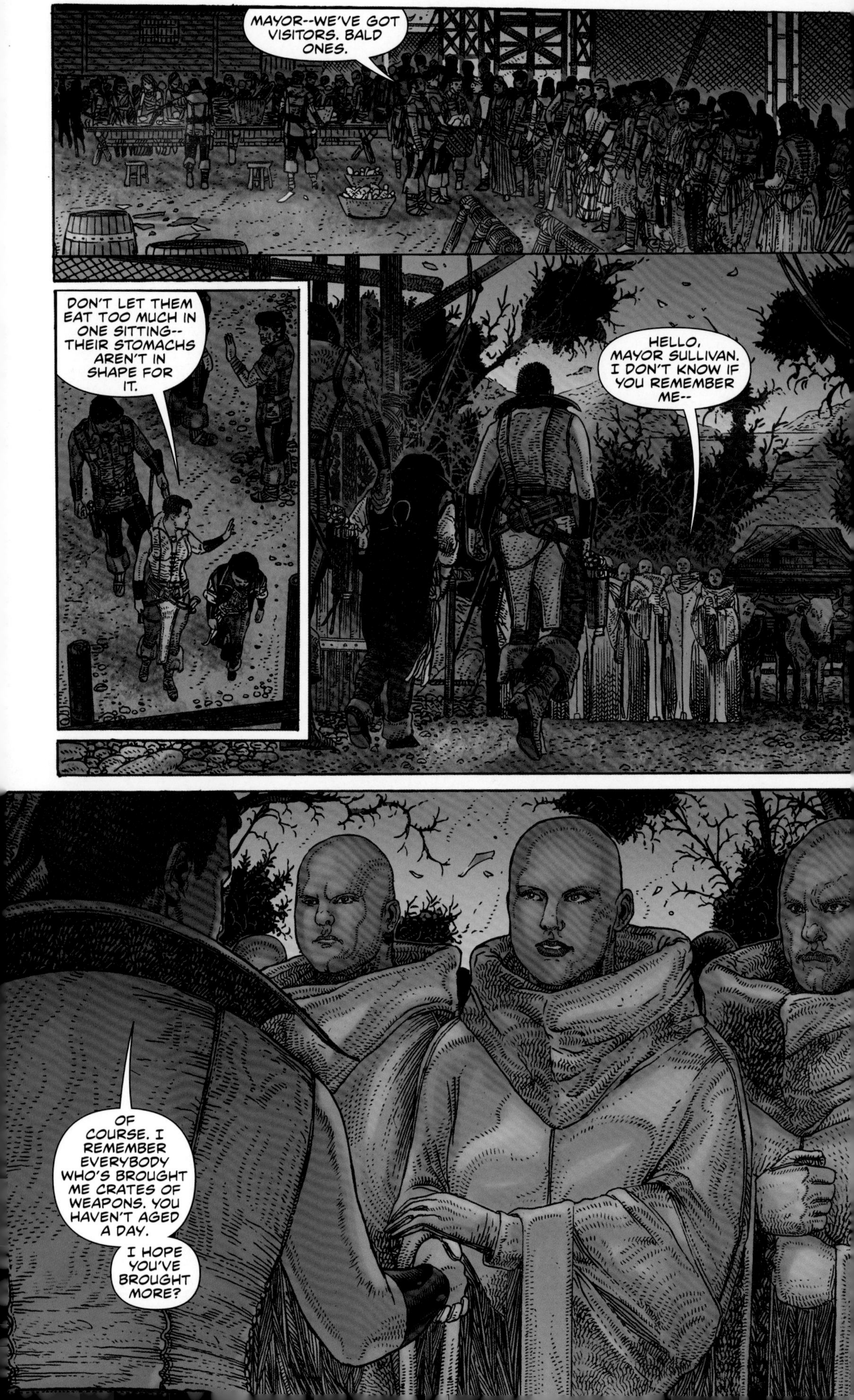
MAYOR--WE'VE GOT VISITORS. BALD ONES.
DON'T LET THEM EAT TOO MUCH IN ONE SITTING-- THEIR STOMACHS AREN'T IN SHAPE FOR IT.
HELLO, MAYOR SULLIVAN. I DON'T KNOW IF YOU REMEMBER ME--
OF COURSE. I REMEMBER EVERYBODY WHO'S BROUGHT ME CRATES OF WEAPONS. YOU HAVEN'T AGED A DAY.
I HOPE YOU'VE BROUGHT MORE?

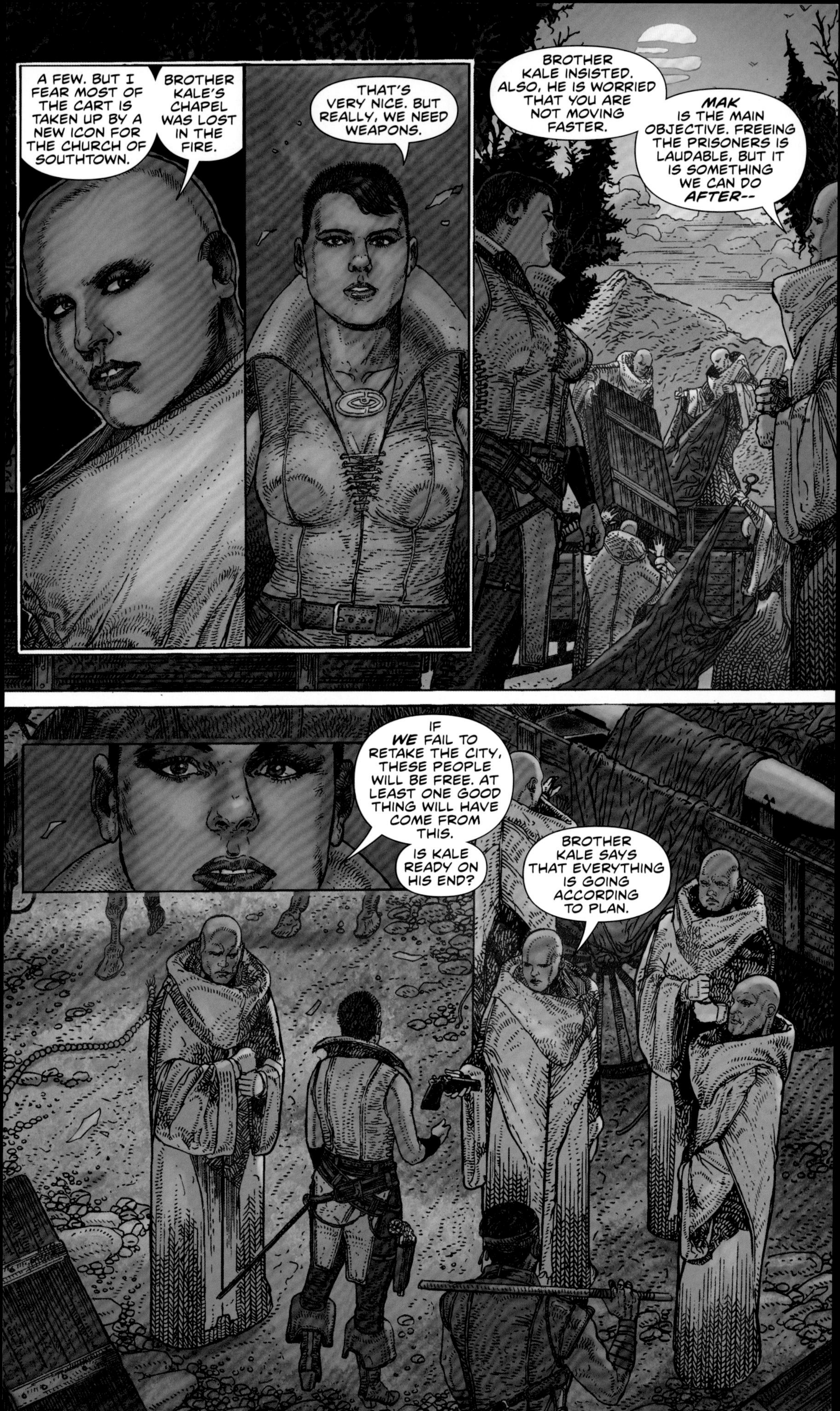
A FEW. BUT I FEAR MOST OF THE CART IS TAKEN UP BY A NEW ICON FOR THE CHURCH OF SOUTHTOWN.
BROTHER KALE'S CHAPEL WAS LOST IN THE FIRE.
THAT'S VERY NICE. BUT REALLY, WE NEED WEAPONS.
BROTHER KALE INSISTED. ALSO, HE IS WORRIED THAT YOU ARE NOT MOVING FASTER.
MAK IS THE MAIN OBJECTIVE. FREEING THE PRISONERS IS LAUDABLE, BUT IT IS SOMETHING WE CAN DO AFTER--
IF WE FAIL TO RETAKE THE CITY, THESE PEOPLE WILL BE FREE. AT LEAST ONE GOOD THING WILL HAVE COME FROM THIS.
IS KALE READY ON HIS END?
BROTHER KALE SAYS THAT EVERYTHING IS GOING ACCORDING TO PLAN.

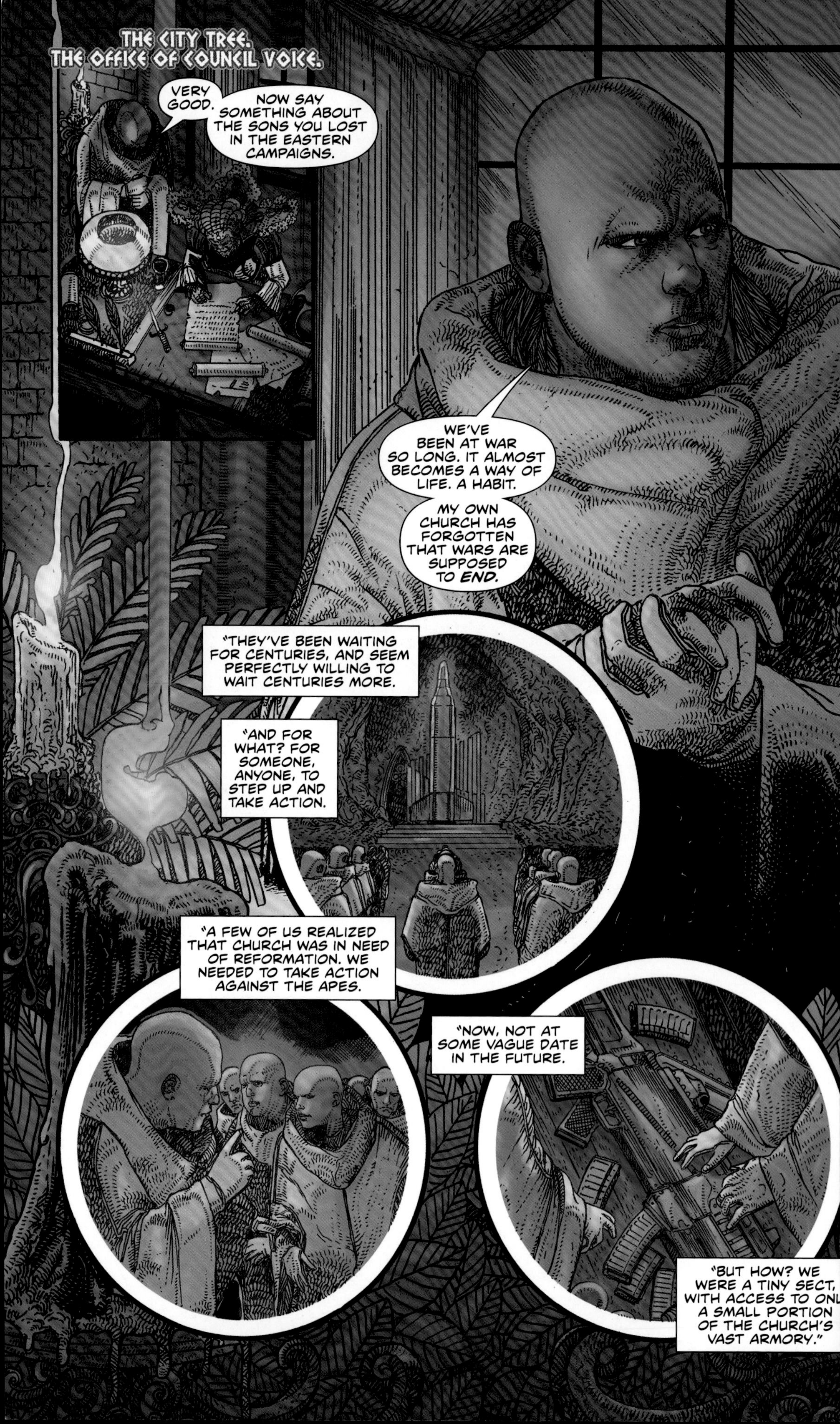
THE CITY TREE. THE OFFICE OF COUNCIL VOICE.
VERY GOOD.
NOW SAY SOMETHING ABOUT THE SONS YOU LOST IN THE EASTERN CAMPAIGNS.
WE'VE BEEN AT WAR SO LONG. IT ALMOST BECOMES A WAY OF LIFE. A HABIT.
MY OWN CHURCH HAS FORGOTTEN THAT WARS ARE SUPPOSED TO END.
"THEY'VE BEEN WAITING FOR CENTURIES, AND SEEM PERFECTLY WILLING TO WAIT CENTURIES MORE.
"AND FOR WHAT? FOR SOMEONE, ANYONE, TO STEP UP AND TAKE ACTION.
"A FEW OF US REALIZED THAT CHURCH WAS IN NEED OF REFORMATION. WE NEEDED TO TAKE ACTION AGAINST THE APES.
"NOW, NOT AT SOME VAGUE DATE IN THE FUTURE.
"BUT HOW? WE WERE A TINY SECT, WITH ACCESS TO ONL A SMALL PORTION OF THE CHURCH'S VAST ARMORY."

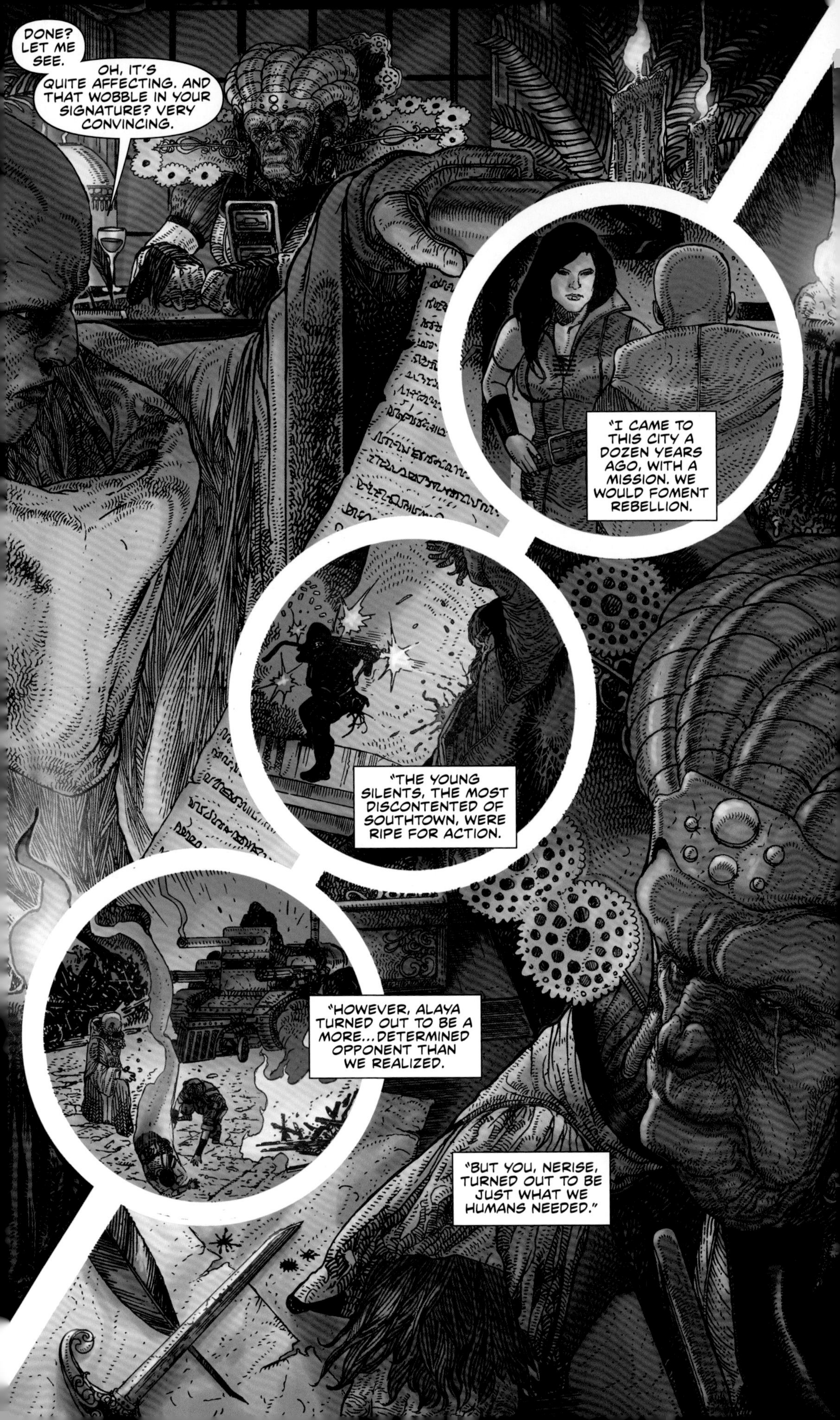

DONE? LET ME SEE.
OH, IT'S QUITE AFFECTING. AND THAT WOBBLE IN YOUR SIGNATURE? VERY CONVINCING.
"I CAME TO THIS CITY A DOZEN YEARS AGO, WITH A MISSION. WE WOULD FOMENT REBELLION.
"THE YOUNG SILENTS, THE MOST DISCONTENTED OF SOUTHTOWN, WERE RIPE FOR ACTION.
"HOWEVER, ALAYA TURNED OUT TO BE A MORE...DETERMINED OPPONENT THAN WE REALIZED.
"BUT YOU, NERISE, TURNED OUT TO BE JUST WHAT WE HUMANS NEEDED."

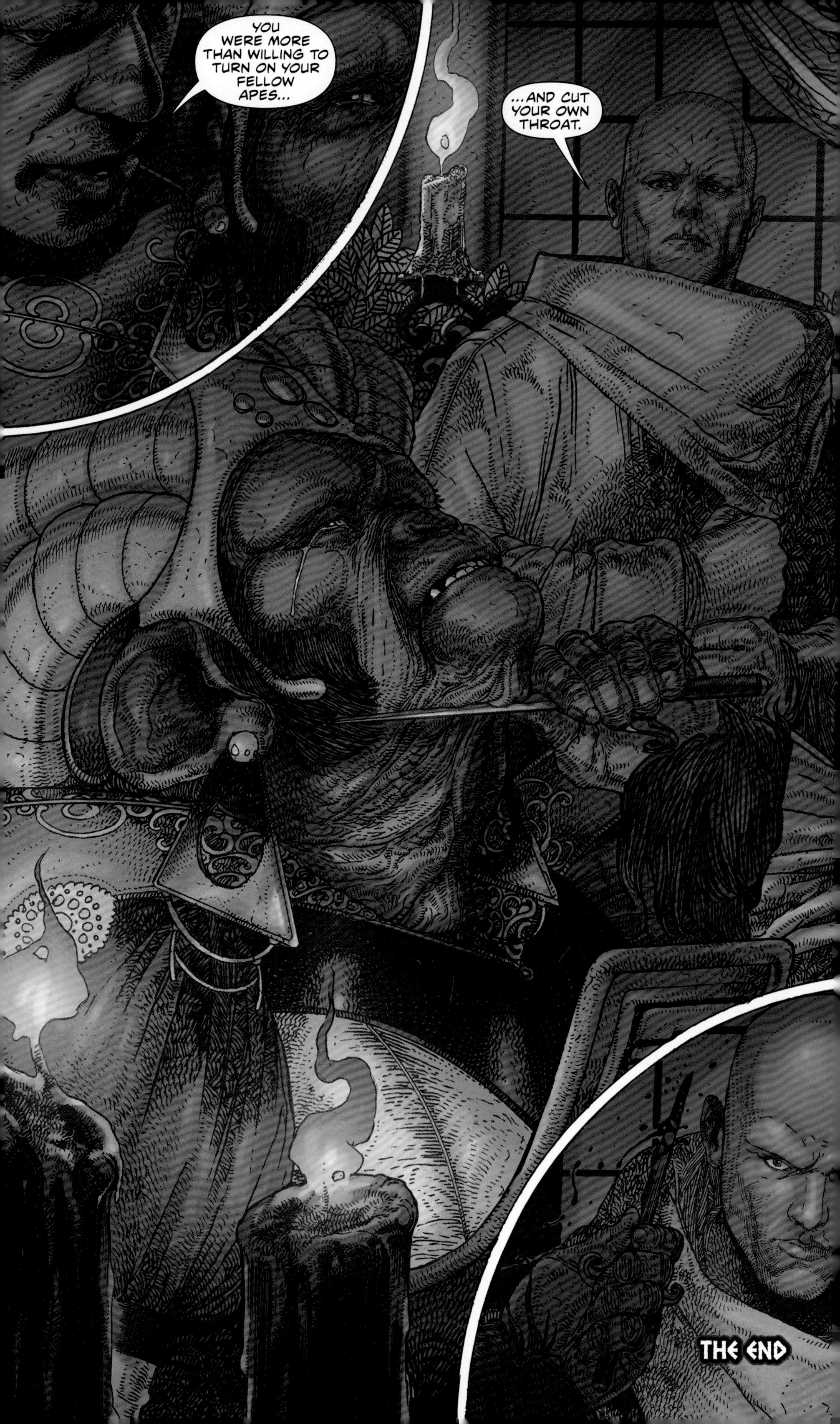
YOU WERE MORE THAN WILLING TO TURN ON YOUR FELLOW APES...
...AND CUT YOUR OWN THROAT.
THE END

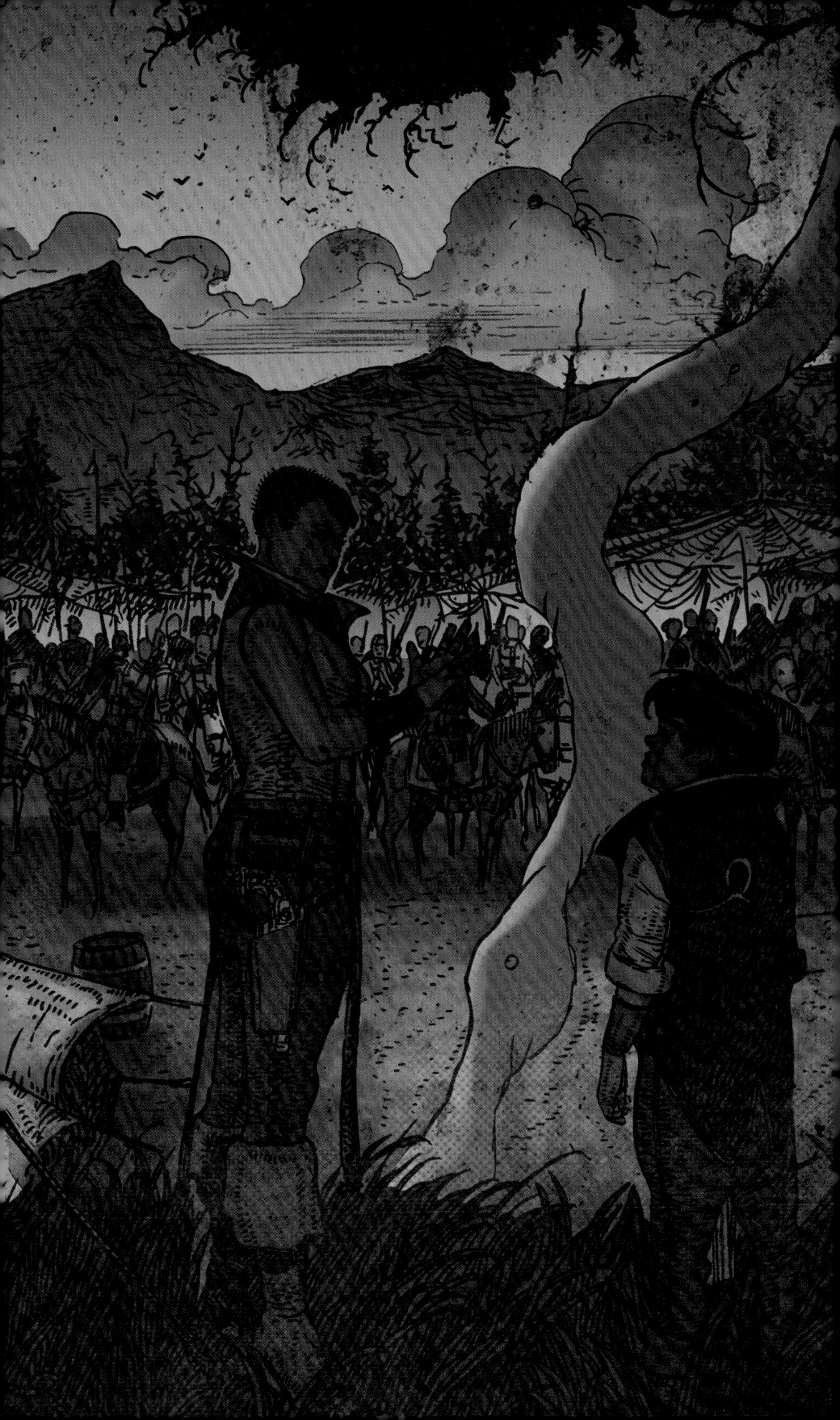

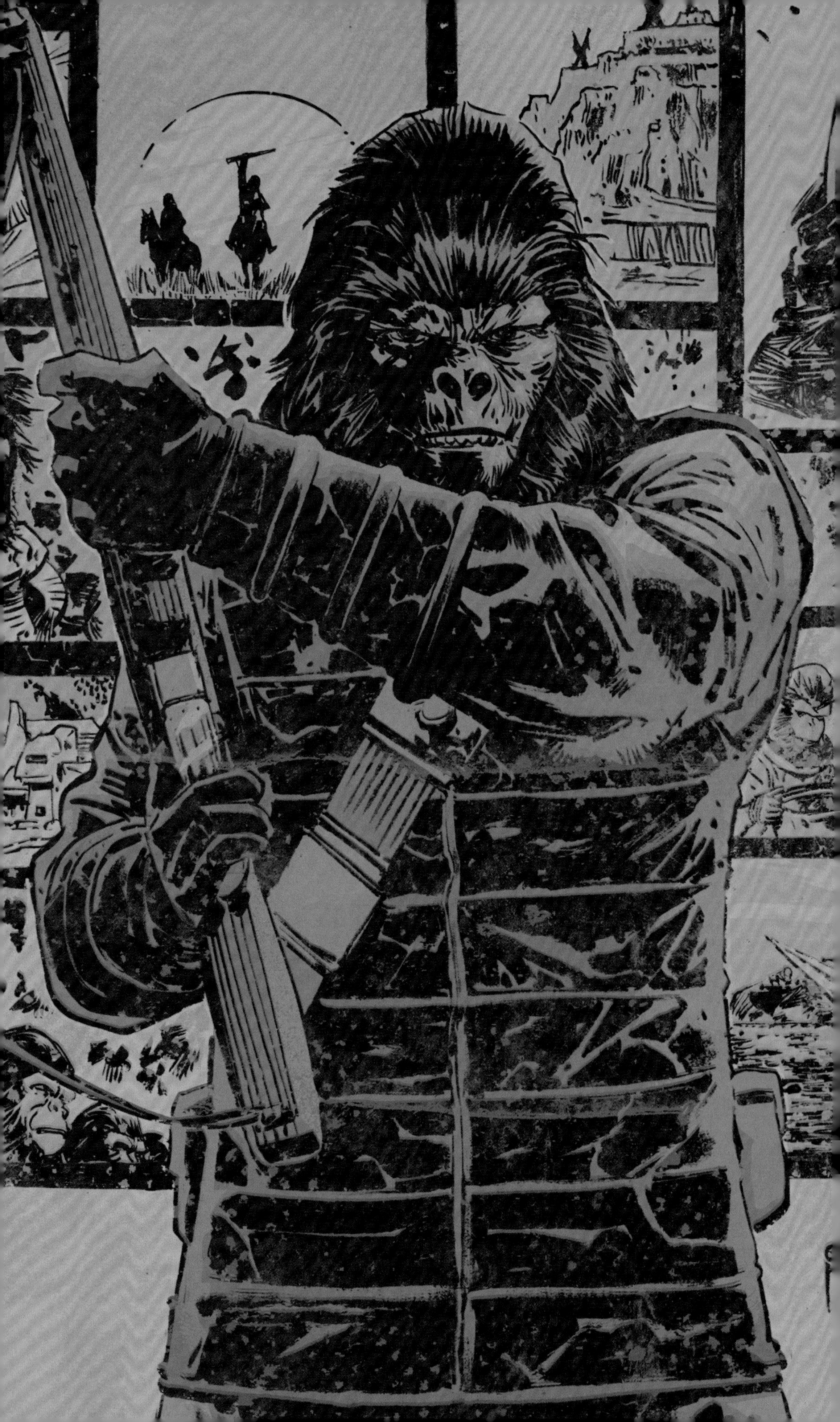

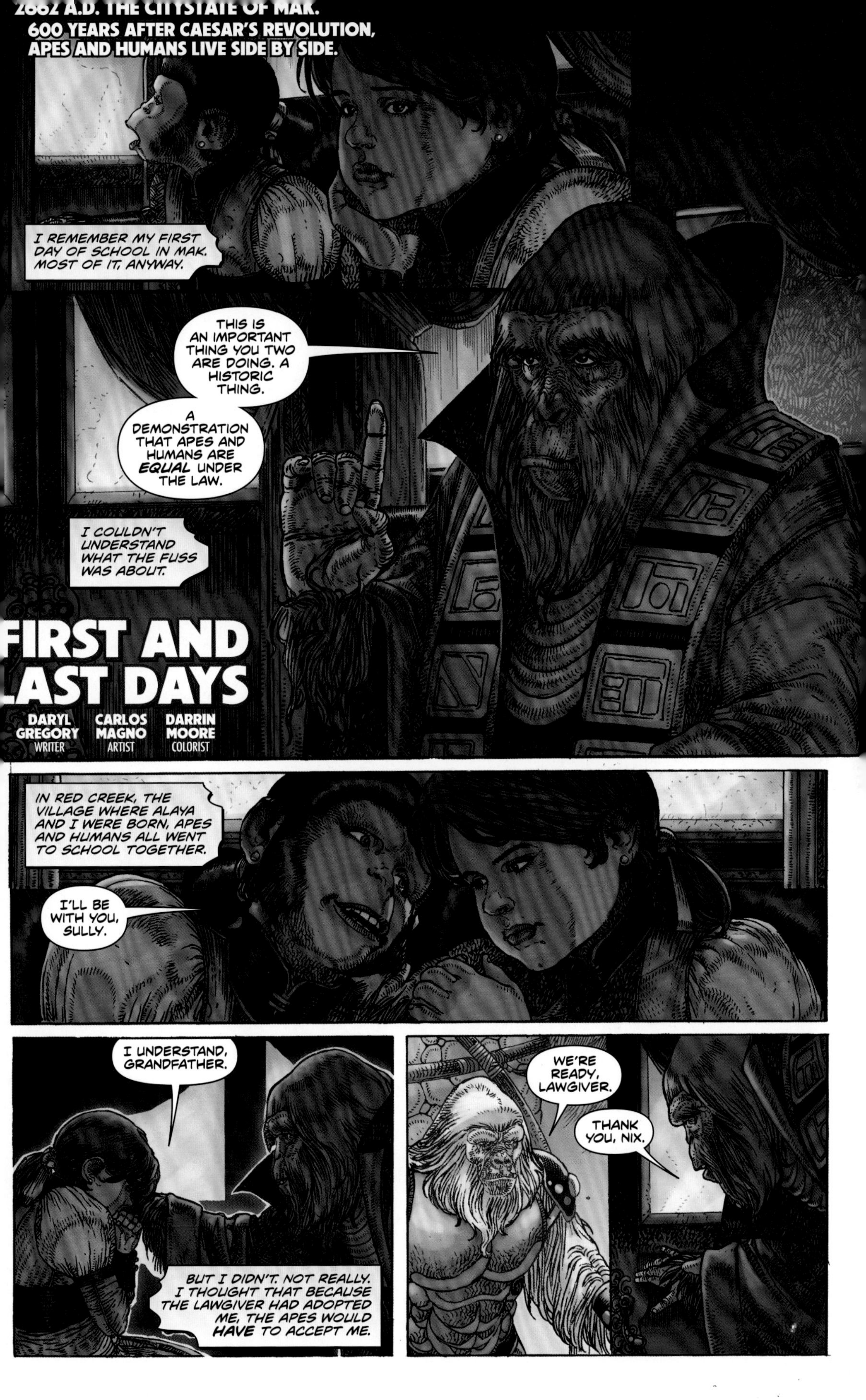
2662 A.D. THE CITYSTATE OF MAK.
600 YEARS AFTER CAESAR'S REVOLUTION, APES AND HUMANS LIVE SIDE BY SIDE.
I REMEMBER MY FIRST DAY OF SCHOOL IN MAK. MOST OF IT, ANYWAY.
THIS IS AN IMPORTANT THING YOU TWO ARE DOING. A HISTORIC THING.
A DEMONSTRATION THAT APES AND HUMANS ARE EQUAL UNDER THE LAW.
I COULDN'T UNDERSTAND WHAT THE FUSS WAS ABOUT.
FIRST AND
AST DAYS
DARYL GREGORY WRITER
CARLOS MAGNO ARTIST
DARRIN MOORE COLORIST
IN RED CREEK, THE VILLAGE WHERE ALAYA AND I WERE BORN, APES AND HUMANS ALL WENT TO SCHOOL TOGETHER.
I'LL BE WITH YOU, SULLY.
I UNDERSTAND, GRANDFATHER.
BUT I DIDN'T. NOT REALLY. I THOUGHT THAT BECAUSE THE LAWGIVER HAD ADOPTED ME, THE APES WOULD HAVE TO ACCEPT ME.
WE'RE READY, LAWGIVER.
THANK YOU, NIX.

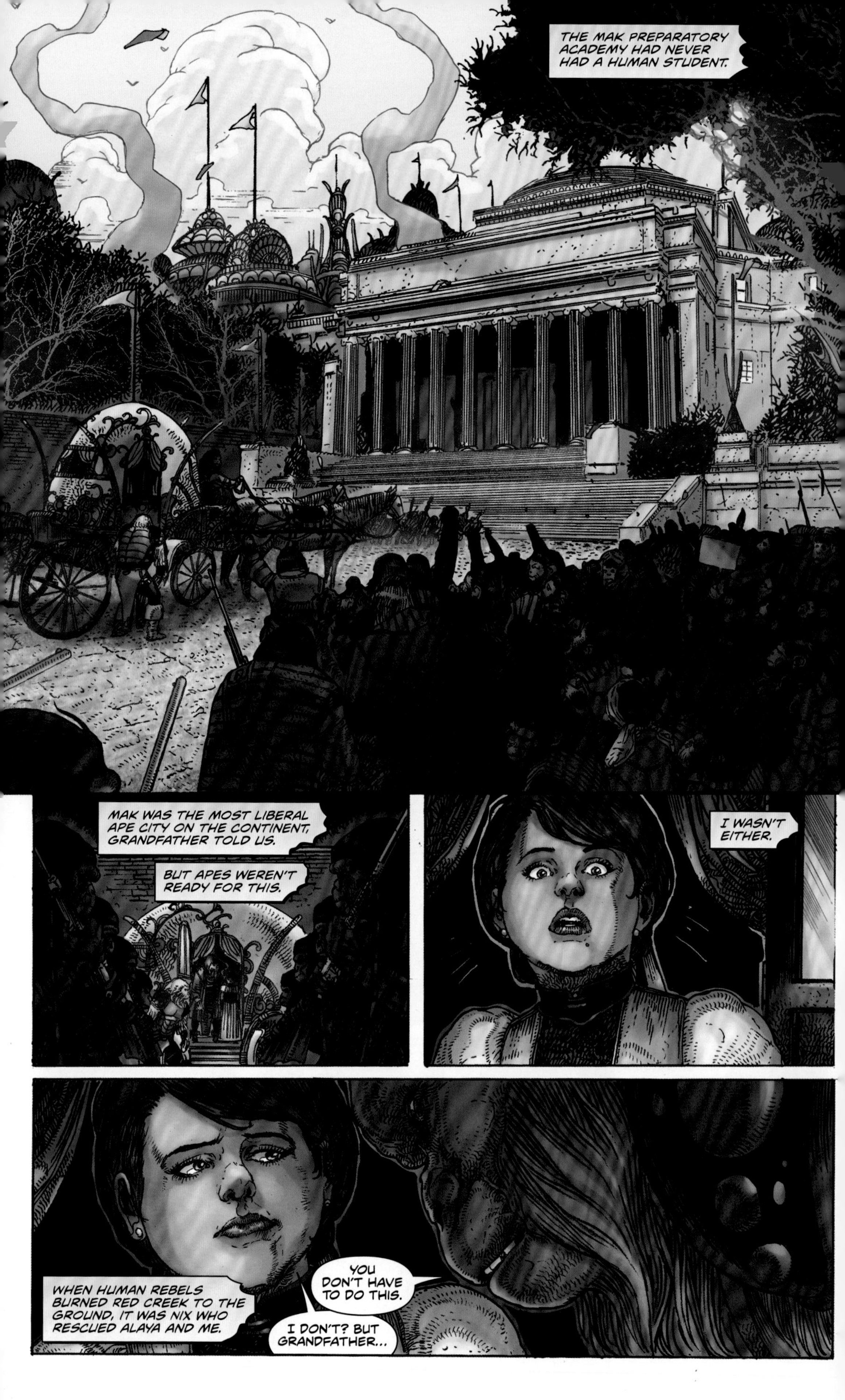
THE MAK PREPARATORY ACADEMY HAD NEVER HAD A HUMAN STUDENT.
MAK WAS THE MOST LIBERAL APE CITY ON THE CONTINENT, GRANDFATHER TOLD US.
BUT APES WEREN'T READY FOR THIS.
I WASN'T EITHER.
WHEN HUMAN REBELS BURNED RED CREEK TO THE GROUND, IT WAS NIX WHO RESCUED ALAYA AND ME.
YOU DON'T HAVE TO DO THIS.
I DON'T? BUT GRANDFATHER...

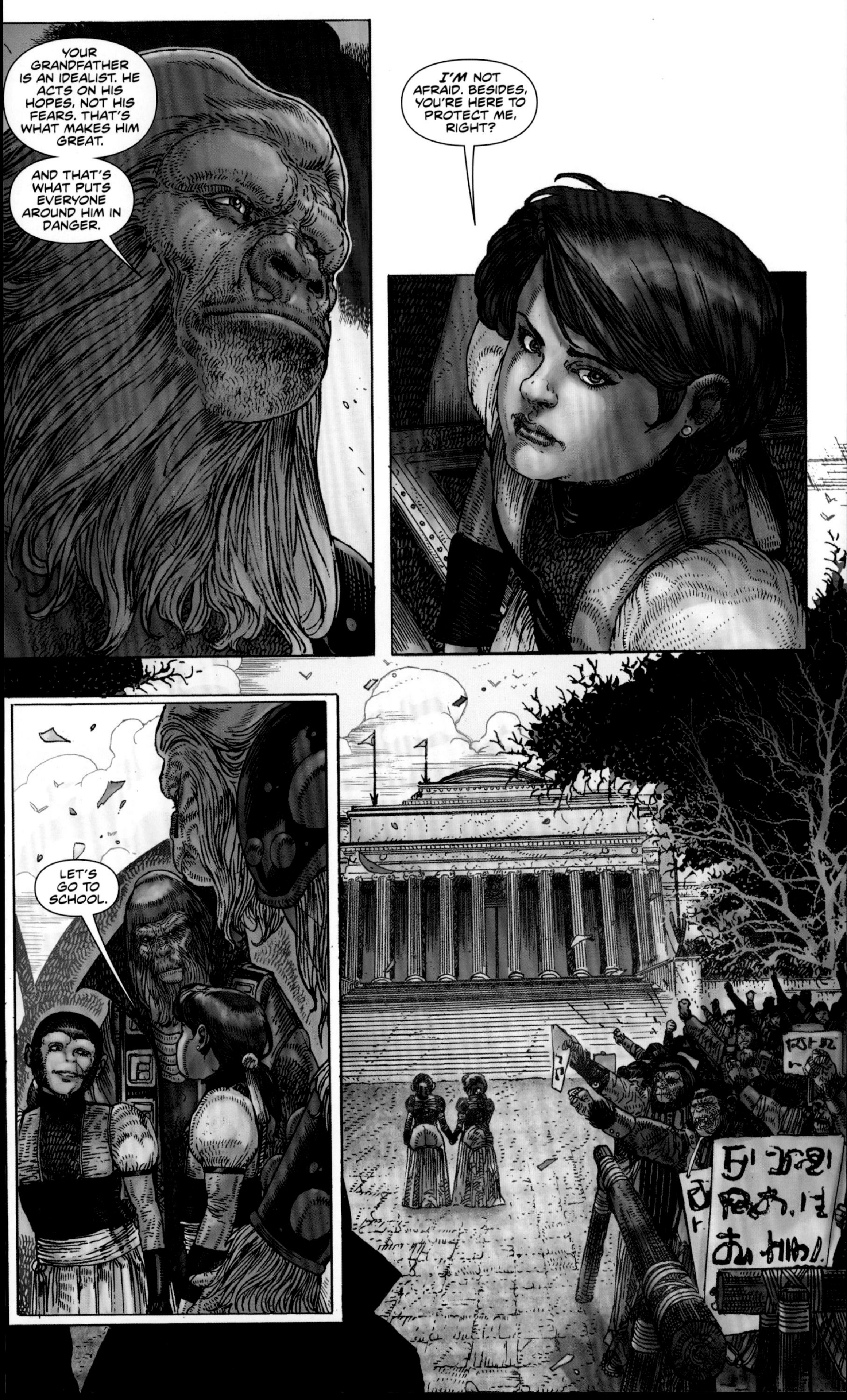
YOUR GRANDFATHER IS AN IDEALIST. HE ACTS ON HIS HOPES, NOT HIS FEARS. THAT'S WHAT MAKES HIM GREAT.
AND THAT'S WHAT PUTS EVERYONE AROUND HIM IN DANGER.
I'M NOT AFRAID. BESIDES, YOU'RE HERE TO PROTECT ME, RIGHT?
LET'S GO TO SCHOOL.

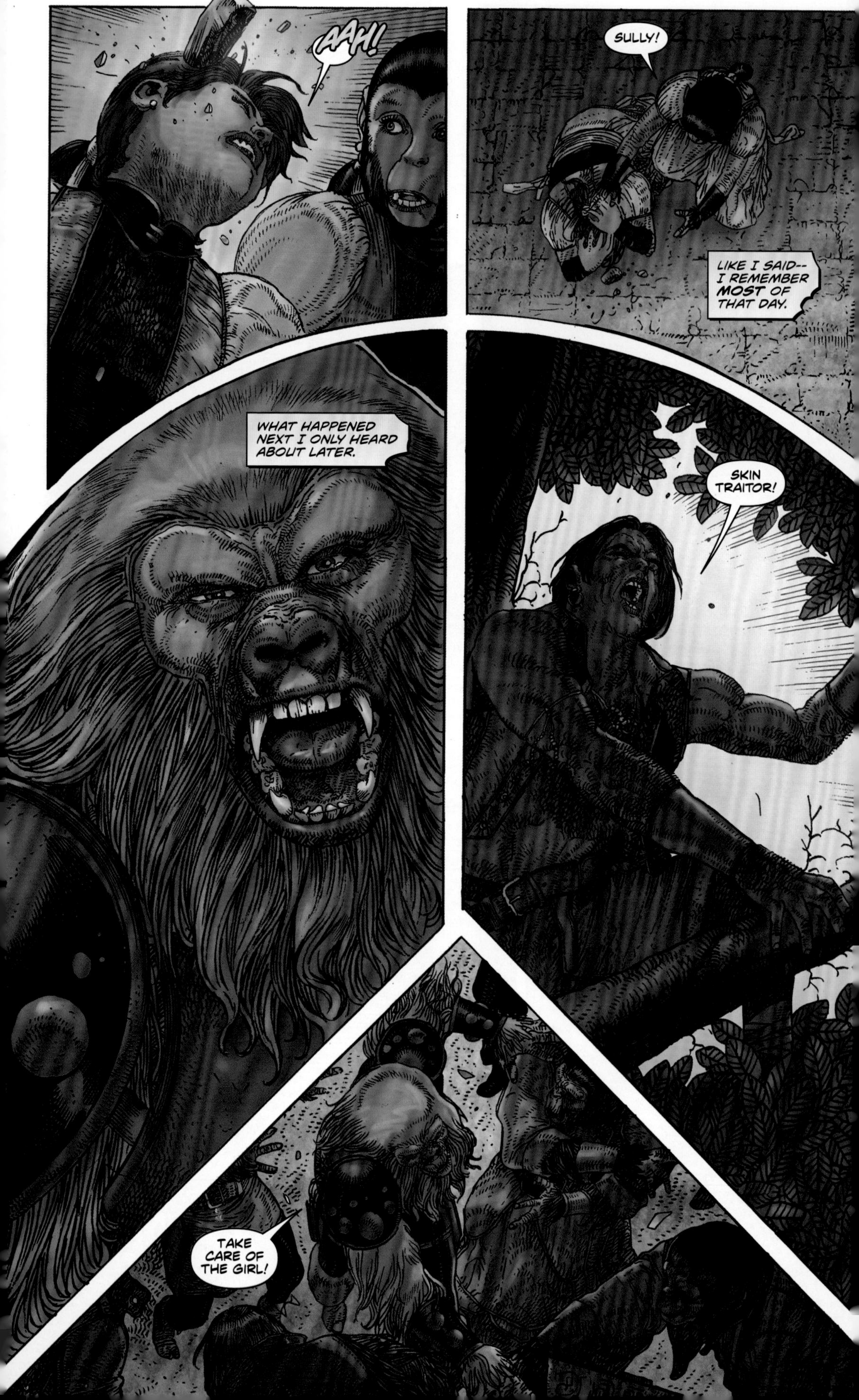
AAH!
SULLY!
LIKE I SAID-- I REMEMBER MOST OF THAT DAY.
WHAT HAPPENED NEXT I ONLY HEARD ABOUT LATER.
SKIN TRAITOR!
TAKE CARE OF THE GIRL!

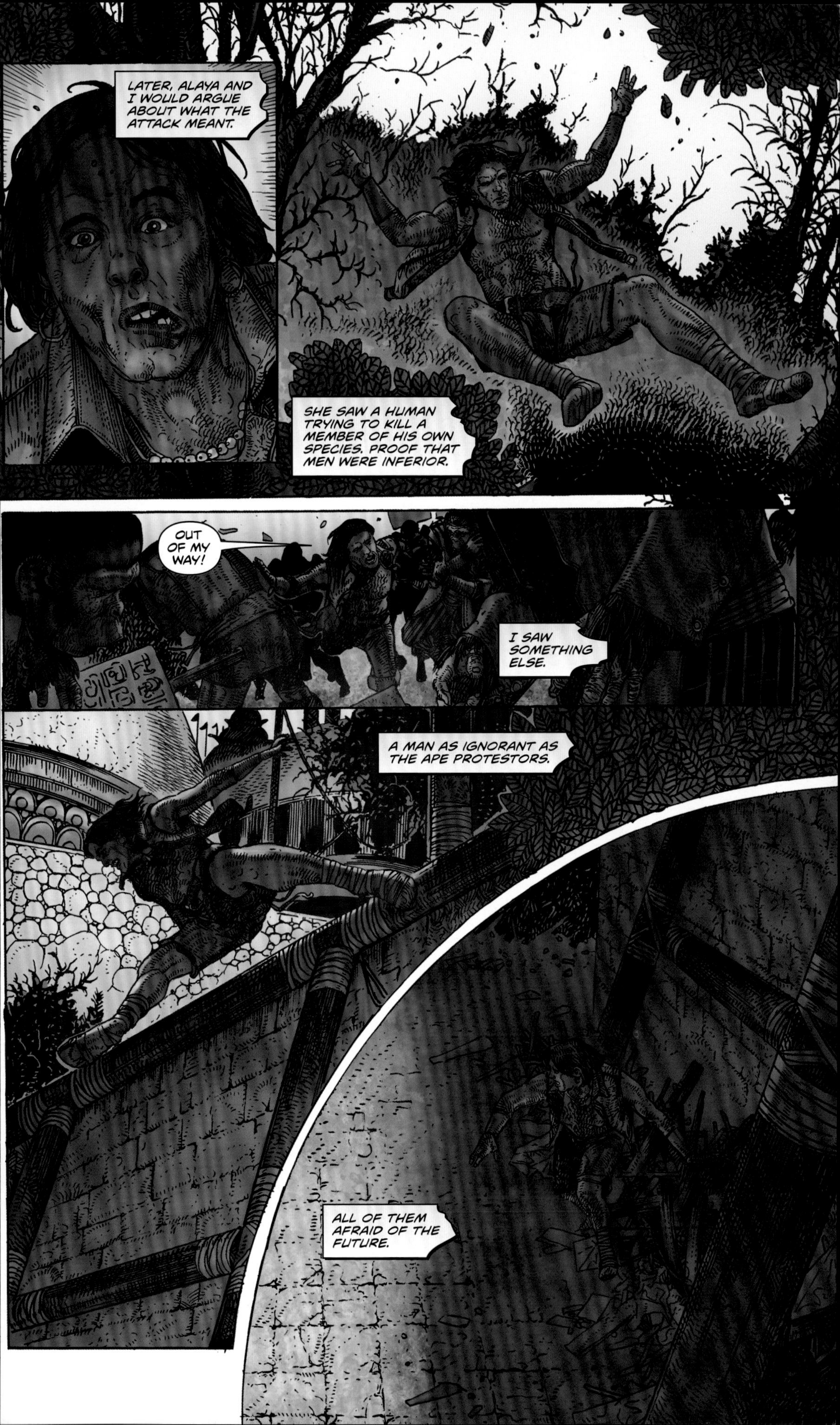
LATER, ALAYA AND I WOULD ARGUE ABOUT WHAT THE ATTACK MEANT.
SHE SAW A HUMAN TRYING TO KILL A MEMBER OF HIS OWN SPECIES. PROOF THAT MEN WERE INFERIOR.
OUT OF MY WAY!
I SAW SOMETHING ELSE.
A MAN AS IGNORANT AS THE APE PROTESTORS.
ALL OF THEM AFRAID OF THE FUTURE.

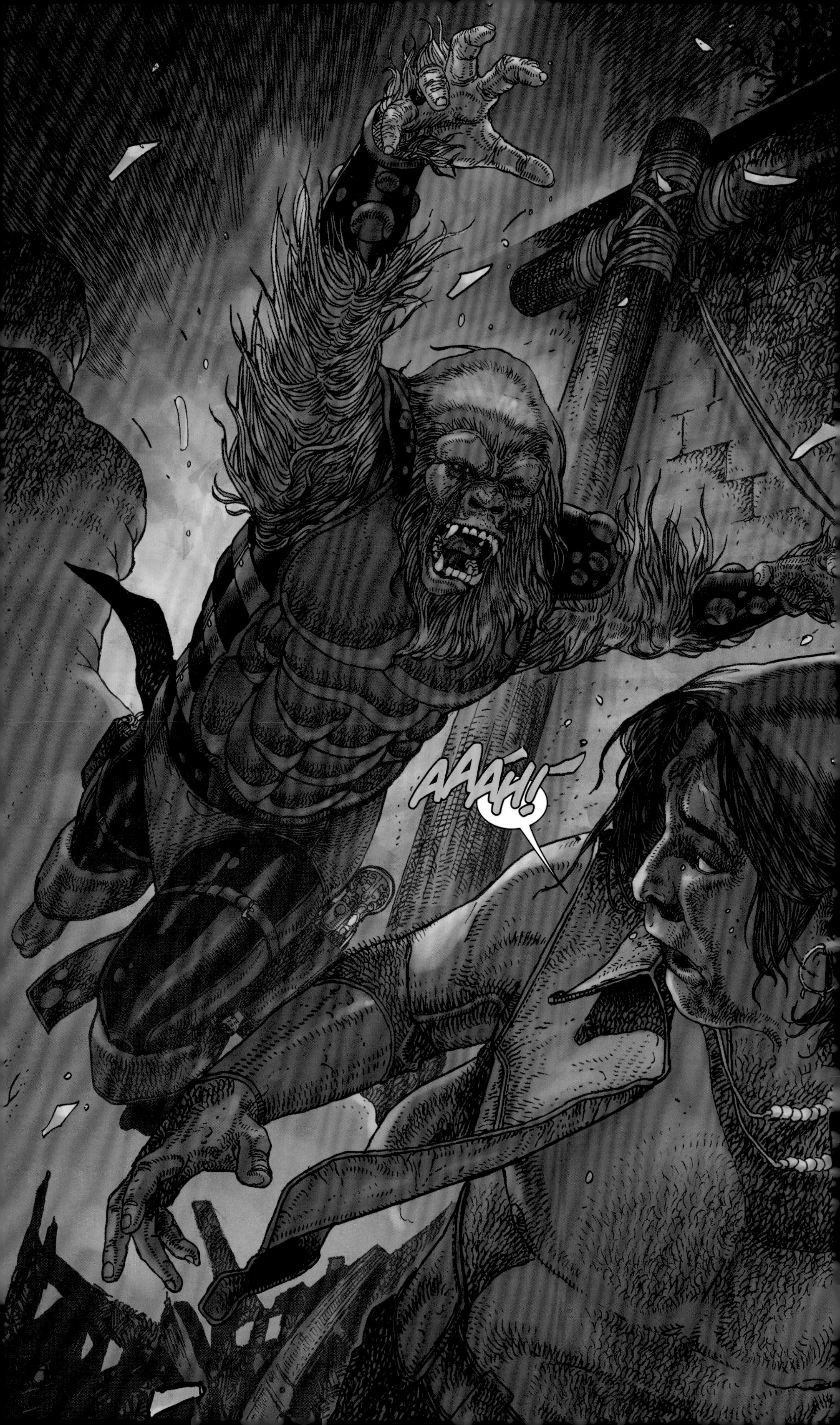
AAAH!

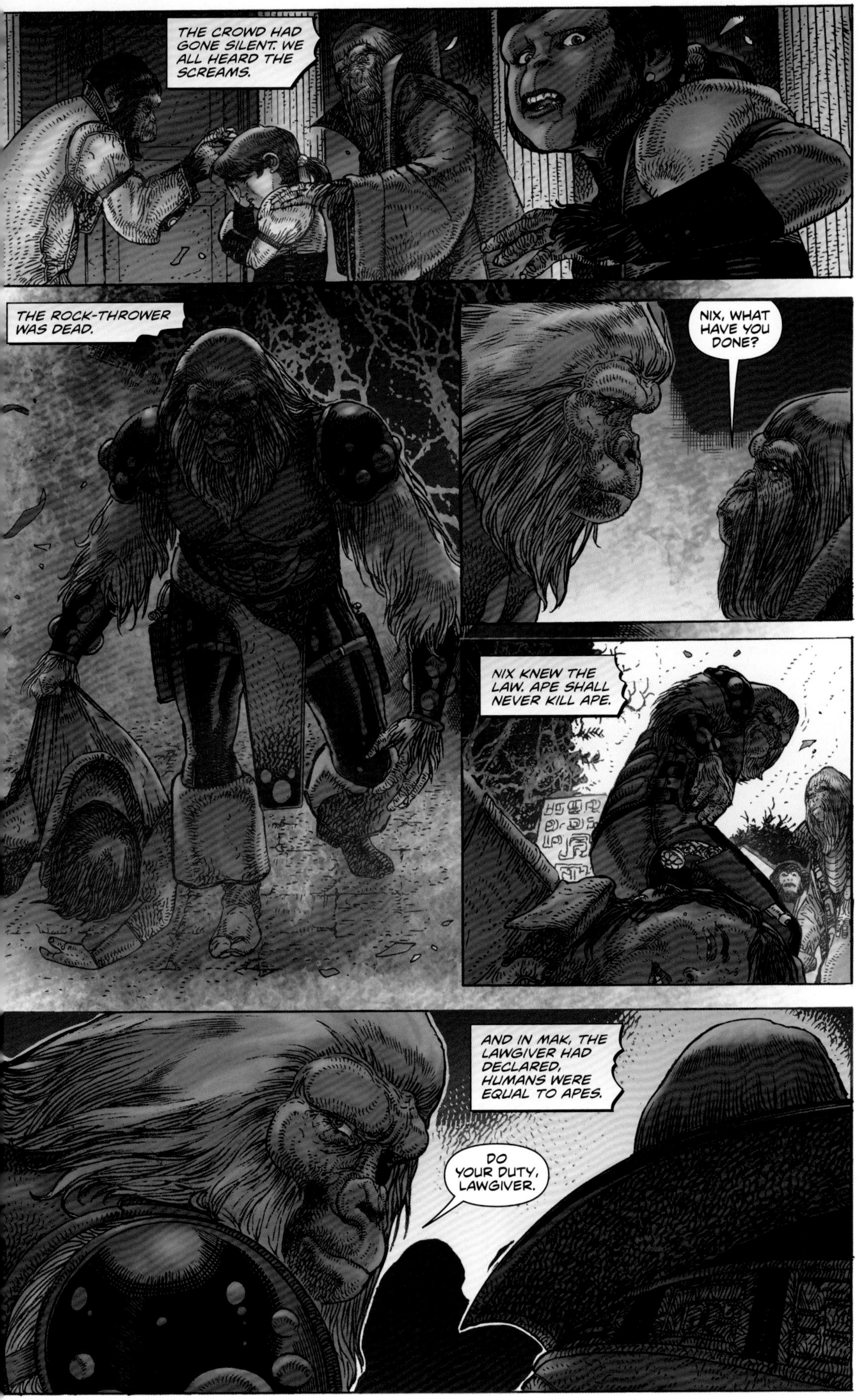
THE CROWD HAD GONE SILENT. WE ALL HEARD THE SCREAMS.
THE ROCK-THROWER WAS DEAD.
NIX, WHAT HAVE YOU DONE?
NIX KNEW THE LAW. APE SHALL NEVER KILL APE.
AND IN MAK, THE LAWGIVER HAD DECLARED, HUMANS WERE EQUAL TO APES.
DO YOUR DUTY, LAWGIVER.

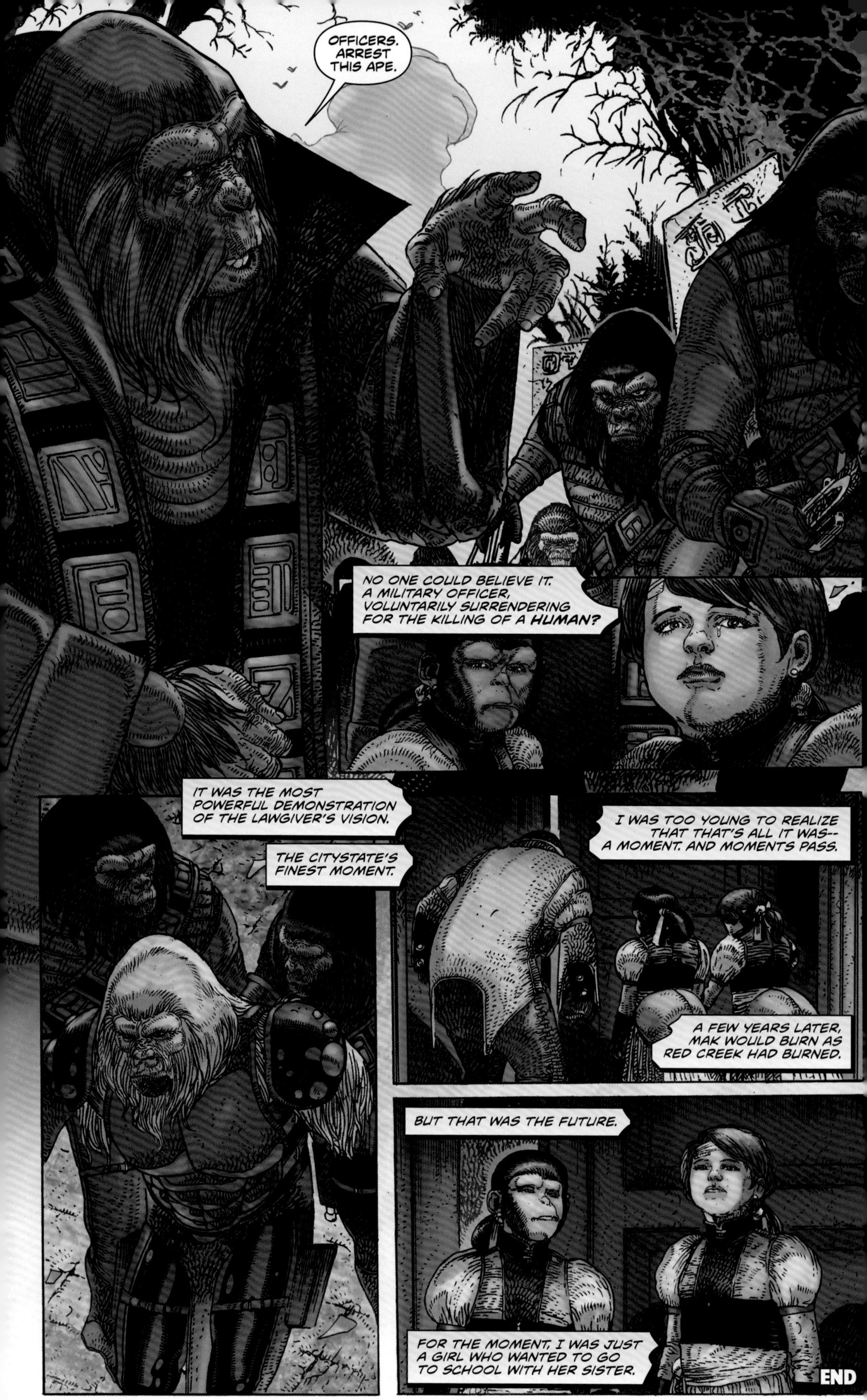

OFFICERS. ARREST THIS APE.
NO ONE COULD BELIEVE IT. A MILITARY OFFICER, VOLUNTARILY SURRENDERING FOR THE KILLING OF A HUMAN?
IT WAS THE MOST POWERFUL DEMONSTRATION OF THE LAWGIVER'S VISION.
THE CITYSTATE'S FINEST MOMENT.
I WAS TOO YOUNG TO REALIZE THAT THAT'S ALL IT WAS-- A MOMENT. AND MOMENTS PASS.
A FEW YEARS LATER, MAK WOULD BURN AS RED CREEK HAD BURNED.
BUT THAT WAS THE FUTURE.
FOR THE MOMENT, I WAS JUST A GIRL WHO WANTED TO GO TO SCHOOL WITH HER SISTER.
END

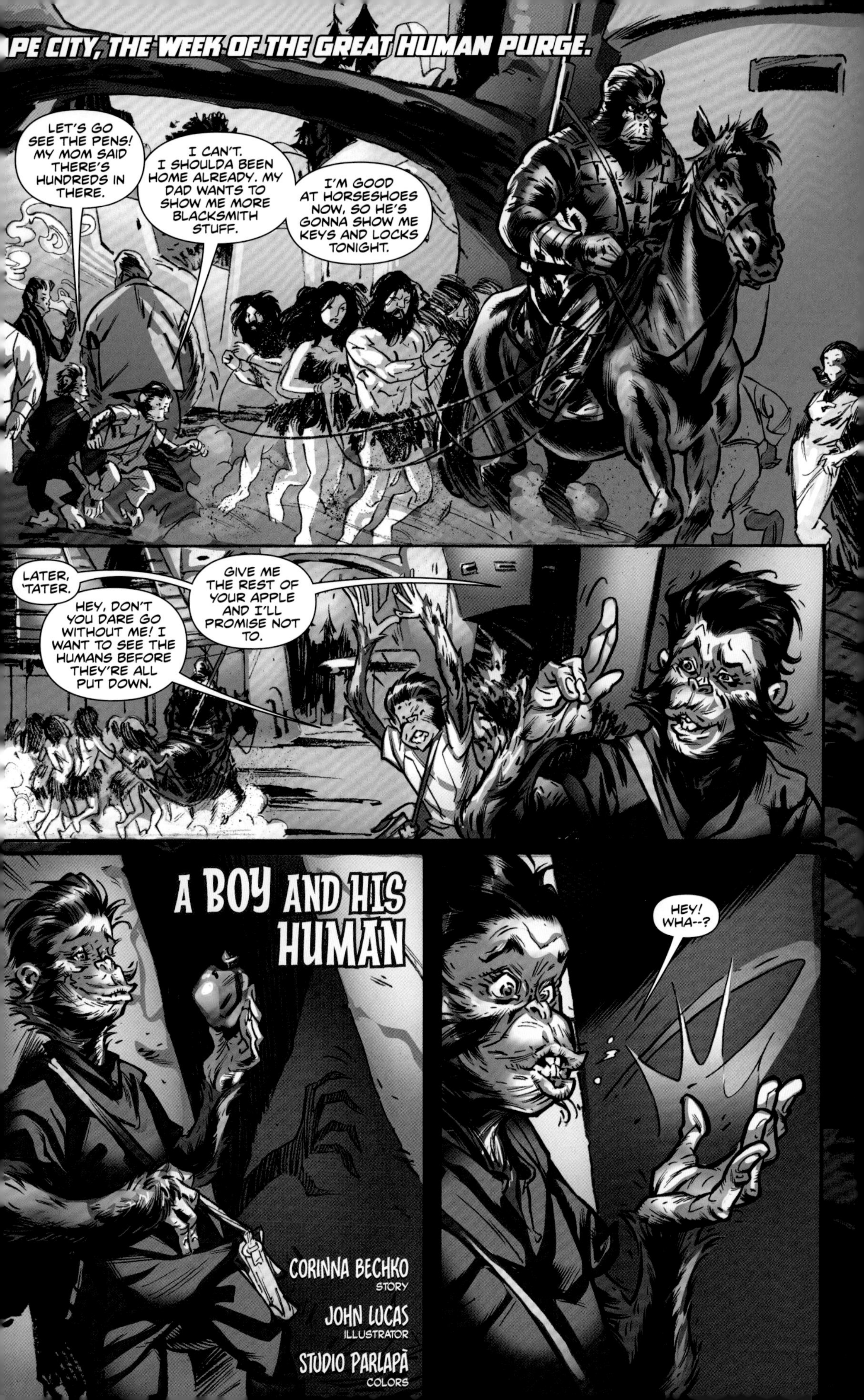
PE CITY, THE WEEK OF THE GREAT HUMAN PURGE.
LET'S GO SEE THE PENS! MY MOM SAID THERE'S HUNDREDS IN THERE.
I CAN'T. I SHOULDA BEEN HOME ALREADY. MY DAD WANTS TO SHOW ME MORE BLACKSMITH STUFF.
I'M GOOD AT HORSESHOES NOW, SO HE'S GONNA SHOW ME KEYS AND LOCKS TONIGHT.
LATER, 'TATER.
HEY, DON'T YOU DARE GO WITHOUT ME! I WANT TO SEE THE HUMANS BEFORE THEY'RE ALL PUT DOWN.
GIVE ME THE REST OF YOUR APPLE AND I'LL PROMISE NOT TO.
A BOY AND HIS HUMAN
CORINNA BECHKO
STORY
JOHN LUCAS
ILLUSTRATOR
STUDIO PARLAPÀ
COLORS
HEY! WHA--?

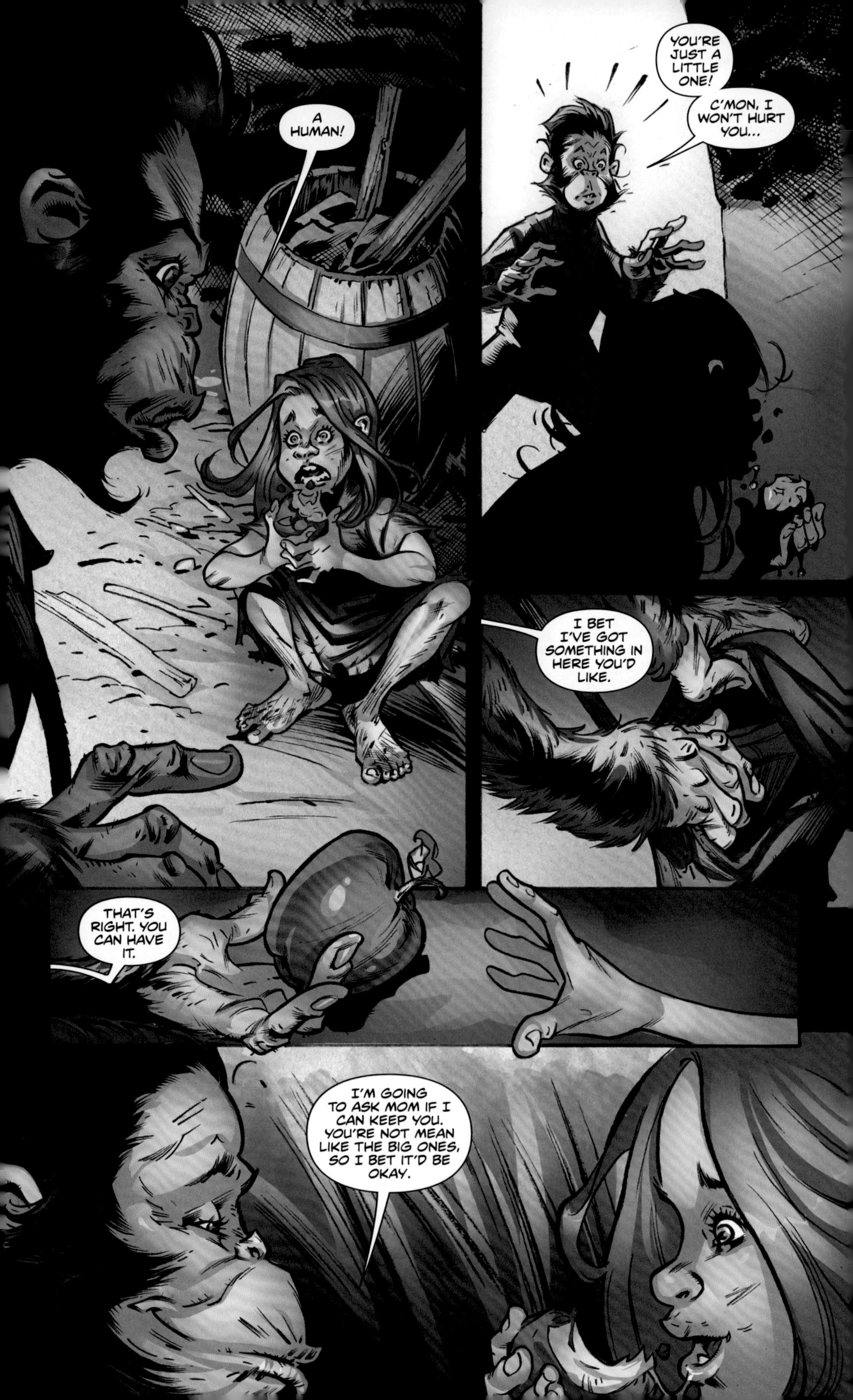
A HUMAN!
YOU'RE JUST A LITTLE ONE!
C'MON, I WON'T HURT YOU...
I BET I'VE GOT SOMETHING IN HERE YOU'D LIKE.
THAT'S RIGHT. YOU CAN HAVE IT.
I'M GOING TO ASK MOM IF I CAN KEEP YOU. YOU'RE NOT MEAN LIKE THE BIG ONES, SO I BET IT'D BE OKAY.

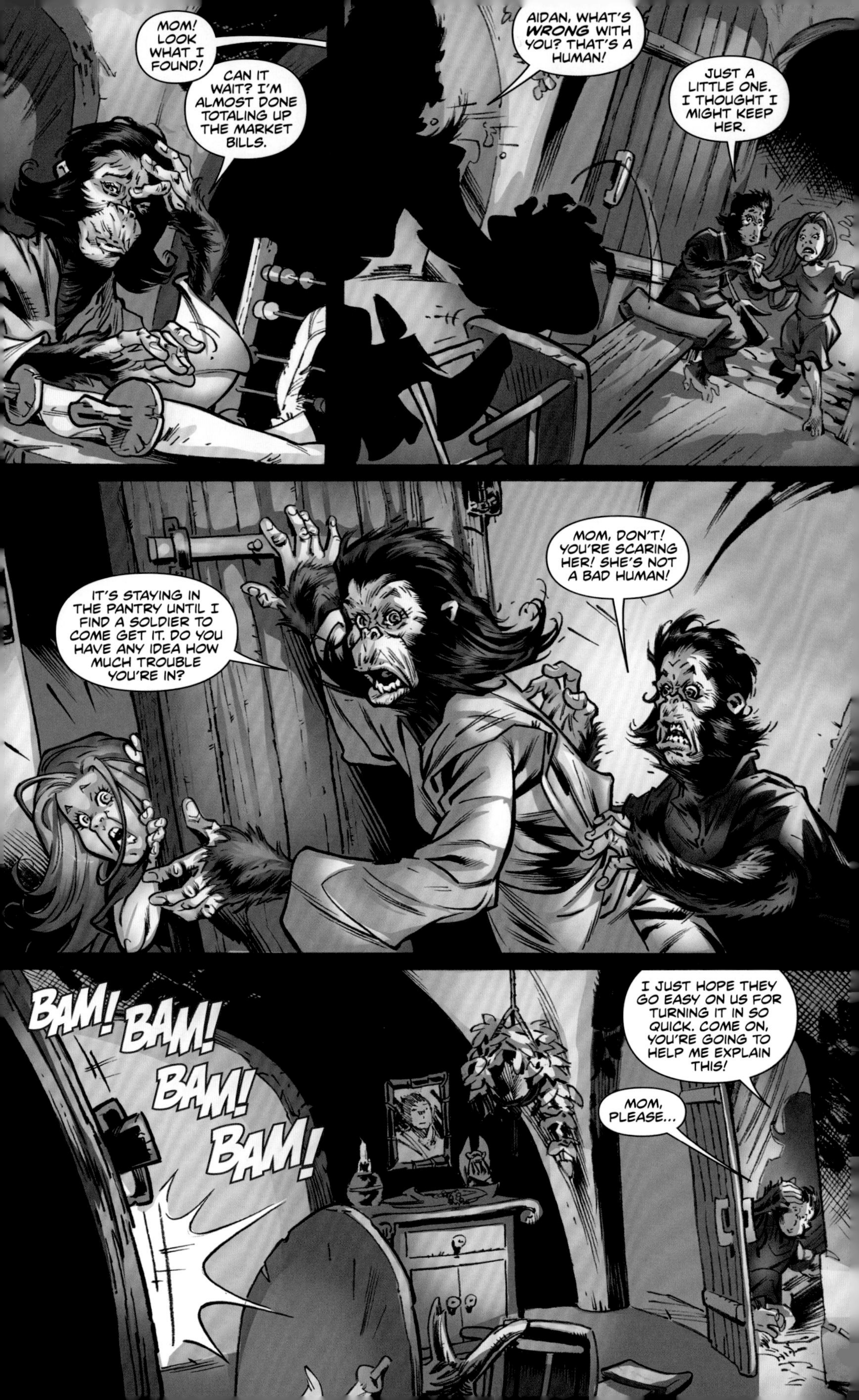
MOM! LOOK WHAT I FOUND!
CAN IT WAIT? I'M ALMOST DONE TOTALING UP THE MARKET BILLS.
AIDAN, WHAT'S **WRONG** WITH YOU? THAT'S A HUMAN!
JUST A LITTLE ONE. I THOUGHT I MIGHT KEEP HER.
IT'S STAYING IN THE PANTRY UNTIL I FIND A SOLDIER TO COME GET IT. DO YOU HAVE ANY IDEA HOW MUCH TROUBLE YOU'RE IN?
MOM, DON'T! YOU'RE SCARING HER! SHE'S NOT A BAD HUMAN!
BAM! BAM! BAM! BAM!
I JUST HOPE THEY GO EASY ON US FOR TURNING IT IN SO QUICK. COME ON, YOU'RE GOING TO HELP ME EXPLAIN THIS!
MOM, PLEASE...

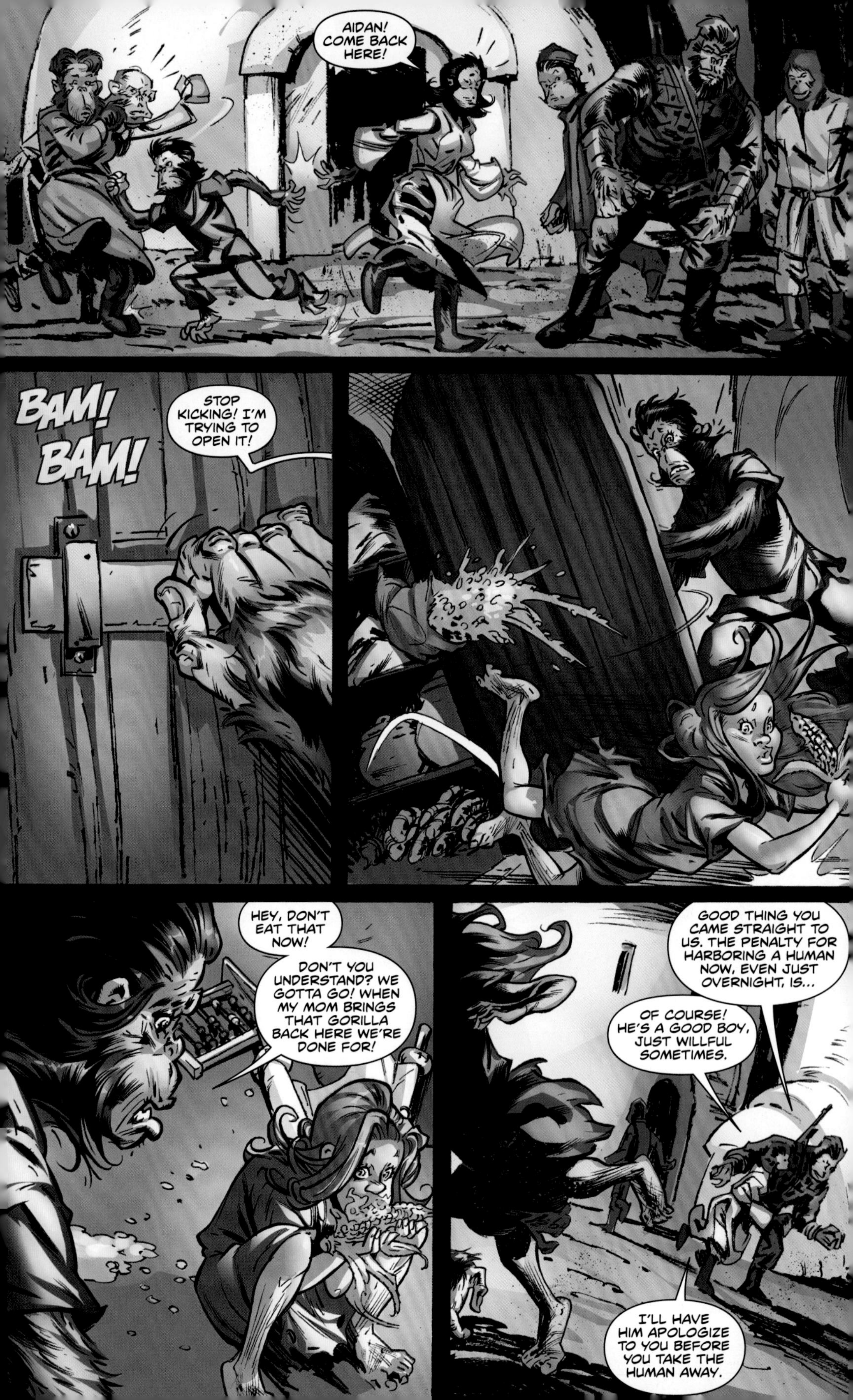
AIDAN! COME BACK HERE!
BAM! BAM!
STOP KICKING! I'M TRYING TO OPEN IT!
HEY, DON'T EAT THAT NOW!
DON'T YOU UNDERSTAND? WE GOTTA GO! WHEN MY MOM BRINGS THAT GORILLA BACK HERE WE'RE DONE FOR!
GOOD THING YOU CAME STRAIGHT TO US. THE PENALTY FOR HARBORING A HUMAN NOW, EVEN JUST OVERNIGHT, IS...
OF COURSE! HE'S A GOOD BOY, JUST WILLFUL SOMETIMES.
I'LL HAVE HIM APOLOGIZE TO YOU BEFORE YOU TAKE THE HUMAN AWAY.

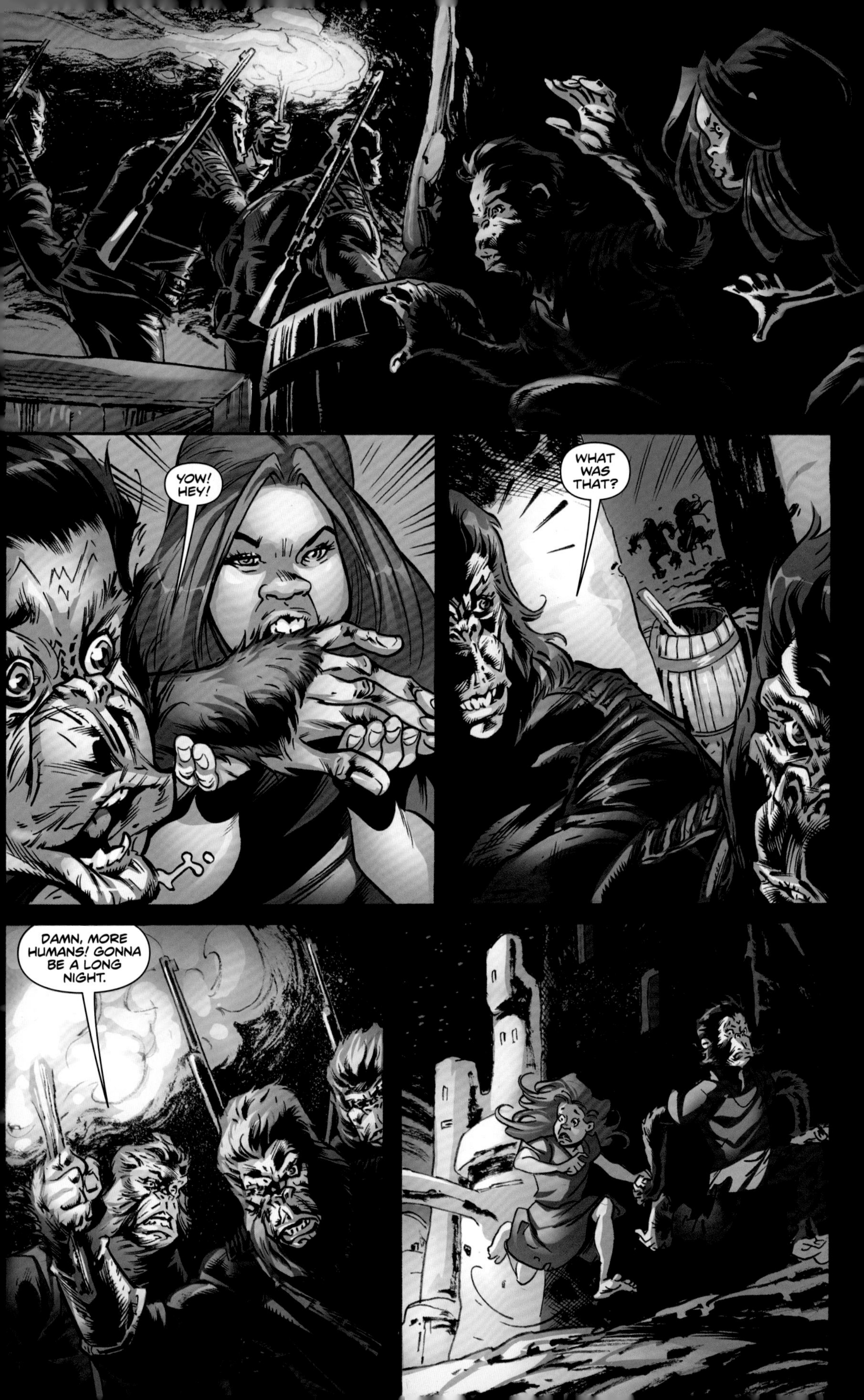
YOW! HEY!
WHAT WAS THAT?
DAMN, MORE HUMANS! GONNA BE A LONG NIGHT.

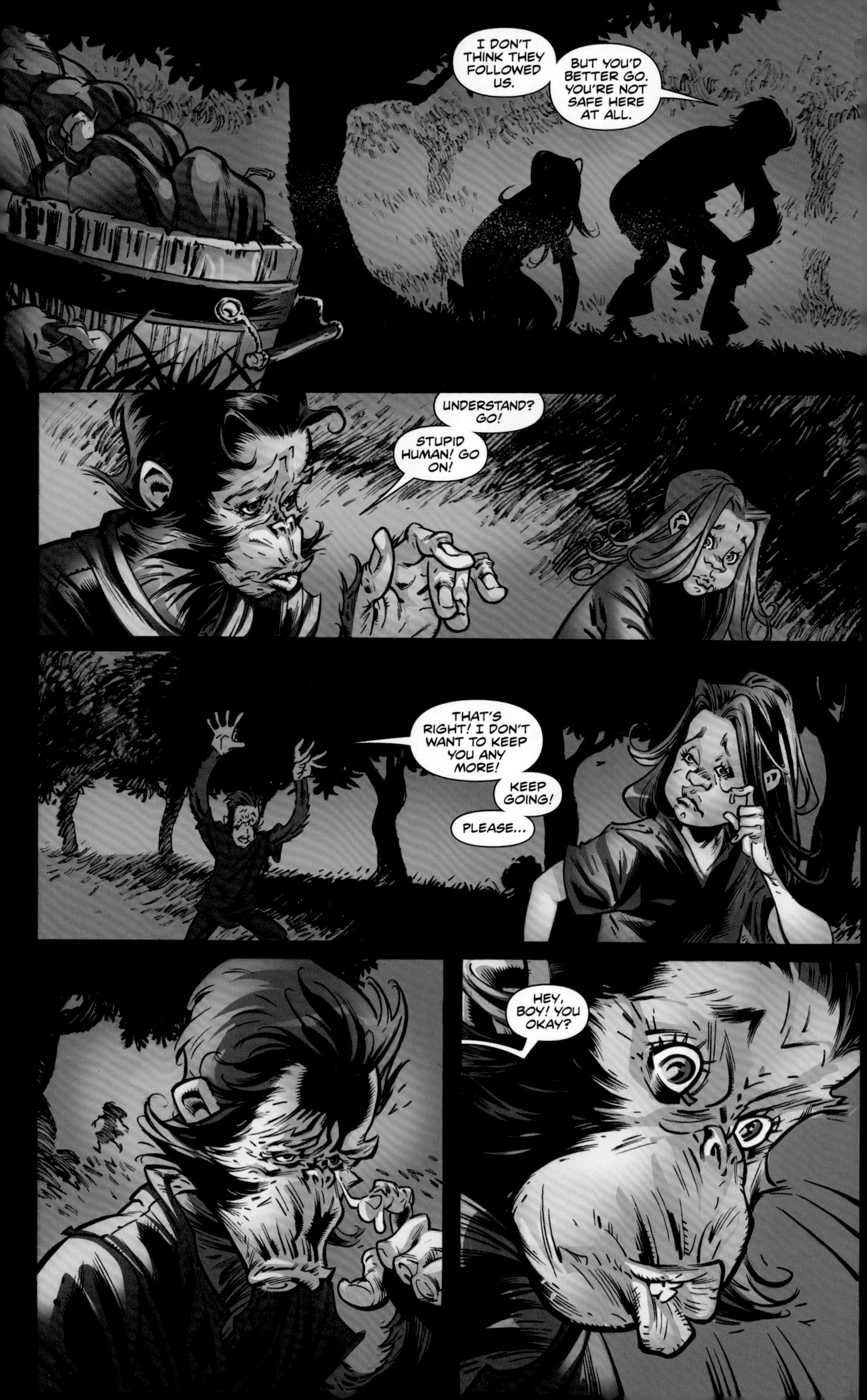
I DON'T THINK THEY FOLLOWED US.
BUT YOU'D BETTER GO. YOU'RE NOT SAFE HERE AT ALL.
UNDERSTAND? GO!
STUPID HUMAN! GO ON!
THAT'S RIGHT! I DON'T WANT TO KEEP YOU ANY MORE!
KEEP GOING!
PLEASE...
HEY, BOY! YOU OKAY?

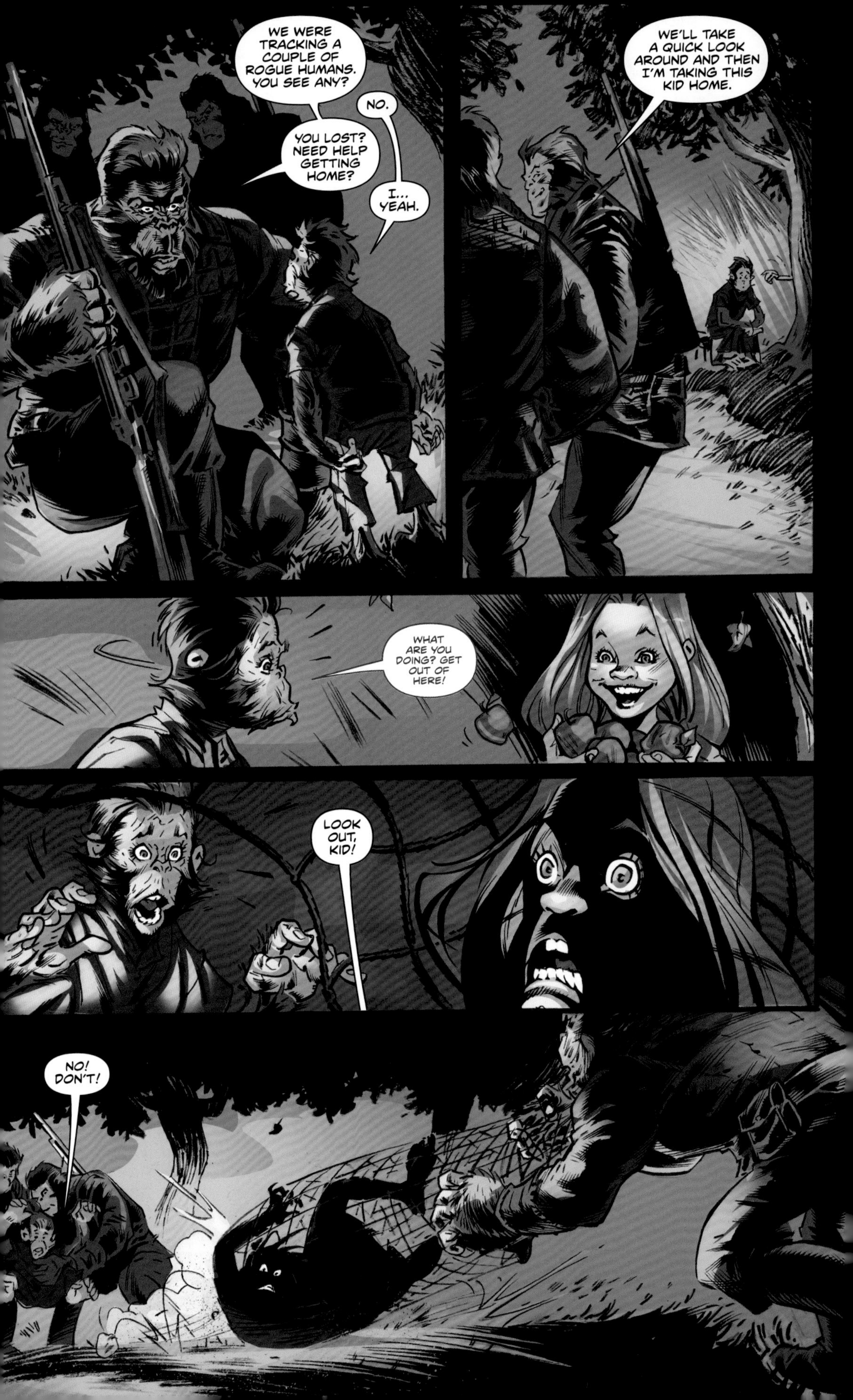
WE WERE TRACKING A COUPLE OF ROGUE HUMANS. YOU SEE ANY?
NO.
YOU LOST? NEED HELP GETTING HOME?
I... YEAH.
WE'LL TAKE A QUICK LOOK AROUND AND THEN I'M TAKING THIS KID HOME.
WHAT ARE YOU DOING? GET OUT OF HERE!
LOOK OUT, KID!
NO! DON'T!

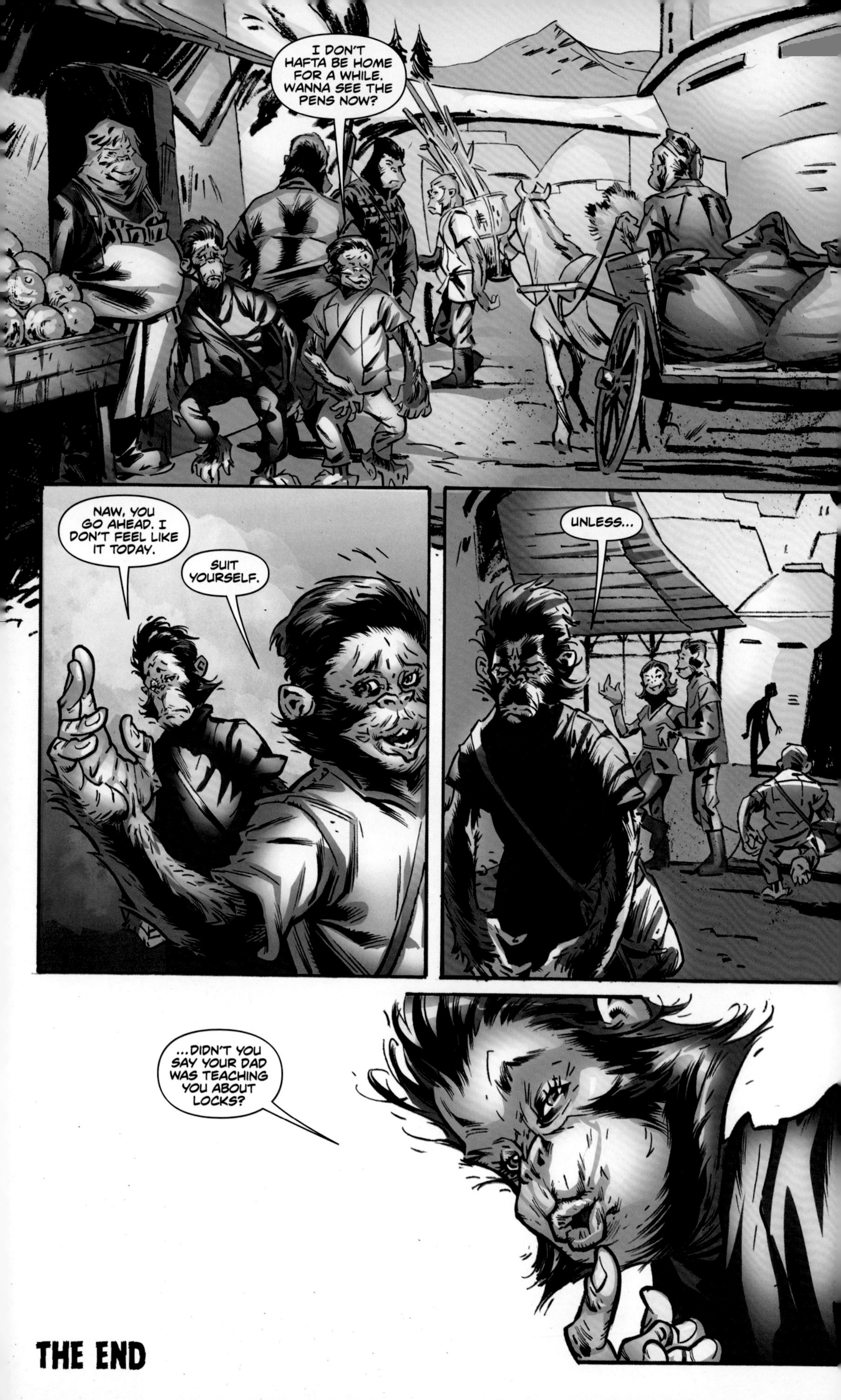
I DON'T HAFTA BE HOME FOR A WHILE. WANNA SEE THE PENS NOW?
NAW, YOU GO AHEAD. I DON'T FEEL LIKE IT TODAY.
SUIT YOURSELF.
UNLESS...
...DIDN'T YOU SAY YOUR DAD WAS TEACHING YOU ABOUT LOCKS?
THE END

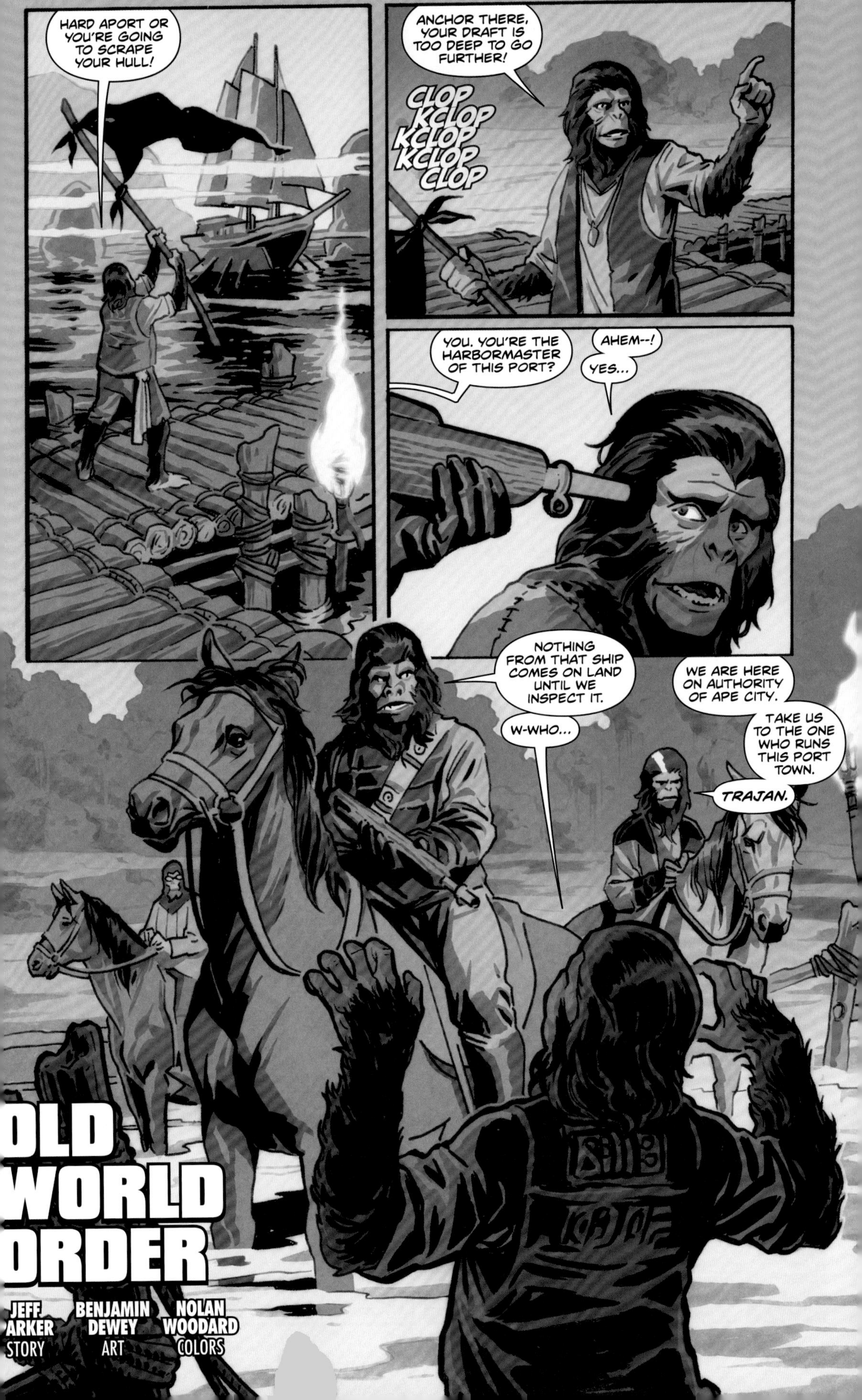
HARD APORT OR YOU'RE GOING TO SCRAPE YOUR HULL!
ANCHOR THERE, YOUR DRAFT IS TOO DEEP TO GO FURTHER!
CLOP KCLOP KCLOP KCLOP CLOP
YOU. YOU'RE THE HARBORMASTER OF THIS PORT?
AHEM--!
YES...
NOTHING FROM THAT SHIP COMES ON LAND UNTIL WE INSPECT IT.
W-WHO...
WE ARE HERE ON AUTHORITY OF APE CITY.
TAKE US TO THE ONE WHO RUNS THIS PORT TOWN.
TRAJAN.
OLD WORLD ORDER
JEFF ARKER STORY
BENJAMIN DEWEY ART
NOLAN WOODARD COLORS

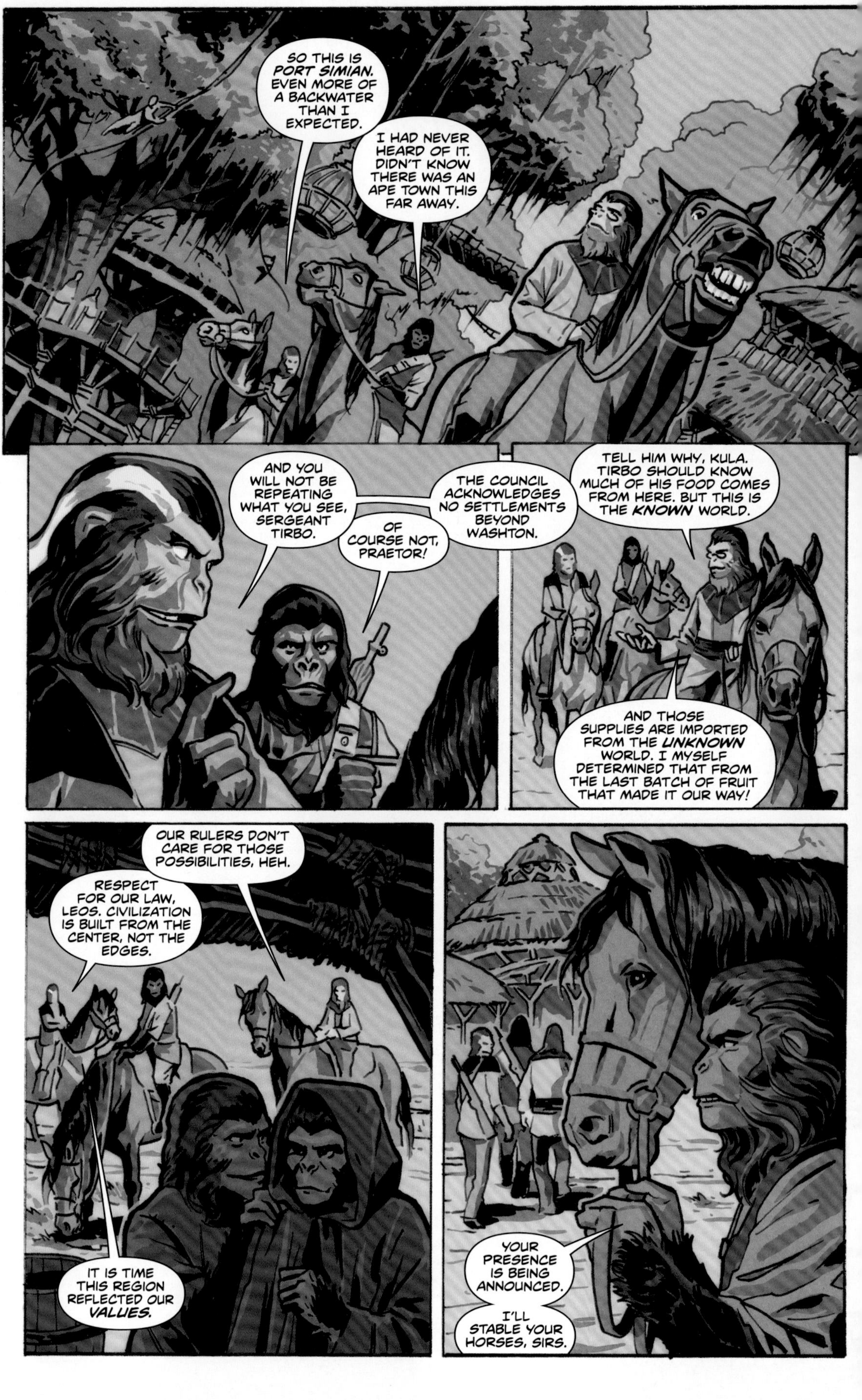
SO THIS IS *PORT SIMIAN.* EVEN MORE OF A BACKWATER THAN I EXPECTED.
I HAD NEVER HEARD OF IT. DIDN'T KNOW THERE WAS AN APE TOWN THIS FAR AWAY.
AND YOU WILL NOT BE REPEATING WHAT YOU SEE, SERGEANT TIRBO.
THE COUNCIL ACKNOWLEDGES NO SETTLEMENTS BEYOND WASHTON.
OF COURSE NOT, PRAETOR!
TELL HIM WHY, KULA. TIRBO SHOULD KNOW MUCH OF HIS FOOD COMES FROM HERE. BUT THIS IS THE *KNOWN* WORLD.
AND THOSE SUPPLIES ARE IMPORTED FROM THE *UNKNOWN* WORLD. I MYSELF DETERMINED THAT FROM THE LAST BATCH OF FRUIT THAT MADE IT OUR WAY!
OUR RULERS DON'T CARE FOR THOSE POSSIBILITIES, HEH.
RESPECT FOR OUR LAW, LEOS. CIVILIZATION IS BUILT FROM THE CENTER, NOT THE EDGES.
IT IS TIME THIS REGION REFLECTED OUR *VALUES.*
YOUR PRESENCE IS BEING ANNOUNCED.
I'LL STABLE YOUR HORSES, SIRS.

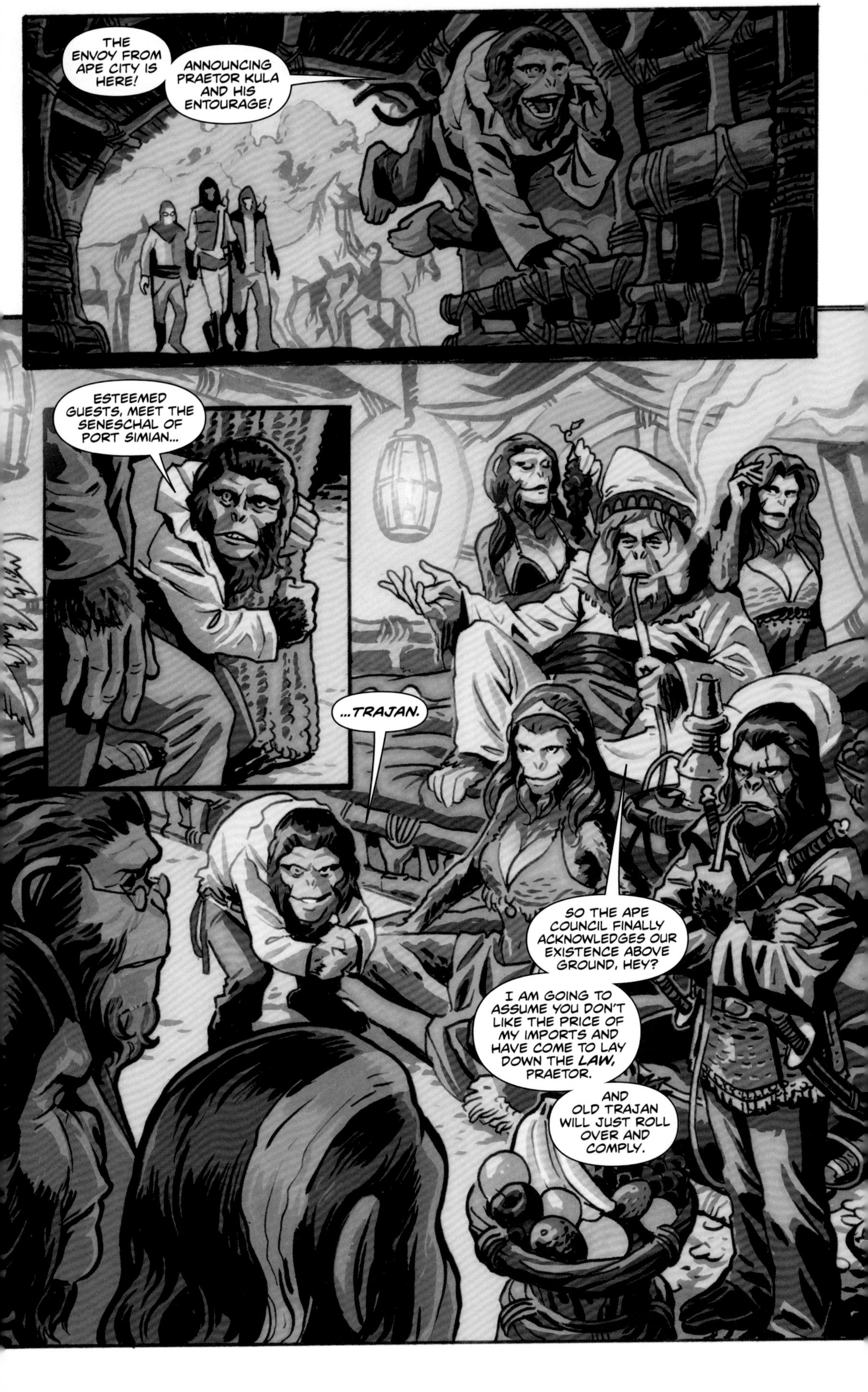
THE ENVOY FROM APE CITY IS HERE!
ANNOUNCING PRAETOR KULA AND HIS ENTOURAGE!
ESTEEMED GUESTS, MEET THE SENESCHAL OF PORT SIMIAN...
...TRAJAN.
SO THE APE COUNCIL FINALLY ACKNOWLEDGES OUR EXISTENCE ABOVE GROUND, HEY?
I AM GOING TO ASSUME YOU DON'T LIKE THE PRICE OF MY IMPORTS AND HAVE COME TO LAY DOWN THE LAW, PRAETOR.
AND OLD TRAJAN WILL JUST ROLL OVER AND COMPLY.

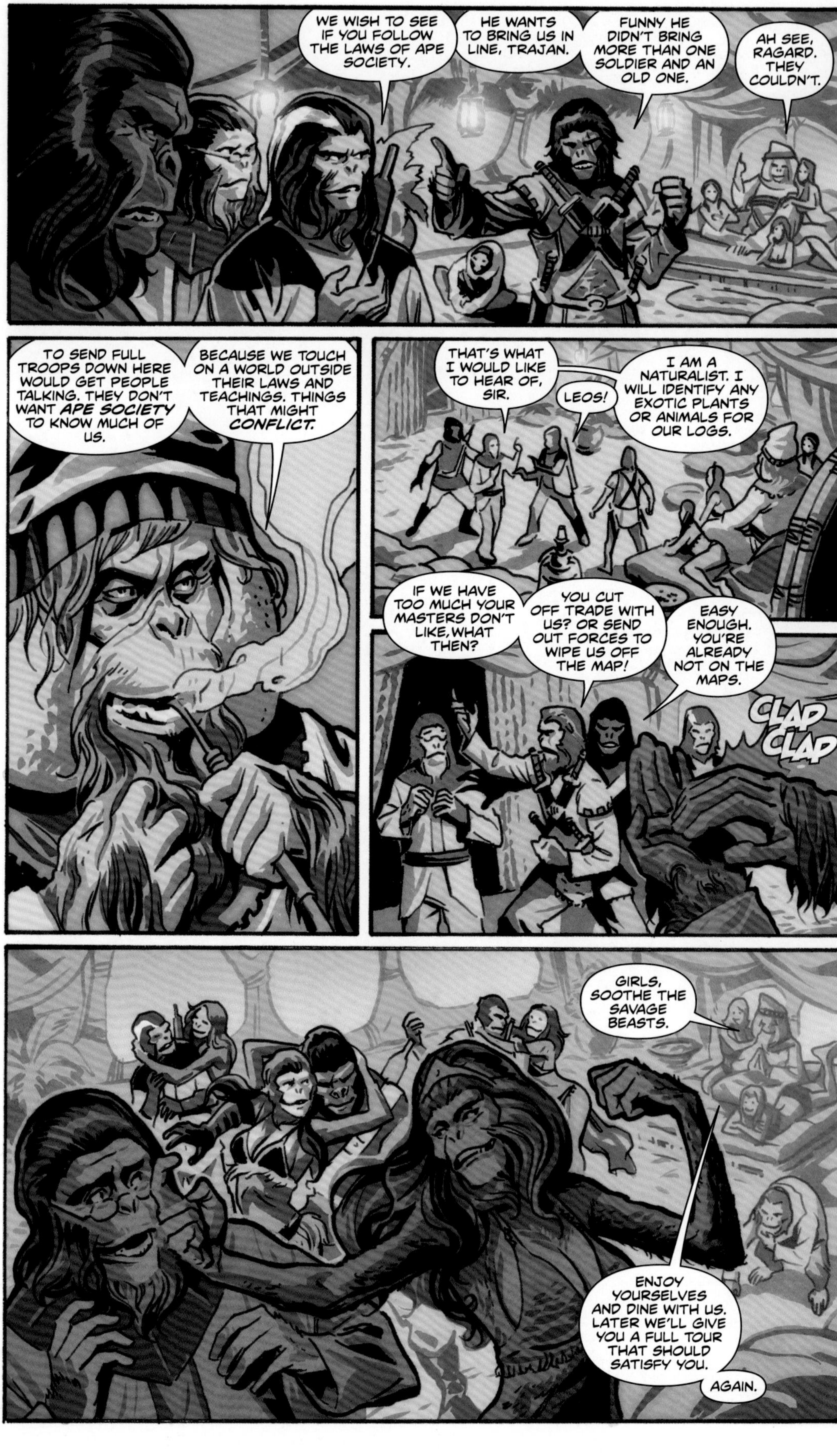

WE WISH TO SEE IF YOU FOLLOW THE LAWS OF APE SOCIETY.
HE WANTS TO BRING US IN LINE, TRAJAN.
FUNNY HE DIDN'T BRING MORE THAN ONE SOLDIER AND AN OLD ONE.
AH SEE, RAGARD. THEY COULDN'T.
TO SEND FULL TROOPS DOWN HERE WOULD GET PEOPLE TALKING. THEY DON'T WANT *APE SOCIETY* TO KNOW MUCH OF US.
BECAUSE WE TOUCH ON A WORLD OUTSIDE THEIR LAWS AND TEACHINGS. THINGS THAT MIGHT *CONFLICT.*
THAT'S WHAT I WOULD LIKE TO HEAR OF, SIR.
LEOS!
I AM A NATURALIST. I WILL IDENTIFY ANY EXOTIC PLANTS OR ANIMALS FOR OUR LOGS.
IF WE HAVE TOO MUCH YOUR MASTERS DON'T LIKE, WHAT THEN?
YOU CUT OFF TRADE WITH US? OR SEND OUT FORCES TO WIPE US OFF THE MAP!
EASY ENOUGH. YOU'RE ALREADY NOT ON THE MAPS.
CLAP CLAP
GIRLS, SOOTHE THE SAVAGE BEASTS.
ENJOY YOURSELVES AND DINE WITH US. LATER WE'LL GIVE YOU A FULL TOUR THAT SHOULD SATISFY YOU.
AGAIN.

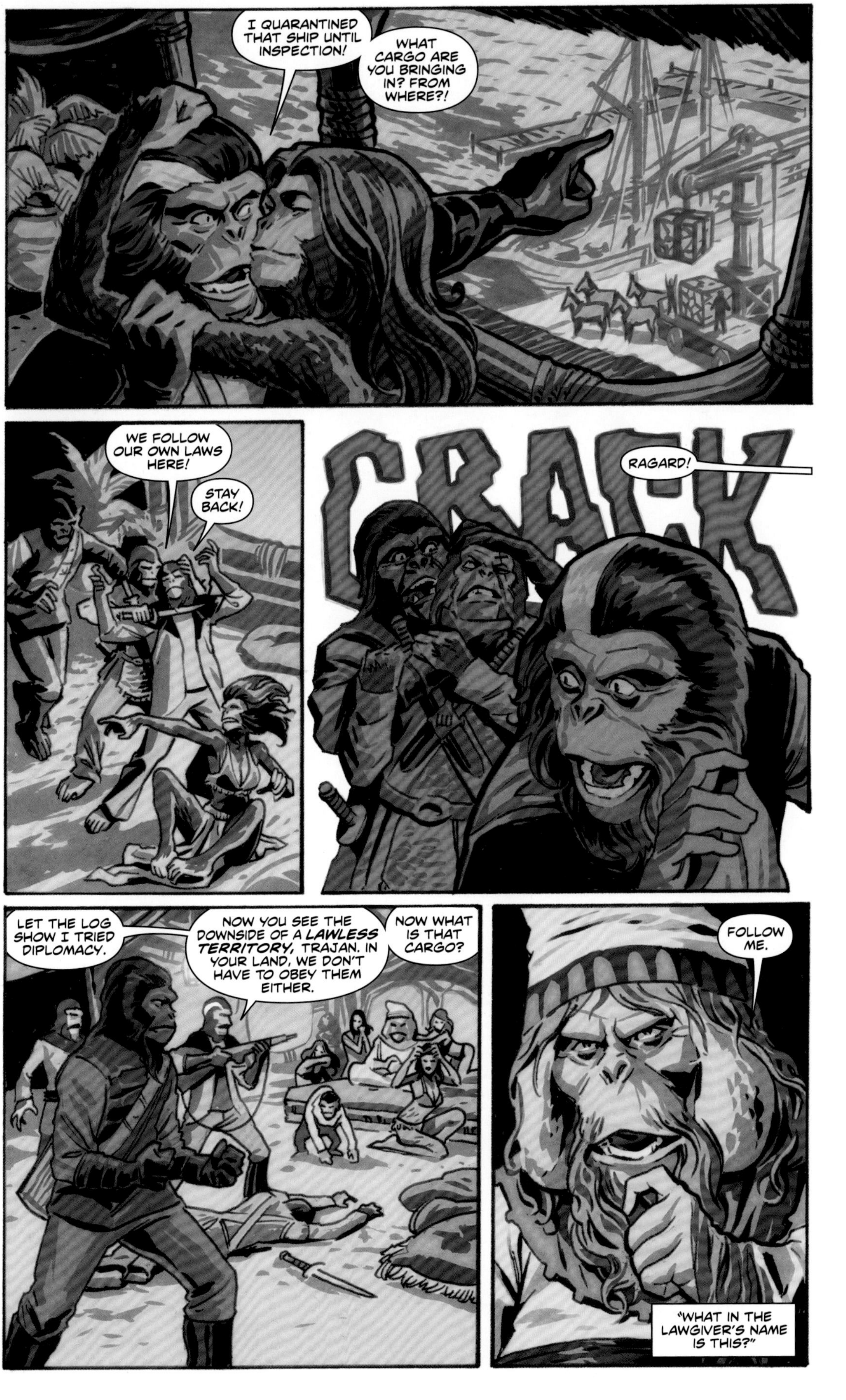
I QUARANTINED THAT SHIP UNTIL INSPECTION!
WHAT CARGO ARE YOU BRINGING IN? FROM WHERE?!
WE FOLLOW OUR OWN LAWS HERE!
STAY BACK!
CRACK
RAGARD!
LET THE LOG SHOW I TRIED DIPLOMACY.
NOW YOU SEE THE DOWNSIDE OF A LAWLESS TERRITORY, TRAJAN. IN YOUR LAND, WE DON'T HAVE TO OBEY THEM EITHER.
NOW WHAT IS THAT CARGO?
FOLLOW ME.
"WHAT IN THE LAWGIVER'S NAME IS THIS?"

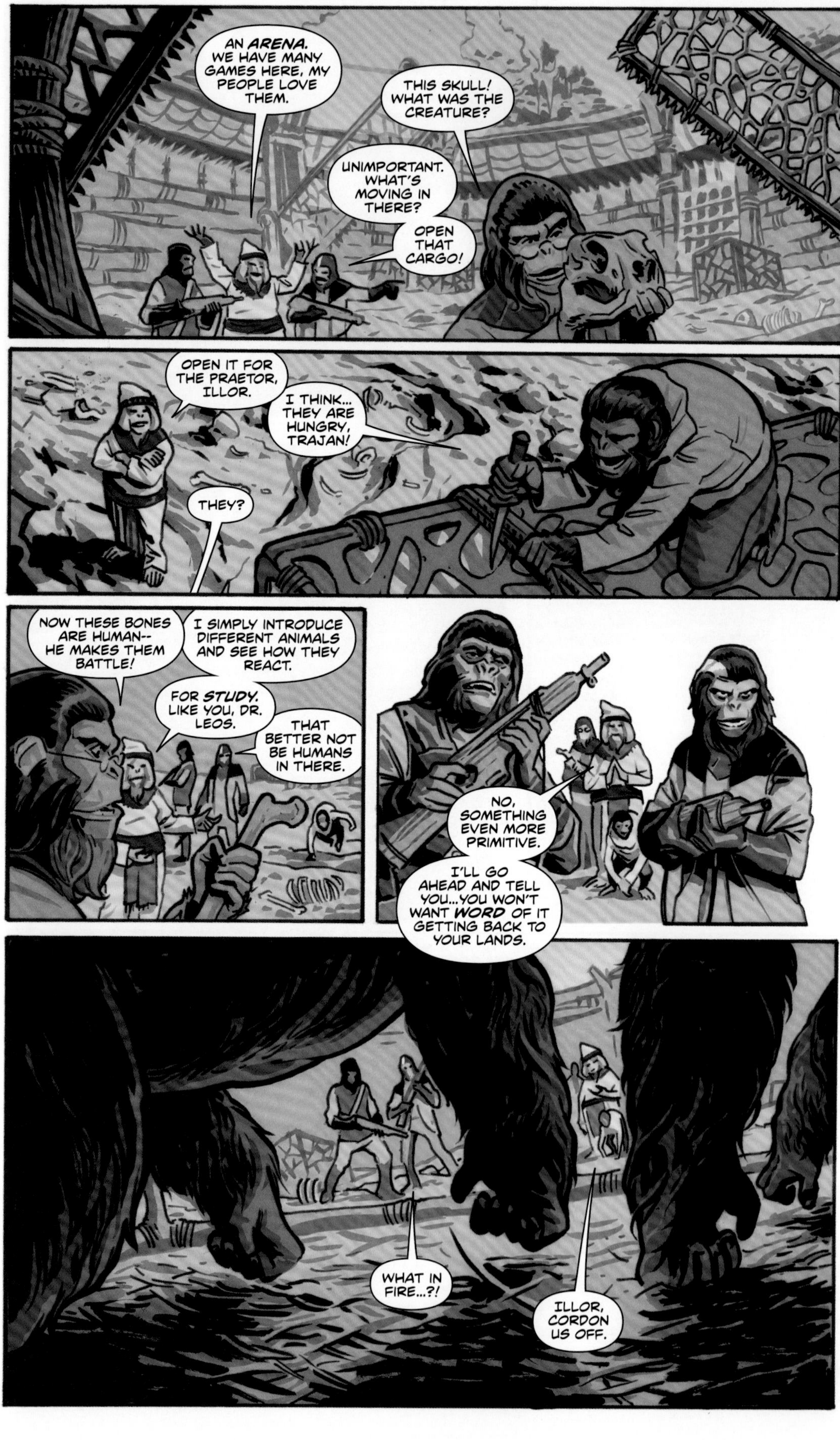
AN ARENA. WE HAVE MANY GAMES HERE, MY PEOPLE LOVE THEM.
THIS SKULL! WHAT WAS THE CREATURE?
UNIMPORTANT. WHAT'S MOVING IN THERE?
OPEN THAT CARGO!
OPEN IT FOR THE PRAETOR, ILLOR.
I THINK... THEY ARE HUNGRY, TRAJAN!
THEY?
NOW THESE BONES ARE HUMAN-- HE MAKES THEM BATTLE!
I SIMPLY INTRODUCE DIFFERENT ANIMALS AND SEE HOW THEY REACT.
FOR STUDY. LIKE YOU, DR. LEOS.
THAT BETTER NOT BE HUMANS IN THERE.
NO, SOMETHING EVEN MORE PRIMITIVE.
I'LL GO AHEAD AND TELL YOU...YOU WON'T WANT WORD OF IT GETTING BACK TO YOUR LANDS.
WHAT IN FIRE...?!
ILLOR, CORDON US OFF.

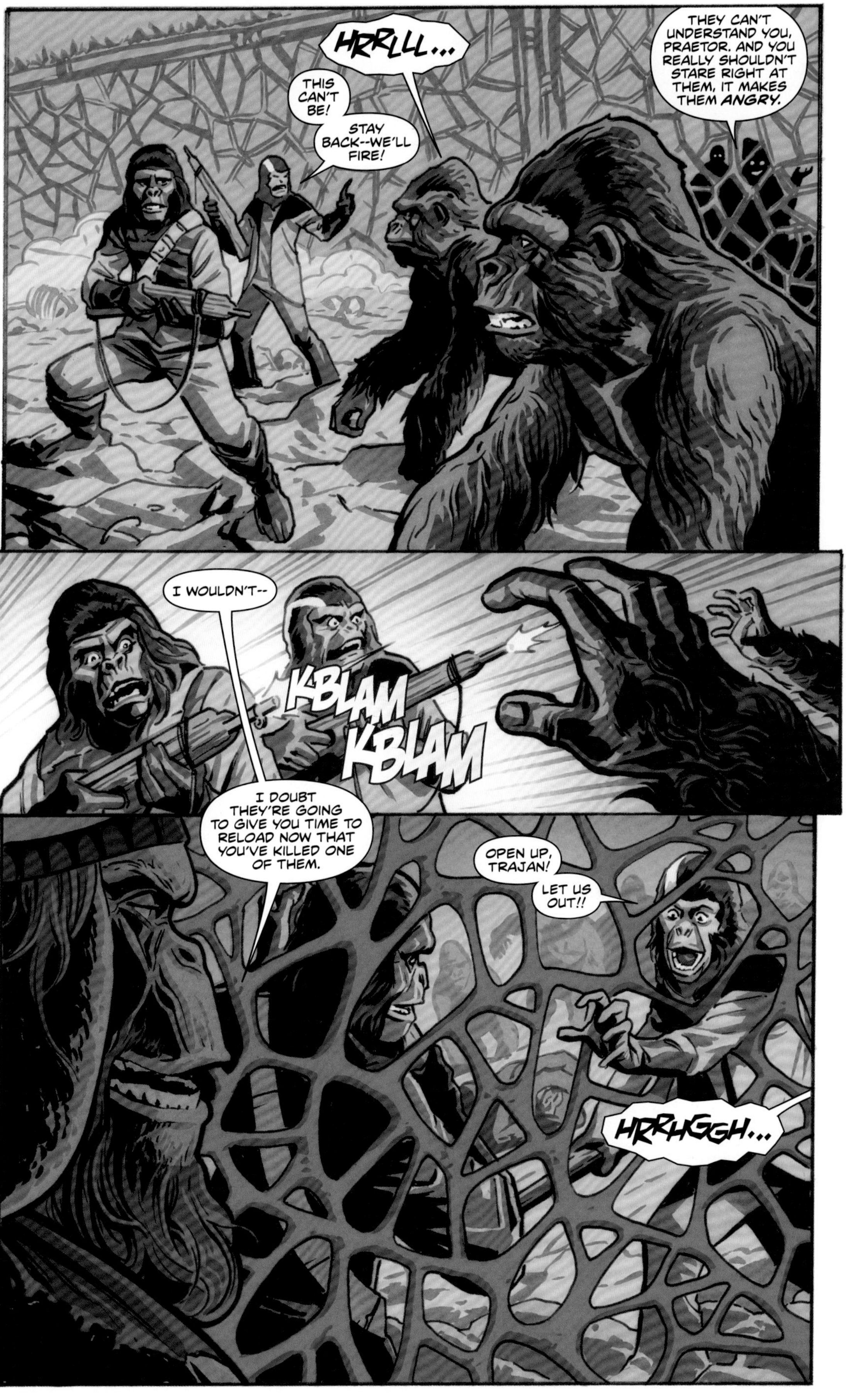
HRRLLL...
THIS CAN'T BE!
STAY BACK--WE'LL FIRE!
THEY CAN'T UNDERSTAND YOU, PRAETOR. AND YOU REALLY SHOULDN'T STARE RIGHT AT THEM, IT MAKES THEM ANGRY.
I WOULDN'T--
KBLAM
KBLAM
I DOUBT THEY'RE GOING TO GIVE YOU TIME TO RELOAD NOW THAT YOU'VE KILLED ONE OF THEM.
OPEN UP, TRAJAN!
LET US OUT!!
HRRHGGH...

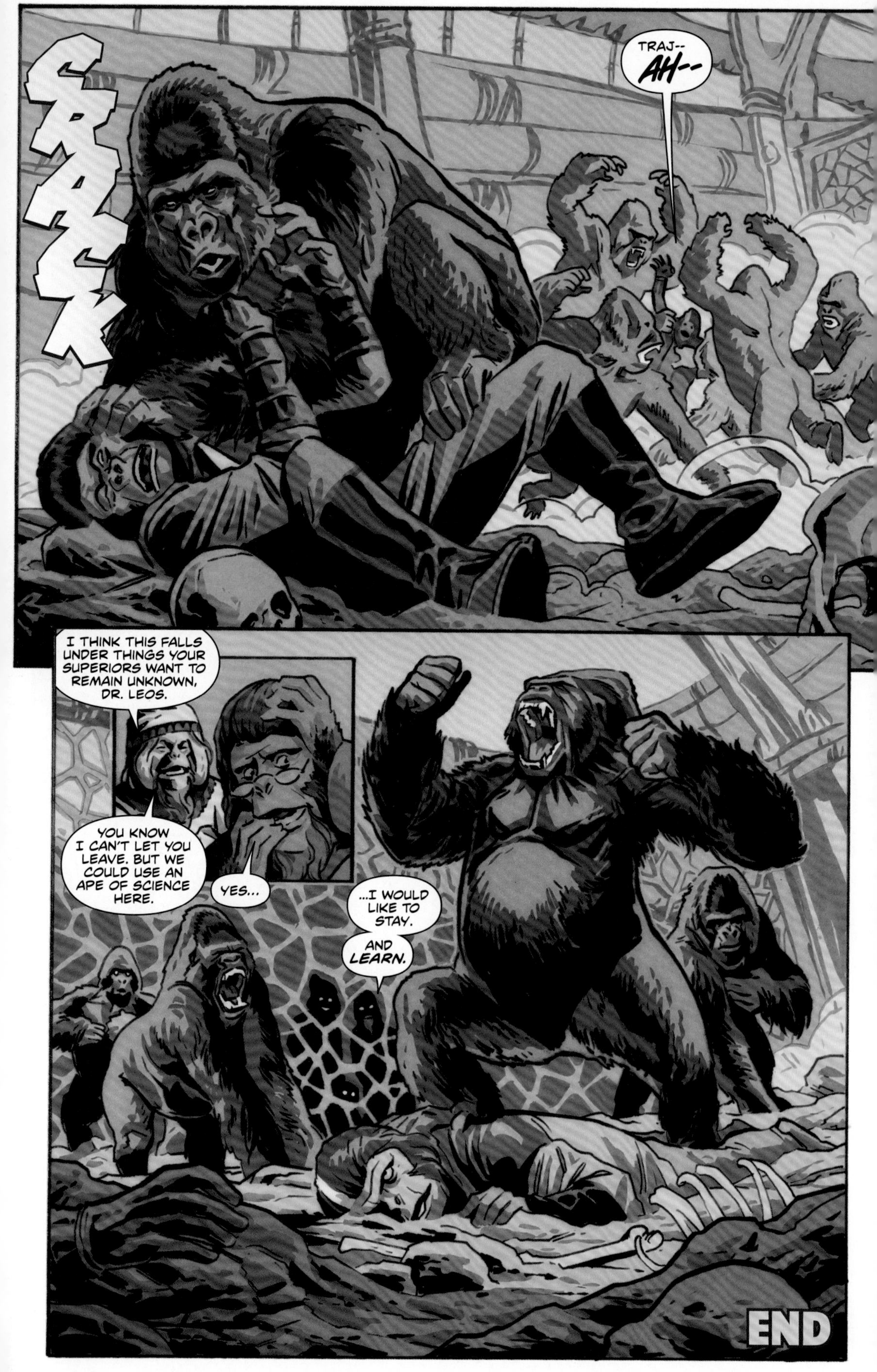
CRACK
TRAJ-- AH--
I THINK THIS FALLS UNDER THINGS YOUR SUPERIORS WANT TO REMAIN UNKNOWN, DR. LEOS.
YOU KNOW I CAN'T LET YOU LEAVE. BUT WE COULD USE AN APE OF SCIENCE HERE.
YES...
...I WOULD LIKE TO STAY.
AND LEARN.
END

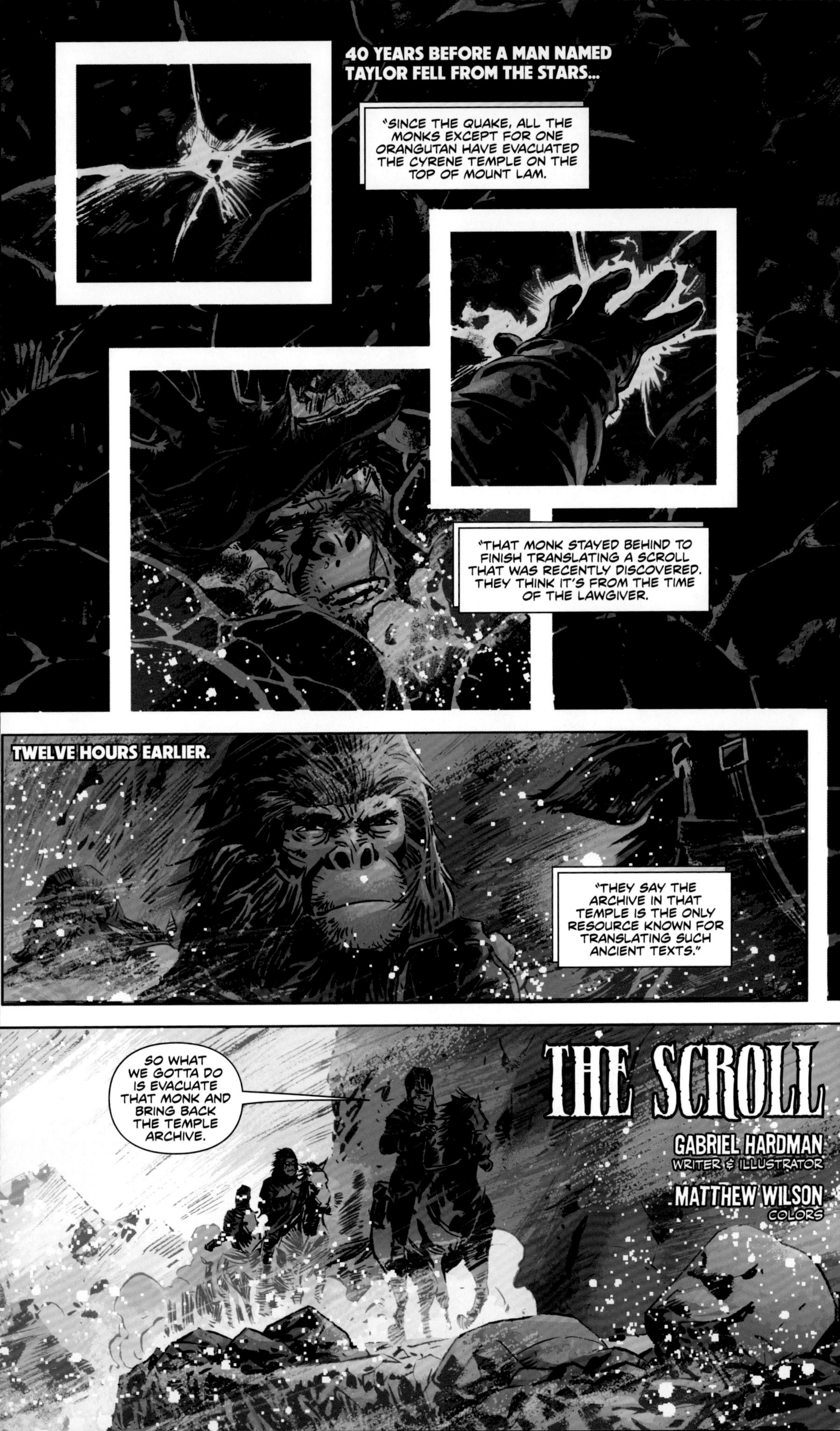

40 YEARS BEFORE A MAN NAMED TAYLOR FELL FROM THE STARS...
"SINCE THE QUAKE, ALL THE MONKS EXCEPT FOR ONE ORANGUTAN HAVE EVACUATED THE CYRENE TEMPLE ON THE TOP OF MOUNT LAM.
"THAT MONK STAYED BEHIND TO FINISH TRANSLATING A SCROLL THAT WAS RECENTLY DISCOVERED. THEY THINK IT'S FROM THE TIME OF THE LAWGIVER.
TWELVE HOURS EARLIER.
"THEY SAY THE ARCHIVE IN THAT TEMPLE IS THE ONLY RESOURCE KNOWN FOR TRANSLATING SUCH ANCIENT TEXTS."
SO WHAT WE GOTTA DO IS EVACUATE THAT MONK AND BRING BACK THE TEMPLE ARCHIVE.
THE SCROLL
GABRIEL HARDMAN
WRITER & ILLUSTRATOR
MATTHEW WILSON
COLORS

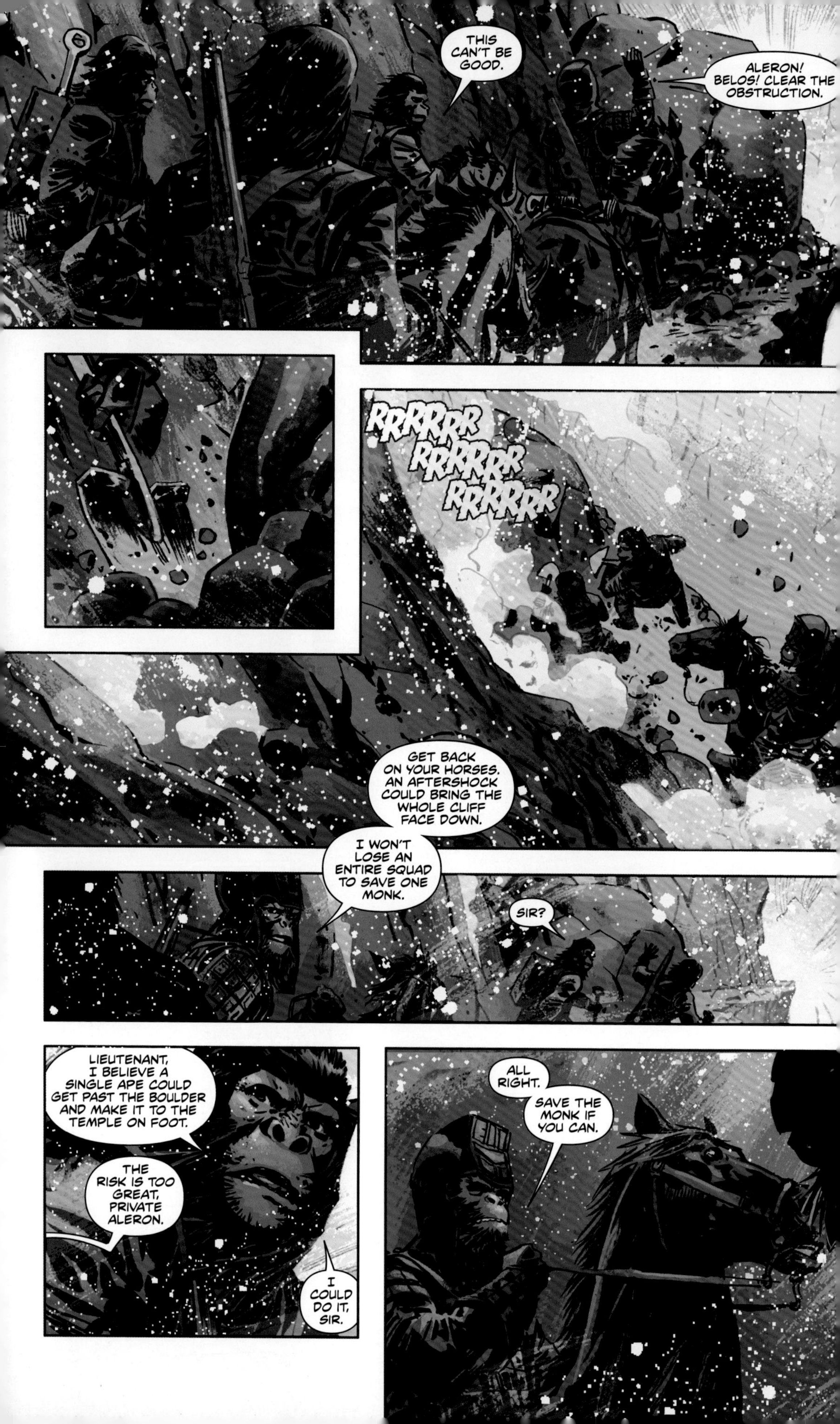
THIS CAN'T BE GOOD.
ALERON! BELOS! CLEAR THE OBSTRUCTION.
RRRRRR RRRRRR RRRRRR
GET BACK ON YOUR HORSES. AN AFTERSHOCK COULD BRING THE WHOLE CLIFF FACE DOWN.
I WON'T LOSE AN ENTIRE SQUAD TO SAVE ONE MONK.
SIR?
LIEUTENANT, I BELIEVE A SINGLE APE COULD GET PAST THE BOULDER AND MAKE IT TO THE TEMPLE ON FOOT.
THE RISK IS TOO GREAT, PRIVATE ALERON.
I COULD DO IT, SIR.
ALL RIGHT.
SAVE THE MONK IF YOU CAN.

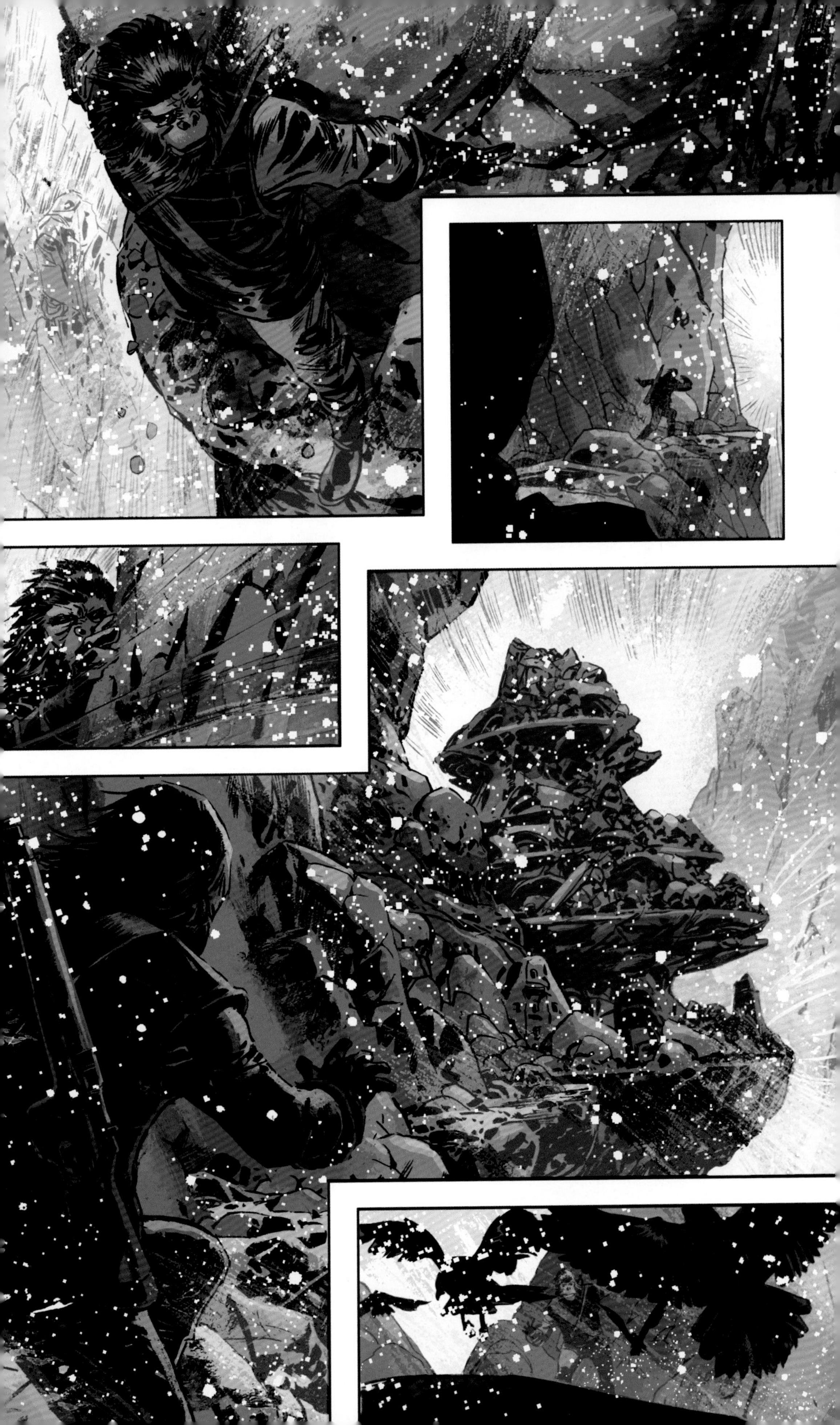

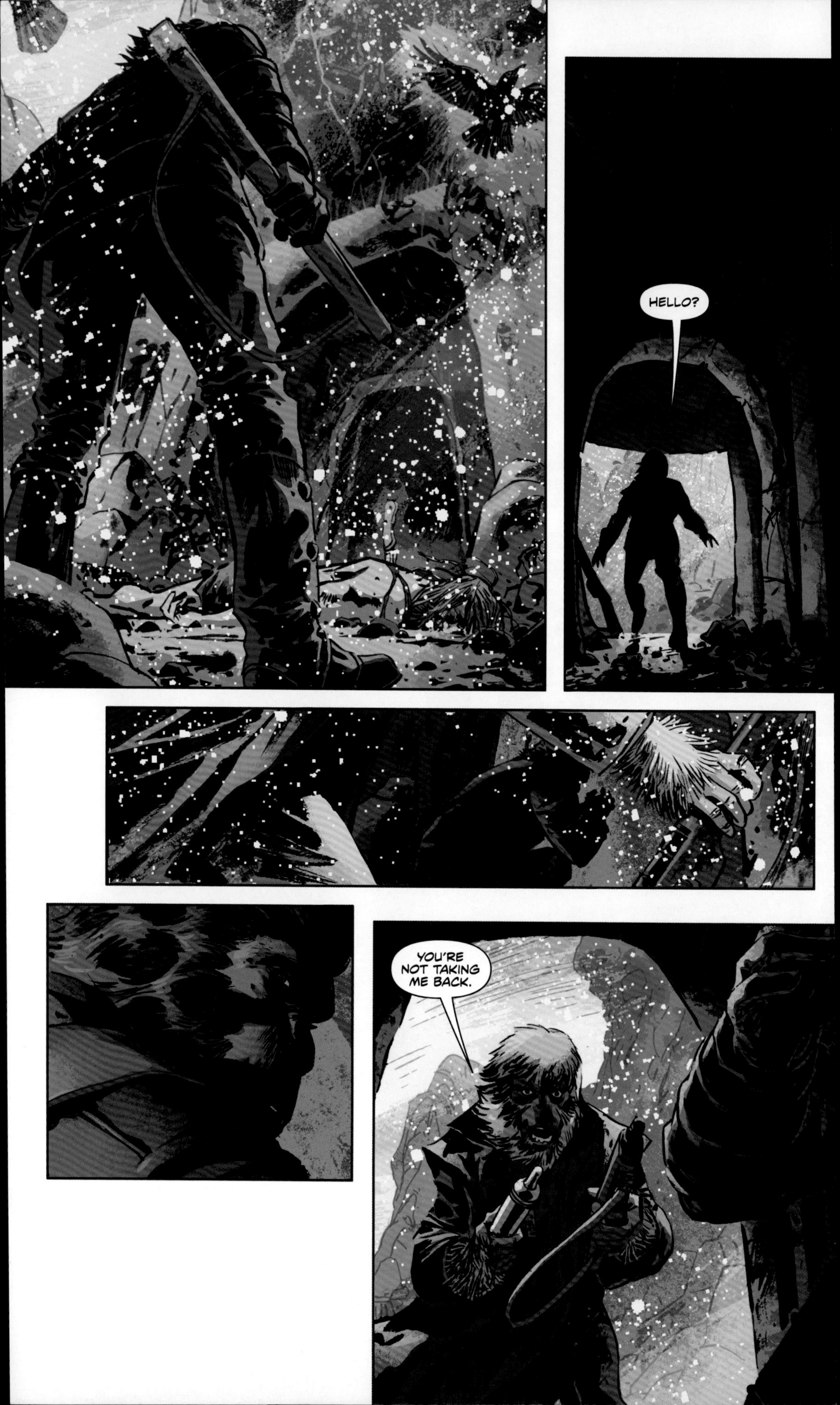
HELLO?
YOU'RE NOT TAKING ME BACK.

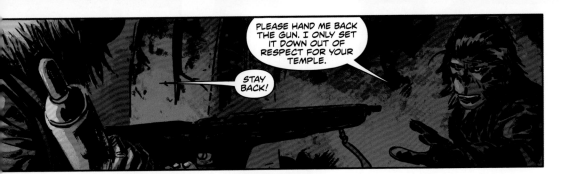

PLEASE HAND ME BACK THE GUN. I ONLY SET IT DOWN OUT OF RESPECT FOR YOUR TEMPLE.

STAY BACK!

I'M ALREADY A MURDERER. I'M DAMNED NO MATTER WHAT I DO.

KILLING AN ANIMAL ISN'T MURDER.

THAT'S RIGHT, YOU WOULDN'T KNOW.

I CAUGHT THE HUMAN RAIDING THE LAST OF MY FOOD RESERVES. HE TURNED TOWARD ME. MAYBE TO ATTACK, MAYBE TO RUN.

I HAD THE KNIFE IN MY HAND...

WHAT'S IN THE SCROLL, FATHER? WERE YOU ABLE TO TRANSLATE IT?

I DID... I DID AFTER...

FATHER?

NO!

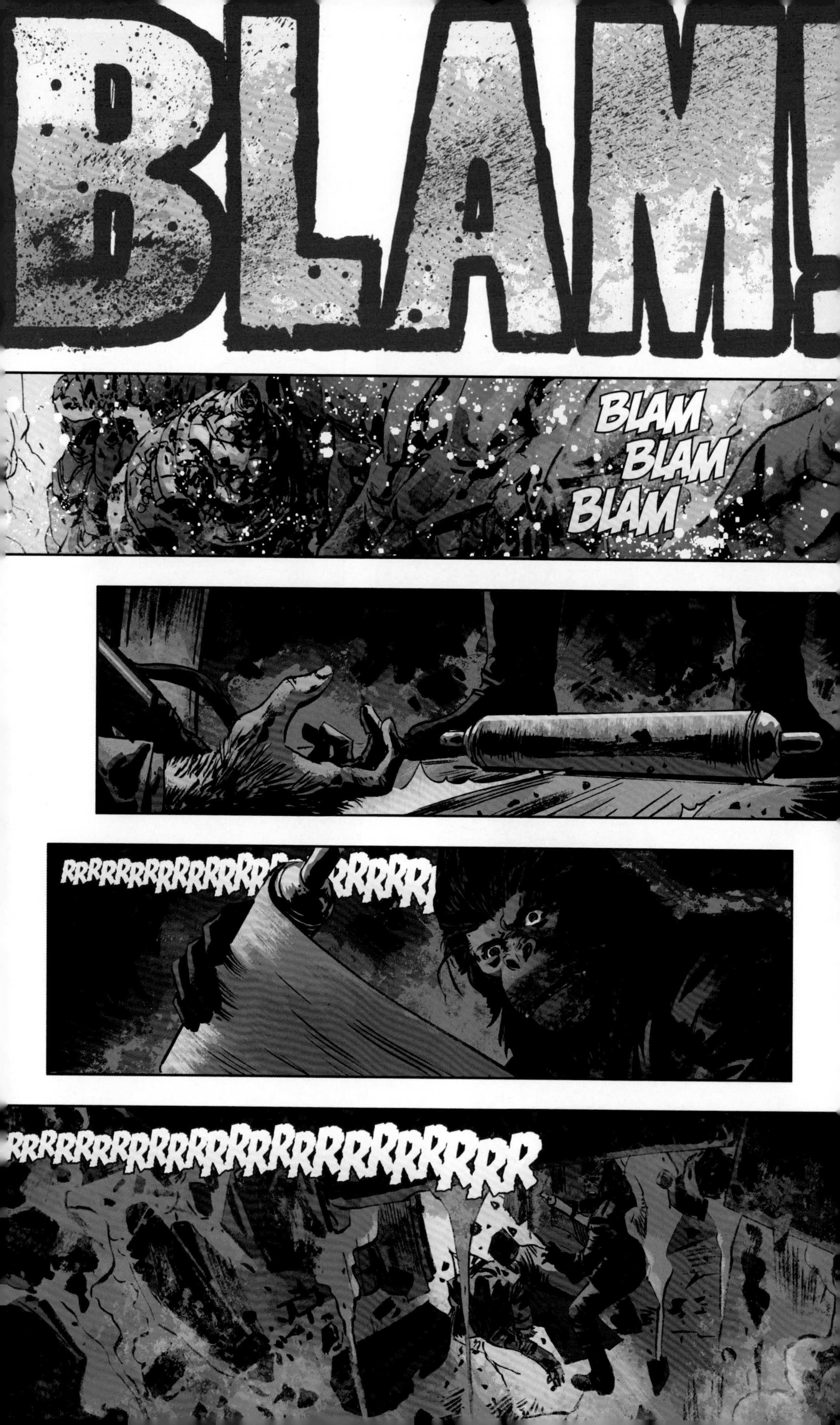
BLAM!
BLAM
BLAM
BLAM
RRRRRRRRRRRRRRRR RRRRR
RRRRRRRRRRRRRRRRRRRRRRR

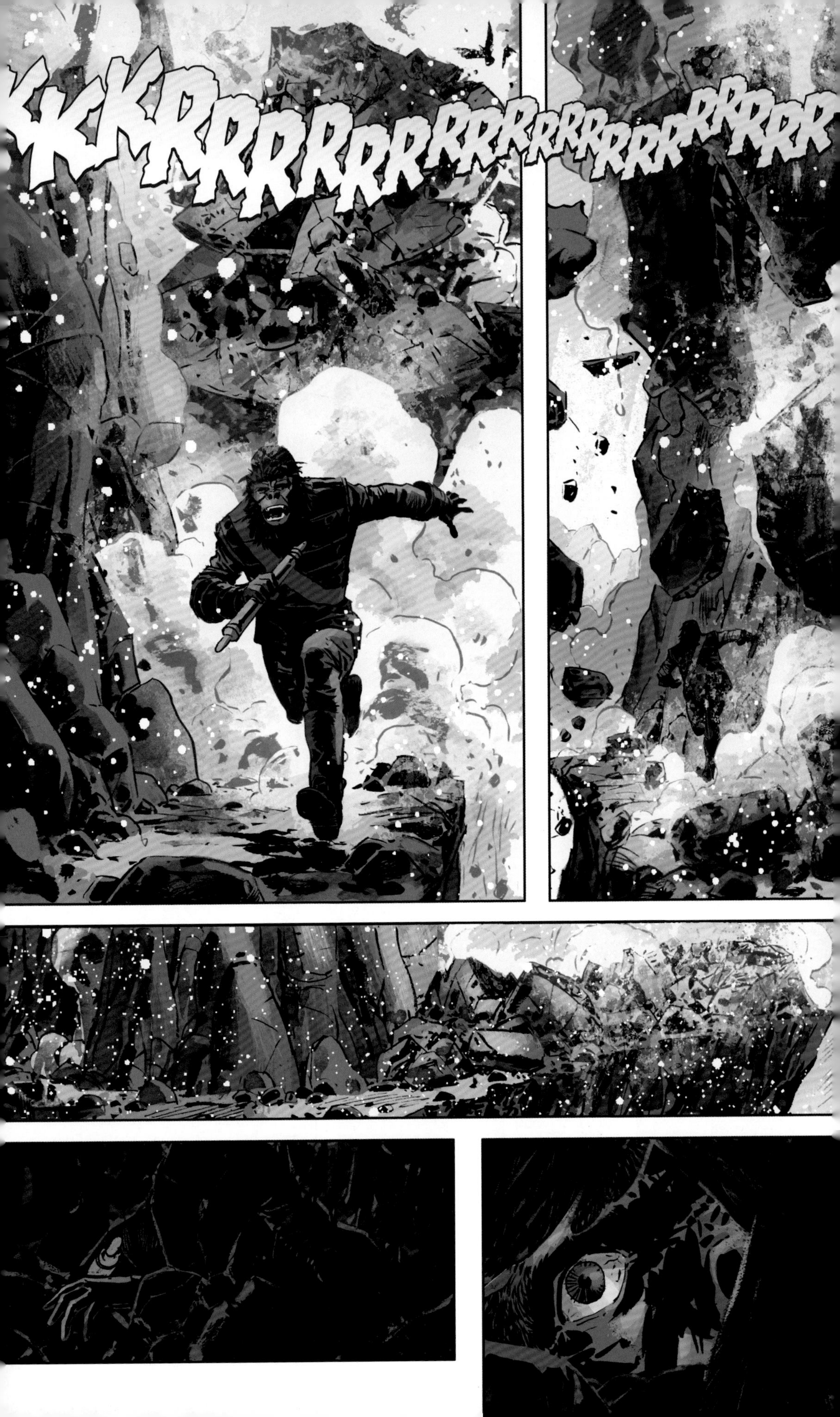
KKRRRRRRRRRRRRRRRRRRRRRRRRR

AARRGGHHH!

FWIP FWIP

WHAT'S THAT?

"DUE TO THE EXTRAORDINARY INITIATIVE YOU SHOWED ON MOUNT LAM..."

...THE COUNCIL HAS AGREED TO ADVANCE YOU AS A CANDIDATE FOR OFFICER TRAINING.

THANK YOU, COUNCILOR TENEBRIS. I'M HONORED. BUT...

...WHAT WILL HAPPEN TO THE SCROLL? I WAS TOLD--

SADLY THE SCROLL WAS AN OBVIOUS FORGERY.

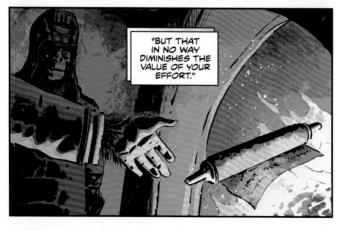

"BUT THAT IN NO WAY DIMINISHES THE VALUE OF YOUR EFFORT."

AND THE LAWGIVER SAID, "APE AND MAN SHALL LIVE TOG N FRIENDSHIP AND SHARE DO VER THE WORLD IN PEACE."

END

PLANET OF THE APES

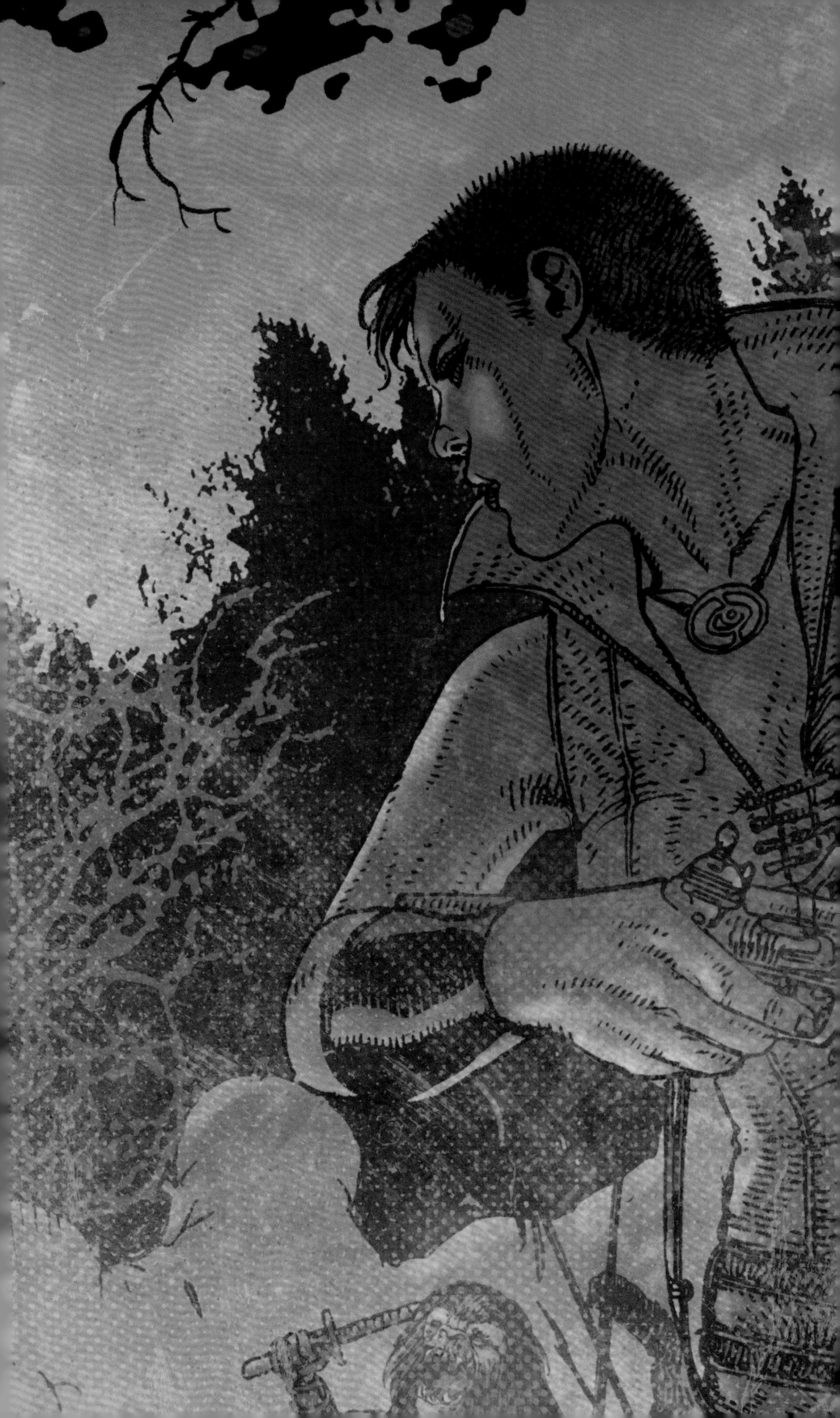

COVER GALLERY

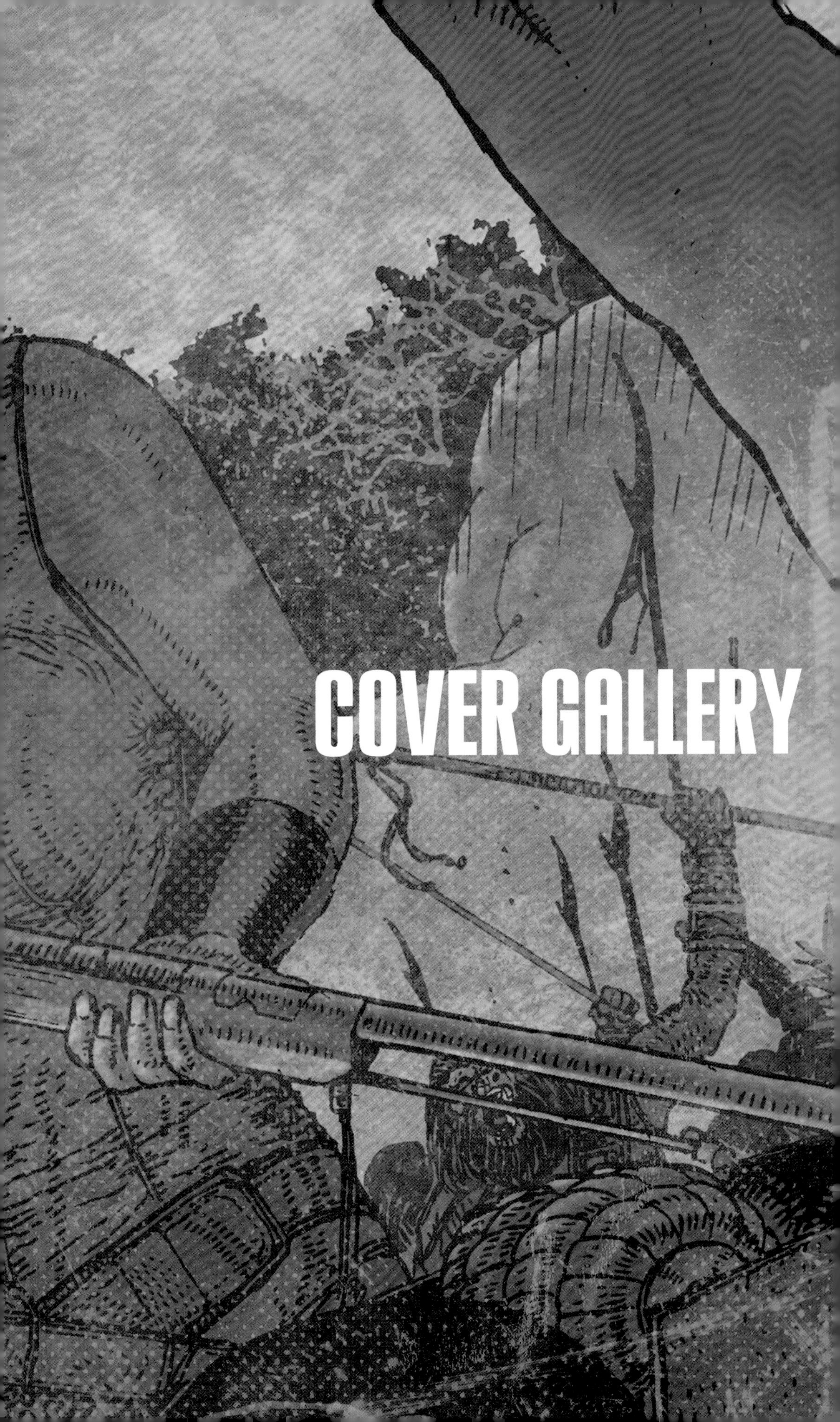

COVER 13A: DAMIAN COUCEIRO
WITH COLORS BY NOLAN WOODARD

COVER 13B: MARC LAMING
WITH COLORS BY NOLAN WOODARD

COVER 14A: CARLOS MAGNO
WITH COLORS BY NOLAN WOODARD

COVER 14B: DAMIAN COUCEIRO
WITH COLORS BY NOLAN WOODARD

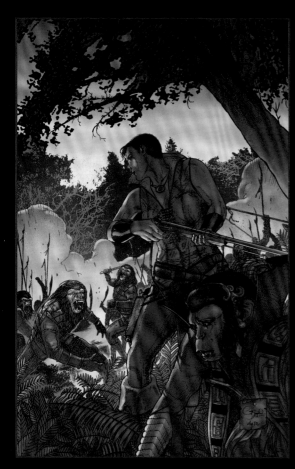

COVER 15A: CARLOS MAGNO
WITH COLORS BY NOLAN WOODARD

COVER 15B: DAMIAN COUCEIRO
WITH COLORS BY NOLAN WOODARD

COVER 16A: CARLOS MAGNO
WITH COLORS BY NOLAN WOODARD

COVER 16B: DAMIAN COUCEIRO
WITH COLORS BY NOLAN WOODARD

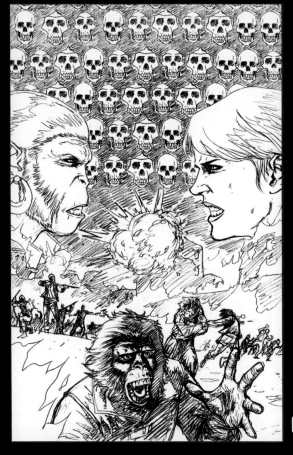

COVER 13C: DAMIAN COUCEIRO

COVER 14C: CARLOS MAGNO

COVER 15C: CARLOS MAGNO

COVER 16C: CARLOS MAGNO

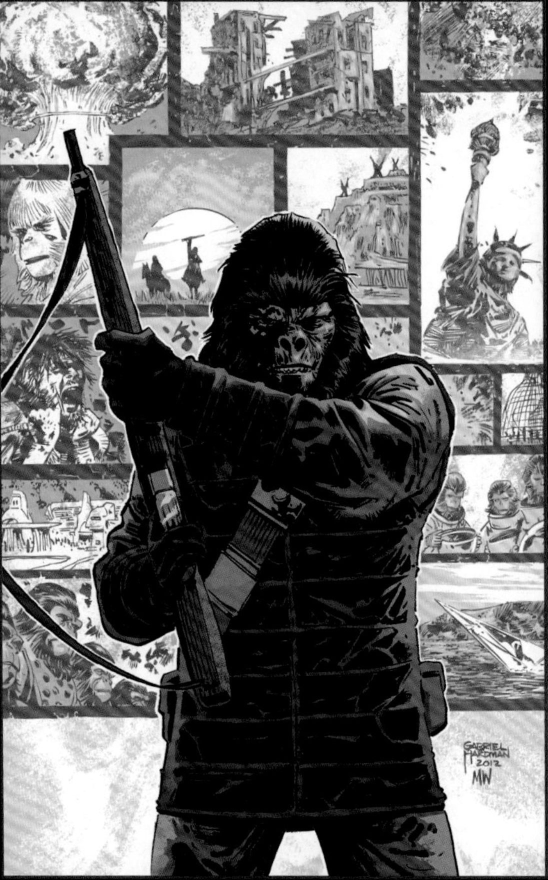
GABRIEL HARDMAN 2012
MW

PLANET OF THE APES ANNUAL

COVER 1A: GABRIEL HARDMAN

WITH COLORS BY MATTHEW WILSON

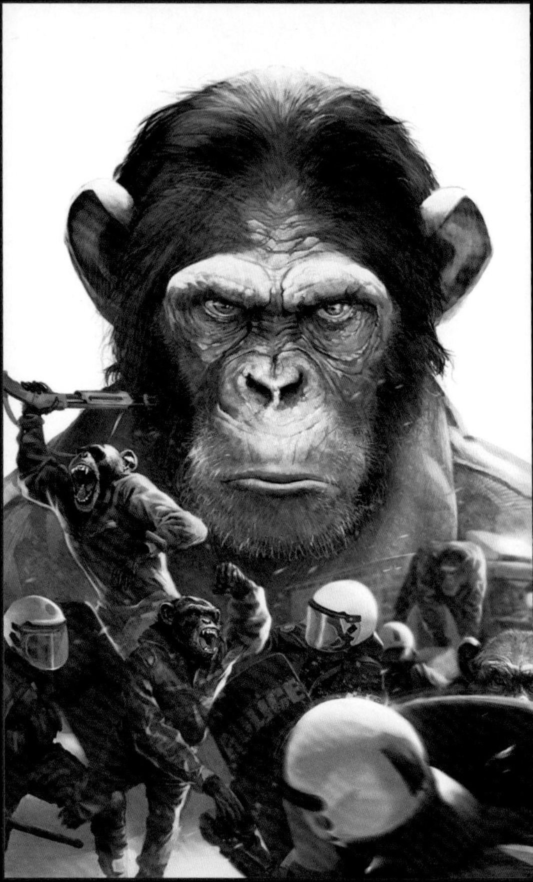

PLANET OF THE APES ANNUAL

COVER 1B: RAEL LYRA

**PLANET OF THE APES ANNUAL
COVER 1C: CHRIS SAMNEE
WITH COLORS BY MATTHEW WILSON**

**PLANET OF THE APES ANNUAL
COVER 1D: ZIRA PHOTO VARIANT**